ADVENTUROUS IDEALISM

ALFRED HENRY LLOYD, 1864–1927

Adventurous Idealism—the
Philosophy of Alfred Lloyd

Evelyn Urban Shirk

GREENWOOD PRESS, PUBLISHERS
NEW YORK   1968

To

MARY JANE AND URBAN SHIRK

my mother and father

PREFACE

THE name of Alfred Lloyd was first made known to me by Professor Herbert W. Schneider, of Columbia University, who sensed the importance of an independent study. During the preparation of this book I have been in frequent consultation with Professor Schneider and Professor Joseph L. Blau, also of Columbia University. I have had the benefit not only of their pervasive knowledge of American philosophy, but also of numerous fertile insights and criticisms which they have given me.

On a visit to the University of Michigan in 1947 I had the good fortune to meet the philosopher's widow, Mrs. Margaret C. Lloyd, and daughters, Dean Alice C. Lloyd, of the University, and Mrs. William P. Jesse. Their hospitality, delightful conversation, and unstinted coöperation I recall with great pleasure. Professor Lewis G. Vander Velde, Director of the Michigan Historical Collections, supplied me with clues to biographical and academic material concerning Lloyd. Mrs. Jane T. Lemish and Mrs. Mary Welch, of the Collections staff, provided invaluable aid in my use of the unpublished Lloyd manuscripts.

With Professor Roy W. Sellars, of the University of Michigan, and the late Professor DeWitt H. Parker I have had highly profitable conversations about Lloyd's thought. Professor Sellars and the late Professor C. B. Vibbert gave me the benefit of comments on the completed manuscript. Professor A. Cornelius Benjamin, of the University of Missouri, very generously permitted me to examine his set of Lloyd's lecture notes. I am thankful to Miss Margaret I. Smith, Chief Reference Librarian at the University of Michigan, and to Dr. Joseph Ratner for bibliographical assistance. Professors Oscar J. Campbell, Irwin Edman, Horace L. Friess, James Gutmann, Marjorie H. Nicolson, and John H. Randall, Jr., all of Columbia University, read the final manuscript and contributed many useful suggestions. Dr. Frank E. Robbins, Director of the University of Michigan Press, has been helpful in many ways. Miss Grace E. Potter, Associate Editor of the Press, has contributed greatly toward whatever readability the book may have.

I wish to take this occasion to express my gratitude to the members of the Department of Philosophy at Columbia University, who have been my friends and teachers for a long time. To my first teacher of philosophy, Professor Marie T. Copp, of Wilson College, I owe a very special and permanent debt which it is not easy to express. My husband, Professor Justus Buchler, of Columbia, has tolerated my interminable soliloquies on Lloyd and has more than once rescued me from obscurity in phrase and idea.

E. U. S.

TABLE OF CONTENTS

NOTE

Words and phrases quoted directly or indirectly from Lloyd or from other authors are in double quotation marks. Words and phrases which I wish to distinguish for some other reason are in single quotation marks.

Introduction

For about three years, from 1891 to 1894, John Dewey, George Mead, and Alfred Lloyd were together at the University of Michigan. What the mutual influences were is a problem in itself, as yet unanswered. But the fact remains that this association symbolizes the kindling of a new spark in American philosophy and in the thought of the twentieth century. All three were idealists, yet none remained wholly in the idealistic tradition. Each went his separate way and expressed the new direction in an original manner. Lloyd, for reasons which I shall explain, exercised only local influence and has remained virtually unknown. In the succeeding chapters I shall try to construct his system of philosophy and define his philosophic contribution.

In 1927 Lloyd, known in his own environs primarily for his more than common administrative ability, died and was buried with honors befitting one who had served as acting president (February–October, 1925) of the University of Michigan. The memorials speak of his unusual tolerance and his broad sympathies, which had endeared him to students and faculty alike. The *Michigan Alumnus* for May 21, 1927, attests his remarkable personal qualities by the statement that he "had not an enemy on the Campus." These qualities seem to have been candor, integrity, and personal (if not philosophic) simplicity.[1]

But in his capacity of philosopher Lloyd seems almost

1

entirely isolated from his contemporaries. Even a memorial written by his intimate colleagues[2] devotes itself entirely to a panegyric of his personal morality and character. It is significant that these colleagues choose to treat Lloyd as a man rather than as a philosopher. But, curiously, they call attention to his moral worth scarcely at all by reference to his published work; instead they confine themselves mainly to quotations from the private youthful outpourings of his "Notebooks," written as a diary of his student days in Germany. The "Notebooks" were devoted principally to religious assertion and confession of faith. In the memorial Lloyd's colleagues omit those statements which indicate that his faith was, even then, far from traditional and more than an embryonic manifestation of a naturalism in religion developed by Lloyd in subsequent articles. The labors so little recognized, not only in these tributes but throughout Lloyd's life, were not, for the most part, either religious or administrative. His philosophic output included five published books, over seventy published articles, and much unpublished material, including a full-length work, "History of the Humani," particularly close to his heart.

Lloyd's sympathies were as broad and his interests as wide as his hospitable metaphysics might suggest. He wrote about aspects of experience as diverse as the meaning of the physical sciences and the purpose of academic fellowships, the religion of the agnostic and the proper functions of a League of Nations. War, peace, logic, immortality, chance, education, negation, and cultural history, all were submitted to his perspective. He wrote on every branch of philosophic inquiry with the sole exception of technical aesthetics, which he virtually ignored. Though he speaks in a significant context of an "artistic phase" of culture,[3] his only contribution to this field as a discipline is a hilariously comic, but unpublished, article.[4]

Familiar as he was with other disciplines, particularly mathematics and biology, a master of what might broadly be called the history of ideas in general and the history of philosophy in particular, Lloyd's philosophic power reveals itself in his treatment of other thinkers. Hostile to purely destructive criticism, Lloyd attempts to "fulfill"[5] older thinkers by developing their internal meanings and showing their significance for the present. He is dominated by ideas, and is never beset by egoism or the urge for intellectual display. Able to appreciate and vitalize concepts far removed from his own, he exemplifies the humble spirit of the teacher. A tempered humor and a charming humanism pervade his work. Humor, in fact, plays a role in his metaphysics, and the humanistic spirit is closely connected with the substance of his ideas.

Lloyd's articles appear in philosophical, psychological, scientific, theological, historical, and educational journals. Yet direct intellectual exchange with his contemporaries appears to have been small. Protesting against thinking "in chorus,"[6] he indeed succeeded in being alone and unheard in his solo. Since the function of the philosopher is to fulfill rather than overthrow, Lloyd seldom writes polemic. But even occasional thrusts at Dewey and James, designed to establish that pragmatism and idealism—as Lloyd presented it—were in considerable harmony,[7] produced little response. James, apparently, found Lloyd "unassimilably obscure."[8] No man could have been more intellectually alone and yet have shared more fully and creatively in the process which later became recognized as marking the emergence of American thought from its European chrysalis.

Reasons for Lloyd's isolation are not difficult to assign. On any first reading he is a tremendously difficult writer, though an irresistibly suggestive one. He is, says Professor Schneider, "extremely abstruse, ironical, and subtle . . . an unusually independent thinker."[9] E. S. Bates, writing in the *Dictionary of American Biography*, says that Lloyd had a "highly original dialectic," that both his thought and his terminology were too original to be easily grasped, that his reasoning was difficult to follow, and that his fondness for paradox often rendered him obscure. Yet Bates feels im-

pelled to note that *The Will to Doubt* (1907), as an answer
to James's *The Will to Believe,* "though much more profound
. . . never obtained a fraction of the influence of that far-
reaching essay."[10]   In his major works, *Dynamic Idealism*
(1898) and *Philosophy of History* (1899), as well as in most
of his articles, Lloyd's ideas appear in an excessively concen-
trated form.   Furthermore, three of his five books were published between 1897 and 1899 (*Citizenship and Salvation*
came out in 1897), and it is mainly in his scattered articles of
the next quarter century rather than in the books themselves
that the ideas receive their expansion and development.

Lloyd's work is a remarkable exhibition of an architec-
tonic never systematically developed.   At first sight each
piece, excluding perhaps *Dynamic Idealism,* seems to be
about anything and everything, and, taken separately, the
pieces give the impression of a viewpoint in bits and fragments scattered throughout thirty-five years of endeavor.
But from the vantage point of his total work, what first
seem to be isolated fragments turn out to be essentially consistent with one another and to exhibit differing aspects of
a system.   Lloyd's thought intrinsically is a closely related
web of ideas involving many themes and innumerable sub-
themes.   Despite his insistence on the "divided labour"[11]
of the universe, Lloyd does not permit his philosophy to
divide it.   Each piece suggests one of Anaxagoras' seeds, for
although each is a complete whole, it contains suggestions
and implications for all the rest.   Lloyd understands systematization to be the mark of philosophy.[12]   But however
coherent his philosophy is on close scrutiny, its categories
become explicit only gradually throughout his work.   Whatever segment of Lloyd's thought the reader approaches
presents, at once, a psychologically incomplete picture and
a logically overcomplete one.   Concepts are employed and
interconnections are suggested which actually presuppose
knowledge of his entire system in order to be fully meaningful.   Insufficient explication is given in any one article to
justify its assertions.   To break into any part of Lloyd's

house requires knowledge of the entire floor plan. For this reason, if for no other, Lloyd could not keep his journal readers with him.

But the real difficulty even for serious readers springs from still another cause. While he suffers from the inability to say all at once, a disease of systematic thinkers, a complication develops in Lloyd which manifests itself as intense impatience with the statement as truth bearer: to be metaphysically whole and complete, in the sense of being all-inclusive, a philosophy must necessarily distrust language for its partiality and discreteness. If Lloyd's philosophy is to be really whole, his language must stagger under its metaphysical load of paradox and poetry. As he puts it, "Truth . . . hath not where to lay its head,"[13] and Lloyd consistently refuses to compromise it even by pillowing it on his own speculation. Since the metaphysical presuppositions upon which his thought rests are never fully exposed, a dilemma faces any expositor. Until Lloyd's philosophy is violated—until it is set forth systematically and explicitly—it remains an enigma.

Lloyd's language presents many problems. Born of an era when older categories were being discarded, he often retains and utilizes them in new ways to suggest the lineage of his ideas and to provide historical continuity. Perhaps had he not been so literal in his conviction that new ideas are old ones redefined, and had he been content to part with old language more radically, he might long ago have taken his place in the history of American philosophy. To the question whether philosophy should get a new vocabulary for its new wares, his answer is negative, because a devised language robs philosophy of its relation and responsibility to life.[14]

At the same time, in an attempt to capture the nature and meaning of dynamic activity in general and of life in particular, Lloyd actually does develop a language of his own. His categories not only aim at fertility and generality, but attempt to shock his readers into a new cultural and philosophic awareness by means of provocative formulation and unexpected analogy. The coupling of old and new terms makes his meaning particularly elusive. Even when he uses philosophically familiar terminology, Lloyd adapts it to his own purpose, and the resultant meaning is almost incredibly subtle.

Lloyd's literary devices usually spring from metaphysical considerations. He deliberately uses analogy with great abandon and considerable generalizing insight because it is a foundational concept in his theory of organism. He generalizes readily because this is the philosopher's special forte. He shocks with paradoxical phrase because this corrects for the deficiencies of earlier views. He uses broad and only implicitly defined terminology because this defines insight. He incorporates a large draught of humor into his most serious work because wisdom is impossible without it. But the unsympathetic reader, the overliteral, and the devoid of humor can easily miss the many dimensions of awareness that Lloyd's thinking attempts to elicit and illustrate.

In his own day Lloyd fell between readers. Older terms like "the whole," "the one and the many," the "negation process" repelled bright young pragmatists, while newer ones like "dimensionality," "mediation," and "focussing" disturbed the conservatives. Titles like "The Passing of the Supernatural," "When Gods Are Born," and "The Duplicity of Democracy" could seem alien and even impious, while "The Logic of Antithesis" and *Dynamic Idealism* could suggest one more derivative of Hegelianism. That anomaly "An Elementary Course in the Metaphysics of Psychology"[15] seemed to appeal to no one at the turn of the century. Although unconventional and even revolutionary sentiments lurked behind forbidding phraseology, these were quite lost on the *avant-garde* of new thinking in America.

Lloyd's thought can hardly be said to exhibit periods in the usual sense. Though the bulk of his work is homogeneous and there is no alteration of his basic position, there is change of emphasis at various times in his life and considerably greater involvement of each idea with every other as his work progresses.   His major ideas, presented in embryo in the two basic books, are not altered but merely explored and elaborated in his later work.   Even the earliest articles,[16] in fact even the "Notebooks" (ca. 1889–91) indicate the direction of his views.   Up to his last, posthumously published, article[17] he is tortuously articulating the same philosophy.

Lloyd is not a self-conscious litterateur.   He may or may not have been aware of the fact that the style and the form of his writing denotatively reproduce his metaphysics!   Each book or article is a microcosm, a small world, an ordered example of his entire system in miniature—provided one knows the key.   Each is a system within a system, a term in a series forming a larger system.   Although every article is inherently connected with every other, each is unique and individual.   Each contains its own particular version or view of the whole system.   As ideas are presented in new contexts and are juxtaposed, they give the effect of restless motion. Not only do Lloyd's ideas move forward, they move sideways as well; they not only develop but they become more interrelated.   Their movement exhibits the metaphysical process they seek to define.   Lloyd acts out his methodology as well: pun, hilarious example, high-spirited phrase, and outlandish manipulation of terminology all contribute to what he calls "the high comedy of philosophy."   Recognition of his humor, unfortunately, depends almost entirely on familiarity with the general structure of his thought.

This collection of interrelated and abbreviated ideas communicated largely by suggestion presents as many problems for the expositor as for the reader.   The mere selection of major themes presents a problem.   Lloyd's thought is so full categorially that it can be approached in many ways. For this philosophy of 'interrelatedness' the order of presentation is, in one sense, arbitrary.   It has seemed to me best, however, to analyze the most general of Lloyd's categories first and to develop the exposition by showing how they can be applied and illustrated.   I beg the indulgence of both Lloyd and the reader for a dull beginning, springing from the optimistic faith that the sequel may be the more lively if the foundation is properly laid.

The task I have posed in the following chapters is to systematize Lloyd and make him intelligible, and thereby to fill a major gap in the history of American philosophy. This is a large enterprise, and only in passing can I indicate Lloyd's significance in the development of twentieth-century ideas and trends. Nor is there room to compare him in any detail with other modern and contemporary thinkers whom he resembles or anticipates. I have selected three major themes —community, process, and truth—in terms of which to explicate the position. I shall try in particular to show the strains and tensions in Lloyd's thought which make him as much naturalist and pragmatist as idealist.

Chapter I is devoted to an account of relational movement, with the emphasis on relation. Chapter II continues this account, with the emphasis on movement. Chapter III shows how the first two chapters apply to an epistemological context. Chapter IV is concerned with the nature of truth and the function of philosophy as distinguished from science. (In one sense, an account of Lloyd's philosophy might well begin with his view of truth, since this prepares the attitude and the spirit in which the reader must submit to his thought. Yet Lloyd's views on truth are derived from his interpretation of community and process, and they seem arbitrary and ill-defined until it is developed.) In Chapters V and VI, I apply all the preceding chapters to the theory of history, society, and conduct: Chapter V develops the theoretical basis for Chapter VI, and Chapter VI concerns what is, in one sense, the culmination of Lloyd's position, namely, a reinterpretation of religious experience. Since "the end of man is action, not thought, though it were the noblest,"[18] these chapters on social philosophy and ethics most suitably bring the book to a close.

II

Lloyd was born on January 3, 1864, in Montclair, New Jersey. A twin, he was one of the five children of Henry Huggins Lloyd and Anna Badger Lloyd. Lloyd's father, always sickly, died of pneumonia when Lloyd was a small boy. The immediate financial necessity into which the young mother of five small children was plunged was relieved by the maternal grandfather, Daniel Badger, one of the contracting engineers for New York City's Grand Central Station. But Mr. Badger's good offices did not last. He suffered the failure of certain business ventures and, when he died, left the young mother once again obliged to assume the struggle against poverty. The family moved to New England, and young Alfred was sent to live with his uncle, the principal of a Massachusetts school, who apparently insisted on the practice of the more rigorous virtues of Puritanism.

From 1881 to 1882 young Lloyd went to St. Johnsbury Academy, in St. Johnsbury, Vermont, for the last year of his secondary-school education. In 1882, when he was preparing for college, a certain Reverend Mr. Fairbanks, of St. Johnsbury, a minister of the Congregational faith, into which Lloyd had been born and in which he was bred, offered to finance him at Dartmouth on the condition that he would enter the Congregationalist ministry. But the boy, apparently fearing even then that he was unable in good conscience to accept a traditional faith and religious professionalism, and unwilling to be morally bound to do so, refused the offer despite his critical need. He decided instead to work his way through Harvard by means of fellowships and tutoring.

Lloyd's undergraduate activities at Harvard reflect his character. He was elected president of the Harvard chapter of the Y.M.C.A. During his incumbency a dispute arose concerning the admission of Unitarians. Lloyd was so disturbed that such a matter should even be an issue that he resigned the presidency. With his resignation his desire for participation in institutionalized religious activity declined. His literary career was somewhat less frustrating. He became a member of the Signet and editor of the *Harvard Crimson* and thereby gained repute for the unique style[19] which he displays throughout his thirty-five years of almost continual philosophic writing.

In 1886 he was graduated from Harvard, *summa cum laude*. The next year he spent at Phillips Andover Academy, inaugurating his teaching career, but apparently under the most unsatisfactory circumstances. His associates recall that he liked to say with his usual satirical humor (always the more lusty when applied to academic matters) that, although his education provided him with competence in Greek and mathematics, he was expected to teach English, Latin, history, botany, physical geography, and physiology.

Lloyd returned to Harvard in 1887 and began his graduate work in philosophy. The great age of Harvard was just beginning, and teaching there at the time were G. H. Palmer, Josiah Royce, William James, Francis E. Abbot, and C. C. Everett. Since Palmer says that the teaching of philosophy at Harvard was historical until 1889,[20] it is possible that Lloyd's interest in cultural and philosophic history and historical method springs from that training.

Much of Lloyd's subsequent development is more understandable when seen in the light of his Harvard teachers. His interest in ethics may have developed from contact with Palmer, who in 1889 gave an analytical course in ethics at Harvard, although Lloyd's ethical views are far removed from Palmer's. One of Lloyd's recurrent themes and one close to his heart, namely, his idea of historical "stages," is really a study in ethical development. Lloyd unites Royce's monism and James's pluralism in a new and original form, never abandoning allegiance to either. His organicist theism may well have been influenced by Abbot.

Although as a student Lloyd seems to have profited principally from association with Royce and James, he never forgot Everett and his book *Poetry, Comedy and Duty*.[21]

He says that he no longer recalled the contents of the book which supplied him with the title for a certain article,[22] but it may be that he remembered more than he thought. Everett's book concerns itself with *necessary* tragedy, which, because necessary, loses its sting. It supports the thesis that whatever is necessary is good by rationalistically obscuring the difference between the cause of evil and the fact of its blight on experience. Everett's position is an exhibition of the very thing from which Lloyd's "new idealism" never fully recovered.[23] Insofar as Everett's book might have been subtitled, 'Anti-intellectualism, Cosmic Humor and Earnest Candor,' it is clear that Lloyd owes *something* to Everett, despite the fact that Lloyd can be called an anti-intellectualist only in a very narrow sense. If there is a strain of anti-intellectualism in Lloyd's theory of truth, it is an accidental by-product of a view that aims to be *more comprehensively* intellectual. In any case, Lloyd's views on this and many other matters resist easy application of traditional categories.

After a year of graduate study Lloyd was awarded the Walker Fellowship,[24] which from 1889 to 1891 took him to Göttingen, Berlin, and Heidelberg. During this period Lloyd wrote his introspective "Notebooks." It is significant that in these "Notebooks" Lloyd rarely mentions either his teachers or his philosophic activities at the time. Both in what was included and in what was omitted, the "Notebooks" are excellent witnesses to the fact that his later work reflects German influence only incidentally and with considerable rebellion. Only one teacher, Kuno Fischer, is mentioned, and then merely in connection with a description of what Lloyd considered a crude and inappropriate birthday ovation by the students. Whatever effect German philosophy had on Lloyd's metaphysics, so much concerned with polarities and historical stages, was greatly modified by his Harvard education and particularly by James's influence. Perhaps the best side comment on this comes from Lloyd himself, when he maintains that while studying on the Continent he found great respect for "Locke, Spencer and others across the Channel" and while at Harvard he was "constantly sent to the works of the great continentals."[25]   His own synthesis was already fermenting.

But throughout his stay in Germany Lloyd was more repelled by German life and culture than impressed with German thought.   While studying Hegel, Fichte, and Schelling on their home ground, his dislike for the Germans as a people seemed to overshadow whatever influence German philosophers had on him, and may have prepared the way psychologically for him to share in an indigenous American philosophy.

In Berlin in 1890 Lloyd wrote an article called "Germany and the Germans" which was published in the *Springfield Daily Republican* about 1899.   Its appearance at that time indicates that his opinions on this score not only remained unchanged some ten years after he wrote the article, but that they would play a part in his understanding of the causes of the war of 1914.   If "Fichte, [the] great Prussian nationalist, and Hegel, [the] great imperialist, translated Kantianism into Prussianism and Pan-Germanism,"[26] it was Hegel who represented that which most revolted Lloyd and from which he consciously rebelled.   In his distaste for *Kultur* and "pan-anything-ism"[27] he wrote that, having become learned, the Germans had ceased to be men.   He disliked the "crudeness, formalism, egoism, curiosity, red tape and rough food" of the Germans, was repelled by their "rudeness, conceit, and mania for system,"[28] and was distressed by their lack of candor, which he thought made them live in a glass and watch themselves live.   Since he saw German life, thought, and culture as merely an ugly necessity, it is evident that his later thinking would consciously repudiate German idealism.

But unconsciously, Lloyd does not entirely succeed.   The "Notebooks" mention a paper (otherwise unknown) entitled "The Virtual Object" which seems to have been written in Germany and which he significantly describes as the search for "the real nature of our nature, the spirit that is behind all." Whatever German influence this may suggest, it is certainly evidence of a deeply religious feeling manifested throughout Lloyd's life and writings. The "virtual object" turns out to be "Christ, who is perfect life and love" and who is "human hope, human struggle and human faith." Even here, the "Christ motive in experience," as the struggle for the fulfillment of ideals, suggests the direction of his later naturalism in religion.

Lloyd returned to Harvard in 1891 to produce a doctoral dissertation which he titled "Freedom," the result of work with Royce, Palmer, and Everett. In the fall of 1891, before the thesis was finished, he was called to the University of Michigan by John Dewey, then chairman of the Department of Philosophy. Here he became an instructor. He received his Ph.D. from Harvard in 1893.

In 1892, during the first year of his instructorship, Lloyd married Margaret Elizabeth Crocker. They had four children, Alice Crocker Lloyd, late Dean of Women at the University of Michigan, and Frederick Thurston, Anna Mary, and Putnam Lloyd.

At Michigan, where Lloyd joined Dewey and Mead, a tradition stemming from G. S. Morris still prevailed,[29] and Lloyd immediately absorbed and digested these new and exciting variations of Hegelian thought, synthesizing them with ideas brought from both Germany and Harvard and probably with some strains of Coleridgean transcendentalism resident in the Michigan background through the influence of President James Burrill Angell.[30] The result was a wave of serious writing begun by Lloyd soon after Dewey and Mead left for Chicago, in 1894. A number of articles and three books appeared in the space of three years, all exhibiting his philosophic originality and power.

Lloyd and Dewey became personal and intellectual companions. Although it is very difficult to measure the comparative influence on either side, Dewey accepts Lloyd as a participant in what he later calls the "new ferment" in thought, in "the reaction against atomic individualism and sensationalistic empiricism" the influence of which "fell in with and reinforced Morris."[31]   In a letter to James written in March, 1903, Dewey says:

I am tremendously glad that you liked his article ["The Savage Mind," by A. W. Moore, of Chicago], and very appreciative of the fact that, liking it, you expressed your satisfaction so generously.   As for *the standpoint,—we have all* been at work at it for about twelve years.   Lloyd and Mead were both at it in Ann Arbor ten years ago.   Did you ever read Lloyd's *Dynamic Idealism*?   I can't see much difference between his monism and your pluralism,—barring a little exaggeration of the plural on its own account, if I may venture.[32]

The letter goes on to describe Mead's part in terms suggestive of some of Lloyd's own formulations:

Mead has difficulty of articulation in written discourse, as you know; but I suppose he is more effective than any man in our Department in giving capable advanced students independent method.   He works himself (and *it*) out mainly in biological terms.   "Life process" is his terminology for the developing reality.

During the three years that Lloyd and Dewey were colleagues at Michigan (1891–94) and sharing the same idealistic idiom, they were both, nonetheless, adapting it to a new position, a fundamentally biological approach, containing the rudiments of pluralism, realism, and pragmatism.   An Aristotelian strain in both the Dewey and the Morris traditions, probably coming through Trendelenburg,[33] provided the Michigan background for and undoubtedly reinforced the Aristotelianism to which Lloyd was exposed in Germany. Although Lloyd's adaptation of the Aristotelian tradition is derived from these impure sources and admixed with other considerations reflecting his German education, it is clearly evident in his definition of 'psychology,' in his biological approach to a conception of process, and in his functionalism.

It is also evident, particularly in Lloyd's later years, that he was aware of the various versions of pragmatism offered at the time, and was particularly alive to their differences and antecedents. Lloyd's own strain of pragmatism is hardly methodological, and he subscribes to pragmatic methodology only with certain reservations; but if pragmatism can be understood broadly as a temper, he can be called a pragmatist, as I shall indicate in Chapter III. In the few places where he specifically concerns himself with the techniques of inquiry, he finds that the answer to a problem must spring from the conditions under which it has been formulated. As he puts it, the answer must be "defined in terms of the demands which the conditions of its rise and articulation have put upon [it] . . . ."[34] But Lloyd is dissatisfied with answers limited by the pragmatic conceptions of meaning and truth. Though he insists that speculative philosophy must rest on scientific knowledge, it must nevertheless rise, in some sense, above scientific specialism and seek a kind of poetic truth which, although verifiable in experience, is broader than any experience. But even while trying to broaden the pragmatic prescription for truth, Lloyd hesitates to violate the strictures imposed by pragmatism. In seeking truth from a *wider* context than science, he would yet repudiate overall absolute truth; for, as he maintains, and reiterates constantly, "a universal relativism, a relativism declaring all things definite to be relative, is not by any means nihilism; it makes nothing unreal; it simply makes reality just not finally and exclusively one of the things."[35]

The Morris tradition played a considerable part in the molding of Lloyd's thought. Morris died in 1889, two years before Lloyd came to Michigan. Dewey says that Morris was concerned with the *meaning* of existence in his objective idealism, that he studied in Berlin with Trendelenburg, and that he was uniting Aristotle and Hegel for his students. Thus Morris returned from Germany to combine a "logical and idealistic metaphysics with a realistic epistemology."[36] Lloyd can be described as doing something of the same kind.

The greatest influences on Lloyd were exercised by Royce and James. Royce's influence is positive and far-reaching and probably well beyond Lloyd's awareness of it. Adequate attention to it would require lengthy and separate analysis. James's influence, on the other hand, although perhaps less systematic, was more immediate and provocative. Lloyd's reactions to James, both for and against, are always intense and produce many statements of concurrence and repudiation. As a result of his study of James's "stream of thought" Lloyd develops a hatred of atomic ideas and of atomic isolation of parts of a universe in general, and formulates a really thoroughgoing relationalism. From James, Lloyd absorbs the idea that an organism must be understood dynamically and actively rather than structurally. Interest in living activity brings Lloyd to an organicism so broad that the distinction between what we ordinarily term 'living' and 'nonliving' collapses. On the other hand, James's pluralism brought Lloyd to a redefinition of both pluralism and monism as principles of explanation rather than as metaphysical descriptions. James's extreme empiricism stimulated Lloyd to take up the cudgels for the other side. Lloyd devoted an article[37] to a gleeful scouring of James's "pluralistic universe" for "paradoxes" which would "expose" what Lloyd considered the narrowness of James's position—an honor which he conferred on none of his other contemporaries. Acting as a sort of devil's advocate, he reveals how seriously and respectfully he took James's views.

In 1894 Dewey left Michigan for Chicago and took Mead with him, leaving Lloyd to work out and express his own particular exhibition of a naturalistic temper imprisoned in a systematic synthesis of various strains. With Dewey's exit Lloyd became assistant professor and, from 1894 to 1896, departmental executive officer. From this time on, at least so tradition has it,[38] Robert Mark Wenley apparently became Michigan's official philosopher, while Lloyd's forte was understood to be administration. In 1899 Lloyd became associate professor and in 1906, full professor. The myth that Lloyd was more successful in an administrative capacity than in a philosophic one persisted, and his administrative duties grew in both number and importance. Lloyd became advisor to students planning to attend Harvard Graduate School. From 1915 to 1924 he was dean of the Graduate School, in recognition of which service the University of California conferred on him an honorary LL.D. in 1924. In 1925, upon the death of President Burton, Lloyd completed Burton's term, as acting president of the University.

But the tasks of university administration were not so pressing that Lloyd had to abandon activity in learned societies. He was one of the original members of Katholepistemiad, the second-oldest faculty club at the University, composed of scholars in a wide variety of fields. It was at this 'institution of universal knowledge' that Lloyd delivered some of his unpublished papers and read his studies on various figures in the history of science. He also belonged to the Research Club, another faculty association devoted to a more effective community among the various scholars of the University. Membership in both clubs indicates Lloyd's broader interests and his pedagogical support of the breakdown of overdepartmentalized education.

Lloyd was first president of the Michigan Alpha chapter of Phi Beta Kappa (1907–9), chairman of the University Committee on Student Affairs, and president of the Harvard Club of Michigan (1909–10). He was an active member of the Western Division of the American Philosophical Association, delivering many papers before it and becoming its president from 1915 to 1916. He was a member of and participated in the activities of the American Psychological Association. At his death he was secretary to the Association of American Universities. So well spaced and widely diversified was Lloyd's participation in intellectual and educational work that his life presents an almost perfect example of the balanced academician.

Among Lloyd's later colleagues at Michigan were R. W. Sellars, DeWitt H. Parker, and C. B. Vibbert. Lloyd also left a host of realistic, naturalistic, and pragmatic students in his wake. Most influenced by him, perhaps, was Charles M. Perry, who, apparently, has written the only philosophical article[39] on Lloyd to date and who, possibly influenced by Lloyd's concept of dimensionality, wrote a work called *Toward a Dimensional Realism*. Students who acknowledge Lloyd's influence are M. Ten Hoor, A. C. Benjamin, and Sellars. Sellars, in his intellectual autobiography, calls himself a realist, naturalist, and humanist,[40] which is a reasonably fair description of Lloyd as well.

Although I should be unwilling to say that Lloyd 'influenced' contemporaries other than, perhaps, Dewey, it is evident that he shared creatively in the climate which made some of the major thinkers of the twentieth century. I should hesitate, however, to suggest more than that many of the problems which concern Lloyd concern them as well.

Though Lloyd's philosophy has idealistic outposts, its reasoned conclusions and permeating attitudes are unabashedly naturalistic. Life is defined as action, interrelationship, and development; ideas become plans of action; supernaturalism in all its guises is repudiated; and truth is found in experimental use. Lloyd functions in the history of philosophy in a way that would have gratified him indeed, namely, as illustrative of a transition, a movement or an exhibition of "inner logic," as he would have called it, within thought which breaks down unqualified traditional labels. As James suggested in a letter to F. C. S. Schiller in April, 1903:

They [Dewey, Mead, and Lloyd] have started from Hegelianism, and they have that temperament (that is, such men as Mead and Lloyd have it strongly) which makes one still suspect that if they do strike Truth eventually, they will mean some mischief to it after all; but still the fact remains that from such opposite poles minds are moving toward a common centre, that old compartments and divisions are breaking down, and that a very inclusive new school may be formed.[41]

And in a letter to Dewey in March, 1903, James says:

What you write of the *new school of truth* both pleases and humiliates me. It humiliates me that I had to wait til I read Moore's article before finding how much on my own lines you were working. Of course I had welcomed you as one coming nearer and nearer, but I had missed the central root of the whole business, and shall now re-read you . . . and try again a hack at Mead and Lloyd of whom I have always recognized the originality, but whom I have found so far unassimilably obscure. I fancy that much depends on the place one starts from. You have all come from Hegel and your terminology *s'en ressent,* I from empiricism, and although we reach much the same goal it superficially looks different from the opposite sides.[42]

Little as James, under the tutelage of Dewey, professes to understand Lloyd, he seems to have touched upon the most significant, if terminologically obfuscated, meaning of Lloyd's philosophy. Historically, Lloyd is a most telling moment in an actual process, a harbinger of trends that dominate present-day thought. Bergson, Peirce, James, Dewey, Santayana, Whitehead, and Alexander not only reflect the same issues that Lloyd found important, but offer solutions strikingly similar to his. Through Lloyd's analyses, couched in categories that are new and surprisingly rich, can be glimpsed, in the very act of developing, such internal relations as those holding between evolutionism and contextualism and between pragmatism and the Kantian tradition. Lloyd's "direct and unreserved"[43] idealism is thus an original reflection of modern themes as well as a major representation of American thought.

Lloyd's career, so illustrative of a life devoted to the energetic search for meaning, came to an end on May 11, 1927. He collapsed while delivering an address before the graduating class of that year on "Some Factors of a Life Worth While" and died a day later of a coronary thrombosis. He had been talking about a central ingredient of his philosophy, the theme of truth as poetry, comedy, and duty. Symbolically, his death illustrated the principal implication of this theme, that the statement of truth is necessarily incomplete.

Unity and Community

1. *The Direction of Lloyd's Thinking*

Born as Lloyd was into an intellectual climate much concerned with the mysteries of biological development and evolutionary process, his most pervasive theme is that of "life" and his most basic concept that of "organism." It is by an analysis of organism that he aims to discover the activities most essential to livingness. However biologically conditioned this approach may sound, it departs from the kind of analysis which might be expected from and which is exemplified by organicisms like that of Spencer.[1] For Lloyd the most basic characteristic of organism is found in the ontological relationship which holds between parts and wholes; and the concepts of life and organism relate not merely to entities in the biological realm, but to any entity whatever.

Perhaps the most fundamental characteristic of an organism is self-movement. Although Lloyd subscribes to this Aristotelianism, he is not content to rest with it. To understand anything as moving is, for him, not merely to see it as fulfilling a function, for movement implies a frame of reference by which we are able to recognize it. We know an object to be physically moving in space by comparing it with something stationary. This commonplace of experience suggests to Lloyd a generalized conception of movement which he calls "organic." Just as physical movement must be understood in terms of the relationships between sensible things, so organic movement or process in general must be understood in terms of the relationships between parts and wholes. Ultimately, to describe life Lloyd must first examine certain ideas associated with the analysis of parts and wholes, for instance, unity and community, which the concept of organism in some sense implies. Thus to describe life, we must begin by describing relationships within and between the things which manifest life.

The fact that Lloyd finds the part-whole relationship the starting point of a philosophy of organism must make it immediately evident that his organicism is not only going to mean something special by the term "life" but is also going to adopt a particular way of dealing with organic relations. Not only does Lloyd make "life" a category encompassing activities far more pervasive than those we customarily understand by the term, since all things exhibit and participate in part-whole relationships, but, further, rather than describe these relationships empirically, Lloyd is going to undertake a kind of metaphysical exploration of the nature of organism. What emerges is a metaphysical account of the meaning of the part-whole relationship rather than a biological account of the nature of organism.

Like all idealists, Lloyd is concerned not simply to recognize the diversification and differentiation of things, but to develop a theory to explain this. Not content with the mere fact that parts compose wholes, he rests his views on a hidden yet influential set of preconceptions. Although the fact of differentiation must in the end be accepted (for Lloyd is an epistemological realist), this acceptance is, in his case, hardly naïve, for he never alters his conviction that we must both discover *what* things are and *why* they are as we find them.

From writings as early as *Dynamic Idealism* (1898) and as late as an article of 1927,[2] it is clear that Lloyd's philosophy of organism rests on a conception of the part-whole relation-

ship which he never makes fully explicit.   Reference to the
part-whole relationship in Lloyd's work is always an indication of a desire to restate fundamental ideas and to recall
first principles; it is always an indication that he feels a need
to return to simplicity and really primary things.   Incomplete as his analysis is, he does not hesitate to offer all sorts
of principles derived from it.   Since every aspect of his
thought is either derived from or intimately related to this
basic theory of organic relationship, and since the understanding of his entire work will be tremendously facilitated
by an account of its role, it is necessary to exhibit the preconceptions, as a kind of least common denominator, despite
the fact that they must be formulated from suggestion alone.
In the next few sections I have devised a terminology and
a conceptual scheme ('the undifferentiated,' 'the differentiated,' and 'the overdifferentiated') which is not that of Lloyd
himself but which, I believe, articulates the latent structure
of his metaphysics.

2. The Undifferentiated

Since, according to Lloyd, the function of philosophy is to
generalize to the greatest degree (the philosopher lives in a
"world-of-things-in-general"),[3] it will be entirely in keeping
with his spirit to begin with the part-whole relationship in
the most general sense.   Lloyd actually holds the view that
there is *some* relation between any given thing and any
other.   The principles of relationship which we are going
to unfold can be peopled by any terms whatsoever.   To
extricate the account from any *particular* subject matter,
let us begin by talking about 'A,' anything—not this or that
named thing but a thing, anything.   And let us first consider it merely in itself, unrelated to anything else.

A mere unrelated A must be understood as an entity
without parts, entirely undifferentiated.   It is therefore
motionless, because motion implies a frame of reference.
The partless A is a void; it is without empirical meaning;
it is a contradiction.   Since nothing can be predicated of it,

nothing can characterize it, and therefore it cannot be said to 'exist,' if we mean by this what any realism means, namely, to have a position in space and time.   Merely being posited linguistically, A cannot be thought of, cannot be conceived; and although it may be considered proper company for Lewis Carroll's "toves," although it may be a term in what Lloyd disparagingly calls "formal logic," which is concerned with "statements" and not with "life," it cannot be a member of Lloyd's life-logic, which has to take lessons from biology[4] and to describe living activity rather than merely to posit terms.   The predicateless A has no place in Lloyd's universe, and hence there is negatively implied the conclusion that an empirical world must be defined as a set of relationships.

Now what I am calling the 'undifferentiated A' plays no direct conceptual role in Lloyd's thought.   It defies predication and stands for zero, for nothing.   It has a partner which I shall call the 'overdifferentiated A' and which plays a more ambiguous part in Lloyd's thought.   The overdifferentiated A stands for absolutely complete being—that anomaly which is so complete that it cannot exist in an empirical world either, that "philosopher's fiction" which also resists predication but which is part of the dream world, the "world in general," in which the philosopher lives.

A pragmatic-minded questioner might ask why Lloyd does not exorcise the undifferentiated A in the first place, when, lacking empirically discoverable predicates, it can only be a meaningless bubble of syllables.   This question will be answered in due time.   But at present let it suffice to say that although he never uses the term 'predicateless A,' he implicitly invokes the concept in specific contexts and calls it by various names.   In an epistemological context he calls it "sensation";[5] in a metaphysical context he calls it "the [wholly] unknowable."[6]   It is unnecessary to describe these conceptions now in order to make the point that they are concrete applications of the notion of a predicateless A and function in exactly the same way.

What, then, does the predicateless A mean in Lloyd's philosophy? On the one hand, he denies its empirical existence, and yet, on the other, he opens all discussions of any type of process or movement by a consideration of it in some form. In the first place, the predicateless A represents a kind of imaginary starting point which any discussion of process must recognize in order to be logically complete. In this sense it operates as a limiting concept necessitated by a consideration of process, because any process is going to involve, for Lloyd, an infinite series of terms which compose it. (In order to explain what I mean by ascribing such a role to this concept, I will return to the matter both in this chapter and in subsequent chapters.) In the second place, it offers a conception of an empirical world in negative terms; it defines the characteristics of existence by showing what they are not. An example of this function is found in the conclusion just drawn, namely, that the empirical world must be conceived in relational terms.

The consequences of Lloyd's denial of the empirical existence of the predicateless A testify to the fact that his version of idealism differs in point of departure from the earlier nineteenth-century versions. Let us examine two of the most significant consequences, namely, Lloyd's nominalistic strain and his relationalism, in order to exhibit those foundations of his thought which are more readily available in their most general form at the present stage in our discussion.

The first consequence originates in the view that, having no parts, A could not "exist." This is a negative way of maintaining that only when it has parts will it be particularized and become an individual. Particularity, therefore, is necessary to existence. The predicateless A cannot exist because it is not an A in particular. In holding the view that each existing entity is particular and unique, Lloyd involves himself in a kind of nominalism. He denies that two things may have a property in common,[7] but asserts that two things may nevertheless share in that they may partici-

pate in one process.   Lloyd's position, which vigorously combats logic as a formal science, attacks the concept of classification.[8]   "The individuality of everything involves the impossibility of any classification of things . . . .   Individuality
requires that no two things be alike,"[9] he says.   He is sus-
picious of the artificiality of class divisions out of respect
for the individual.   We shall later see him developing his
attack on classification whether it be considered as a logical
or as a social device.

Since everything is individualized and unique, classification will, at best, produce only a semiadequate account of
the nature of things.   This, however, is not to suggest that
the notion of class is entirely repudiated, for, on the contrary, Lloyd simply redefines it.   He recognizes that description is impossible without it.   The describer offers only an
inexact kind of truth.   However 'alike' supposedly identical
properties are, they are never identical.   The classifier may
violate the metaphysical individuality in a world *only* if he
does so with the especial license granted him by a scientific
rather than a philosophic enterprise.   Such license merely
gives him the right *scientifically*—but not philosophically—
to unite the ununitable and group the ungroupable.   The
distinction between philosophic and scientific truth which
results will be the burden of Chapter IV, 'Poetry, Comedy,
and Duty.'

The second consequence of denying the empirical existence of the motionless A is Lloyd's relationalism.   Predication can begin only when A has parts and is itself a part of
something else.   To have parts and to be a part of something else is precisely what Lloyd means by the term "organism."   This implies that predication cannot be of things
qua independently existing, but only of "relations between
things."   Since we can only describe things in relation, to
describe a 'thing' means to discriminate a set of relations.
A 'thing' is a concretion of interrelations.   For example, a
table must be defined in terms of its relations to such things
as the room it is in, the books and the cloth on it, and the

reader using it, as well as in terms of its having legs, top, drawers, and so on. And as a moving thing can only be described with respect to a frame of reference, so it turns out now that *any* thing must be described with respect to a frame of reference. It will later appear that 'thing' and 'moving thing' are one and the same. To be and to be in motion are identical.

Lloyd takes care to push his relationalism to its limit by pointing out that any particular quality which we might select and in terms of which we might classify has its particular character only by virtue of the fact that it is united in a *particular relational complex*. Thus anything has its character by virtue of its context and must be described in terms of its relations to that context (which means, among other things, that history will be one of Lloyd's central interests). Epistemologically, for example, the table on which I write has its own particular quality of greenness by virtue of its particular surroundings and its influencing environment, which includes me, the state of my sense organs and my accumulated experience, my memory, and my expectations, all of which I bring to the situation as part of the table's environment.[10] So, ontologically, everything is what it is because of its particular interrelationships. Everything is what it is because of its particular history.

We can now see that Lloyd could distinguish between philosophic and scientific truth and that this distinction is not only a consequence of his nominalism but of his relationalism as well. Because A has to be described with respect to its relations with something else from which it is distinguished, Lloyd is forced into a distinction between truth as partial (truth about the relationship of A's parts) and truth as wider than A (truth about the relations between A and other things). In other words, truth in the special sciences must be distinguished from truth as wider than any of the special sciences (philosophic truth). Although science, too, describes activity and function, its account is always particularly limited. A given science can only describe part of the universe; it cannot encompass all of the other sciences. Disciplines, in other words, must unfortunately be disciplines—overspecial and limited by a narrow context. Lloyd develops the notion of philosophic truth to compensate for the failure of the special sciences to be more than 'special,' to deal with more than "details."[11] Philosophic truth, then, would describe the part-whole relations in some larger sense and wrest neither part nor whole out of some kind of larger, perhaps "total," context. In seeking the real which "dwells in the differences of things,"[12] Lloyd exemplifies his maxim whether he is discussing the problem of knowledge or the history of an idea. Because of this predilection for the concept of relation, his own work tends to examine everything when it examines anything.

3. The Differentiated

Let us return to the device of A to develop the meaning of the differentiated A. When A is a something, when it is differentiated, it becomes a thoroughly diversified unity with infinite predicates. When we say that A is a something, it is equivalent to saying that A *is not B*. To speak meaningfully of A at all, then, is to imply the presence, at least, of some possible contrary, which we shall call 'B.' To say that A is not B entails two consequences. First, A is a whole composed of parts and therefore has an identity of its own. Since A is *not* B, A is a *specific 'this'*—a something—by virtue of the fact that it is composed of parts and that these parts serve in a particular relationship known as 'A.' Being composed of parts, possessing individuality, A is what Lloyd would call an organism. Secondly, since A, in distinguishing itself from B, implies B, the individuality of A implies that A and B are both parts in some other whole, are both in communal relation in some larger unity or frame of reference. (*Why* a larger context is necessary awaits discussion of Lloyd's concept of "infinite series," which defines the relationship holding between A and B, insofar as A is neither B nor C nor D, and so on. But for the moment, it is clear that since A is not B, A and B are both wholes for their own parts and parts in some other whole.)

To say that A has individuality means for Lloyd that it is "active" in a basic and special sense, which, for lack of a better designation, I am suggesting by the term 'organic process.' The organic process or motion which makes A what it is has two interdependent aspects: (1) A is a set of relationships. Each relationship may be called a 'part' of A. A functions as a unity for its parts. It maintains its identity throughout physical alteration. A, then, is distinguished from all other things. It is a 'this' as over against all 'thats.' (2) This differentiation which makes A a whole or a unity implies another differentiation between A as part and other parts in a larger whole. A's relationships not only define A as A but also as not B, not C, not D, and so on. These co-implicative aspects of organic process define A's individuality, namely, its being both whole and part. A is a community of parts and a part of a community. A as differentiated has predicates, relationships.

An examination of the core of organism, namely, the relationship between part and whole, reveals this relationship to be more suitably described as a verb than as a noun. For example, Lloyd says, "The chair, then, *makes* its parts quite as truly as the parts *make* the chair . . . . Relationship, indeed,—and this is the important fact,—means activity. The two, relationship and activity, are one."[13] Lloyd conceives existence as a set of "relating activities" that comprise the persistent organic process in which any organism is involved merely by virtue of its existence and which is, therefore, implied by the nature of individuality, by the very definition of a diversified and pluralistic world. Thus for Lloyd there are no processes which are not relationships—a not uncommon notion—but, as well, there are no relationships which are not also processes—a rather different matter. Lloyd's "relating activities" are to be understood as broader than other common types of relatedness, like logical relatedness in the sense in which *statements* are related as bearing on one another's truth possibilities, physical relatedness in the sense of contiguity in time and space, and epistemological relatedness in the sense in which a Kantian knower relates ideas to his own unity. "Relating activity" as activity must be distinguished from process in the sense of mere physical movement, though, as we shall see, physical process is always one of the factors involved in any process. Lloyd's notion of "relating activity" is a sort of genus, in which the common types of relatedness are the species. The persistence of anything in maintaining, so to speak, both its interior and its exterior relationships, is the generic form of logical, physical, and epistemological relatedness as species.

Lloyd's views of part and whole have not only related unity (roughly 'wholeness') to community (or 'partness'), but have also identified relationship with process. Community and process are the matrices in terms of which Lloyd's thought must be understood. (His identification of the two obviously makes the division between the first and second chapters in this volume artificial, justifiable only by its expediency.)

Let us review the course of the discussion with reference to another matter which can now be made clear. Having begun with the fiction of the undifferentiated A which was not in motion, and having proceeded from there to a discussion of the differentiated A in motion, we may be asked, 'What put it in motion?' This account is certainly not intended as a description of some cosmogony, since that would do violence to Lloyd: ". . . life is an affair of the universe as an organic whole, having neither an origin heretofore nor a destiny hereafter . . . ."[14] Lloyd would vigorously object to the idea that things have a beginning in any sense, whether the questioner means by 'beginning' either a supernatural first mover or a mechanical proximate cause. All 'movers' are inimical to Lloyd's thought, whether they are supernatural and extraempirical or natural and mechanically empirical. Since he conceives even the question "What causes movement?" to be an exhibition of what he calls "mechanicalism," he finds all answers to be so, too, for both question and answers imply that motion is "external" to what is moved. Whether such explanations be couched in the candid and forthright supernaturalism of Aquinas or in what Lloyd understands to be the disguised supernaturalism of the positivism of Comte and Mach, he sees all responses to this kind of question as "creationalism . . . a restless shade" which asks for "a decent burial."[15]   If motion or process is said to have a beginning in any sense, regardless of whether that means a pre-empirical beginning or an ever-present empirical beginning, Lloyd sees the assertion as implying a "spontaneous" and "miraculous" notion of movement.[16] All spontaneous beginnings are what he likes to call "occult,"[17] that is, they imply a lack of relationship between a product and its causes.   Such accounts of motion are by-products of "spiritualism" and the "ouija board mentality."[18]   Consequently, Lloyd describes organic activity as self-activity.

In order to define further the foundations of Lloyd's thought, let us consider certain additional implications of the concept of the differentiated A, namely, (1) functionalism, (2) contextualism, and (3) relativism.

(1) The first implication, functionalism, springs from the fact that, since the relations of a thing to other things, in terms of which it must be described, are activities, the only possible description of a thing is an account of what it 'does'—a description of its functions.   Up to this point Lloyd is Aristotelian in his approach.   But for Lloyd the function of anything consists, at the very least, in organizing itself and in relating itself to other things.   Therefore, the term 'doing' need not mean physical motion, but the persistence of any type of relationship.   Although 'doing' as physical motion is empirically significant, the relational operations of A are for Lloyd metaphysically broader.   They are not physical motion alone and they are often not physical motion at all.   If A represents an animal or a plant, then locomotion and growth will be two of its properties.   But if A represents a stone or a window, neither growth nor locomotion will be

applicable to it, although relating activity (and therefore
"life" in Lloyd's sense)[19] will.   Thus all things, by their mere
existence, share relating activity, but not all things exhibit
that species of it which we understand as locomotion.

Lloyd's notion of organic process, then, is the means by
which he insists that all descriptions, including those of
states of being, must be functional, although his sense of that
term is considerably broader than that of either Aristotle or
Aristotle's pragmatic progeny. Epistemologically, it will
turn out, Lloyd is closer to the pragmatists than his metaphysics might seem to indicate.   But I shall later suggest
that his metaphysics is essential to his version of pragmatism
—a relation which is perhaps questionable in other contribu-
tors to pragmatism, like Peirce or Royce.

To return at this point to Lloyd's nominalistic strain, we
are now able to indicate a further qualification, derived from
his particular adaptation of functionalism, just described.
For Lloyd, to say that A becomes a specific 'thisness' through
activity is equivalent to saying that it gains individuality
when it has a function. In Aristotle's functionalism A is
made both general and particular by its function, insofar
as activity makes it a 'this-here-kind-of-thing.'   In Lloyd's
adaptation, however, function makes the individual thing
absolutely unique; it and only it can have the particular set
of relating activities which it has to a world. Hence, the
thing cannot be a particularized manifestation of a species.
While both Lloyd and Aristotle find that functionality permits us to account for differentiation, for Aristotle there are
universal types of function, whereas for Lloyd each individual functions as a universal type.

(2) The second implication of the concept of a differentiated and individualized A is that the whole-part relationship is understood by Lloyd as contextual. Thus A functions as a whole when looked at from one vantage point,
but as a part when considered from another. A nerve of
my arm may function as a whole (or "inclusively")[20] if the
nature of a nerve cell is the subject matter of inquiry, but

if the subject is the function of the entire arm, the nerves act only as a part (or 'exclusively' if I may supply the correlative term). Inasmuch as A can be either part or whole depending on the perspective, Lloyd must then define *an* organism as a set of active relationships without either physical or fixed boundaries:

If biology only would openly and completely identify individuality, not with any mere physical part, but with an active function or relationship . . . .[21]

A localized physical force is not more seriously self-contradictory than a localized sovereignty.[22]

. . . the living individual [formerly] has been very physically conceived, being determined primarily by spacial and temporal conditions.[23]

An organism, then, cannot be understood spatially or statically, but must be taken "functionally," and its boundaries must be determined in practice. The part gains parthood inasmuch as it collaborates in the function of something else. The whole is a whole only when it is found to be serving as a unity for parts or 'performs inclusively.' As each part becomes a part by sharing in the activities of a larger unity, it relates itself to a larger universe. So Lloyd says that a chair "is really no chair until through active use it is related to things beyond itself."[24] Consequently, the physical boundaries of an organism are never fixed, but depend on the relationships which it sustains to other things.

(3) The third implication is that Lloyd's notion of the infinite relativity of terms implies a theory of the relativity of truth close to certain varieties of pragmatism. On the one hand, A is only A relative to B, C, D, and so on, which are outside itself and in company with which it is a part. On the other hand, A is only A relative to its internal differentiations, in meaningful relation with which it is a whole. That which is a part (or acts part-ly) in one context will be a whole (acting whole-ly) in another. Consequently, determination of the boundaries of A, of the things which give

it individuality and predication, would depend on the question asked, which would, in turn, depend on the vantage point of the observer. Since A is always A relative to something else, 'truth' loses the absoluteness it so characteristically has in idealisms, and Lloyd's relationalism has fathered a fundamental pragmatic notion, namely, the relativity and contextuality of knowledge. An answer to the question 'What is A?' depends upon the context within which the question is framed and, as Lloyd himself puts it in an unpublished article,[25] "depends on the conditions of its asking." Later chapters will elaborate Lloyd's contextualism and relativism.

A further consequence of A's individuality is that a world not only becomes thoroughly intelligible, but that its intelligibility is guaranteed as original and rooted in the very nature of existence. Each empirical A, in order to exist at all, has to have a specific character of a 'this-here' particularity, which in turn means that it possesses an indefinite set of defining characteristics. Individuality rather than type or universality endows Lloyd's organism with intelligibility, because it guarantees that it is composed of indefinite relational characteristics. So A now has a "position,"[26] as Lloyd sometimes refers to it, in the sense that it not only has a place in space but a character, a formal cause. We shall see later that a world of relational configurations is so thoroughly intelligible that there is no 'problem' of knowledge. Instead, the fact of knowing illustrates a necessary metaphysical relation between knower and known.[27]

4. The "Infinite Series"

It will be remembered that the definition of the differentiated A involved two phases of the same situation, namely, A as distinguished from B, which we have just discussed in terms of A's individuality, and A as related to B, which I should now like to consider. Just what does Lloyd's relationalism mean by the notion that the individuality of A implies its contrary, B—implies, in fact, relationship with a total world?   It would seem that contrariety could hardly mean more than the most abstract relatability that anything has to anything else, namely, otherness.   But Lloyd means much more than merely *abstract linguistic relatability*. He does not look at the matter from the standpoint of a logic of terms or term relations, but as a metaphysics of *living things*.   A and B are not terms, but *organisms*. Lloyd's logic, it will be recalled, proposed to take lessons from biology.   The relation of contrariety then, holding for any A, bears witness that any A *must* be metaphysically related to what Lloyd calls an "infinite series" of terms.[28]

When we say that A is distinguished from B—that it is individual and unique—we are really implying, if I may interpret Lloyd's position, that A is not C, not D, not E, and so on.   But where shall we stop?   If we should stop short of infinite degrees of difference between A and B, the serial chains that bind Lloyd's universe together would be broken. Some parts of his world would be disparate from the rest and therefore unintelligible.   Since A is not B, not C, and not D, we are obliged to continue indefinitely.   A is not anything else in the universe; not-A enters Lloyd's system to exhaust the possibilities of difference between A and all else.

To put it another way, since A is distinguished from B, there must be at least some difference between them.   But, since A is unique, however small that difference may appear to be it is always infinite in the sense that A, being unique, is never commensurable with B.   At this point Lloyd's conception of individuality has necessitated that his world be invested not only with A but with A's polar opposite, its "negative,"[29] as he likes to call it, and by virtue of this, his world becomes infinitely differentiated, filled to bursting with cabbages and kings.   A double conclusion results: A is not only infinitely distinguished from the rest of the universe to be just this thing and no other, but it is, as well, divided internally into an infinite number of parts.   With each part of Lloyd's universe becoming serially infinite inside and a part of an infinite series outside, A can now be seen to be exclusively itself only with reference to an infinite amount of difference; A maintains its 'thisness' only by virtue of every other 'thatness' having relations with it. With each entity understood as a small system within an infinite series of other systems, Lloyd's universe is completely unfolded into a restlessly relating, always interrelating series of concentric or tangential systems, which his own literary efforts attempt to duplicate and which he feels his conception of the philosophic enterprise must echo.

5. *Infinity as a Function*

We have seen the need for a notion of infinity because of the place the infinite series plays in Lloyd's thought. It is now possible to describe what he calls infinity as a process, "a principle," or "a function."[30] To treat infinity as a noun instead of a verb would imply that the metaphysical series of relating things is not infinite at all—that it has a beginning and an end and is therefore treated merely as another member of a series, as a part instead of a "whole." Such a series would be infinite in the sense of endless accumulation. To combat this notion of infinity, Lloyd asserts that "infinity [is] a process,"[31] not a thing. It is that activity of *each* thing which makes it not only a unity of its own parts but a part of an infinitely differentiated universe. Since each term functions as a *unity* and not as a *collection* of parts, each functions infinitely in that it not only relates itself to every other term in the series but relates all to a common whole. Infinity, then, becomes a predicate of each term insofar as that term is understood to be related to every other.[32] Infinity is not to be understood as a spatial notion; Lloyd sees this as a contradiction in terms. "Infinity . . . is not a quantity, being an open denial of the very limitations that make quantity."[33] Nor is it to be understood as a mathematical definition of a series without a last term:

Thus a so-called infinite term, a last term or limit, of a series can not possibly be a term of the series . . . . [The infinite] adds

something besides maximum or minimum size to the finite . . . .
[It reveals] something essential to the series, general to all the
terms, and formally different.[34]

Infinity as a principle turns the terms into a "system rather
than a series," turns each term into relations rather than
things, "ratios rather than quanta."[35]   As is consistent with
Lloyd's 'logic of life,' "infinity" connotes the quality of the
relationship holding between terms and is therefore part of
the definition of each term.   Infinity is qualitative—a way of
acting, an adverb[36] modifying existence—and is not to be
understood as an additive or cumulative noun.   Pointing up
the meaning he wants to explore, Lloyd sometimes uses the
term "ratio" for the quality of infinity which the relations of
things manifest, to distinguish it from what he likes to call
"mere mass."   Thus each term in an infinite series of terms
has the quality of infinity in its relationship to other things.
Infinity, Lloyd says, if understood quantitatively,

is only an indirection for [a backhanded innuendo for] (some)
constant relation, . . . or differentiation . . . .   The infinitely
small or great taken quantitatively (or massively) is only sym-
bolic of a uniform process, of an activity under a fixed law, of
a principle immanent in every term of the series . . . .[37]

Infinity is the cement that binds the terms of any series into
a unity:

Projection to infinity seems to me to be only a process by which
the constructive or constitutive principle of a series is positively
asserted *as a principle* . . . abstracted . . . from *all* the particular
cases to which the principle is applicable.   At infinity we have,
not another term or case . . . but the order or system of the
series.[38]

Lloyd attempts to make infinity experiential by maintaining
that it is a property predicable of dynamic system, of organi-
zation-in-process.

    Though I shall do no more with this concept here, it is
one of the keys to Lloyd's metaphysical position.   On the
meaning of this point rests the answer to the question of the

sense in which Lloyd is an idealist. Infinity as a quality of relationship is, for Lloyd, real and experientially guaranteed; yet, in many respects, it is going to function as his 'absolute.' In honor of this concept Lloyd calls his position an "infinitism"[39] rather than either a monism or a pluralism. His view is actually a pluralism in which the 'many' are unified by the function of infinity.

6. Microcosm and Macrocosm

We are now in a position to describe the special adaptation Lloyd makes of the old distinction between microcosm and macrocosm. While the first represents the system of terms extending infinitely "inward" (relationally), the second represents the system extending infinitely "outward" (in process). Both are implied by the nature of individuality. Since the whole-containing part makes sense only qualitatively and functionally,[40] A is a "whole-containing" seed, unifying and organizing its infinite parts, a seed from which they have been developed. Further, since the universe is defined by the same serial process which organizes A, the universe, too, is whole-containing. To put this another way, since A relates itself to all things, A has infinite predicates. That being so, A functions analogously with the universe, to which infinite predicates can also be ascribed. Thus each thing operates analogously with a universe of things. The larger implications of this conception will be unfolded in Chapter V, which, in its turn, will be more meaningful in the light of the present analysis. For example, we shall see that for Lloyd the patterns of individual development and historical development reflect each other. Lloyd's "psychologism" (see Chapter II) will prove to be consistent with his historicism. As he expresses it, the proper study of history is man.

7. The Overdifferentiated

Since infinity now means an ever-constant quality which all relational activity manifests, how can we speak of an A which is *completely* internally differentiated, or yet of an A which is *completely* externally related without violating the meaning of empirical existence as it has been defined?   Both would be overcomplete and therefore deprived of existence in an ever incomplete world.   The 'overdifferentiated A,' as I may call it, functions in Lloyd very much as does the undifferentiated A.   This largest extreme represents the function of infinity hypostatized into an entity: ". . . as last term it is . . . only theoretically possible, never practically so, and is accordingly never found or attained, being only posited, asserted or indicated . . . .   [It must be taken] *cum grano salis.*"[41]   Hence, although it is necessitated by the analysis, as a thing it is a contradiction in terms.   The completed A could not possibly be a movement, an organism, a life.   Thus the infinitely differentiated A is twin to the undifferentiated A in that they are both what might be called 'limiting conditions,' necessary to an account of process but nevertheless empirically fictitious entities.

8. *Intension and Extension*

Since the dual aspects of ontological process by which a 'thing' is seen to be an organism are so basic to Lloyd's thought and represent the most pervasive of all polarities, let me exhibit how varied a part they play by mentioning some of the many analogical term sets he uses for them. Each set is colored by the hue Lloyd feels most characteristic of the particular context.   Although his thought would permit me to start anywhere in enumeration of these sets, the broadest, vaguest, and in one sense the most innocuous terms used to describe these movements are "an upward and outward" and a "downward and inward" movement.[42]   However, the spatial reference makes Lloyd uncomfortable for reasons we shall later discover.   More to his liking, if repeated use is any evidence, are "intension" and "extension,"[43] which, in contrast to the practice of the logic books, he uses to apply to almost anything but verbal terms.   While, understandably enough, the extension of a series is the number of terms in it qua numerical aggregation, the intension of the series represents, for Lloyd, the function of infinity or the "ratio" that each term manifests. Obviously, the full meaning of the function of infinity or what Lloyd means by "unity" is fundamental for the understanding of his thought. So far, perhaps, it has been the only questionable notion in this empirical account of a relational world.

Lloyd's repertoire of analogical terms for the correlative movements which define existence is indefinitely varied; "centripetal" and "centrifugal," "structure" and "function," "impulse" and "compulsion," "spontaneity" and "control," "spendthrift" and "miser," and others will appear as the discussion progresses.

9. *Analogy*

With a serial world now unfolded, the foundations of Lloyd's theory of analogy in the function of infinity as well as the theoretical justification of his literary adaptation of it can be elucidated. The source of Lloyd's conviction that analogous relationships hold between all the terms in a series[44] is found in the fact that each term shares the function of infinity. Since both part and whole act "as a whole" or "function infinitely," the relations maintained by each term are analogous to those maintained by every other. Infinity, we said, is the cement by which all terms are bound together in a continuous process which makes them serial. As a characteristic of each term, infinity guarantees a thread of continuity running through all.

To put it another way, since each term plays a part in the function of a larger series of terms, since A as individual involves A and B in a larger unity, each term in its own individual way echoes the larger operation. Therefore, if the series is infinite, each term has a diverse but analogous part in these serial relations. For Lloyd, "analogous" really means 'one-lawed.' Each term shares the same law in the sense that it operates in the same *way* as do all the others. Infinity is not a term in the series, but is apparently the law of the series present in every term, for a term "is made infinite only serially or gradually, that is only by some persisting function, operation or principle, [which is] the series's unity or law . . . ."[45]   For both Lloyd and Leibniz a thoroughgoing adherence to a *'lex analogiae'* is born of a philosophy of internal relations.   Both attribute individuality to terms only insofar as they are united under a general law.

On the basis of the conviction that everything is related to everything else analogically, Lloyd borrows terminology from any phase of experience to interpret any other.   His selection depends on the psychological suggestibility of the term, its richness of extralogical overtones, and its fruitfulness for interrelating his ideas.   Although as a result no term ever means what one might expect it to mean, and although Lloyd must therefore entirely possess his readers to possess them at all, such license permits him elaborately metaphorical and suggestive writing.

10. *Unity and Community; Monism and Pluralism*

All things, we have seen, function organically insofar as they exist at all.   Since unity and community are mutually implicative[46] and correlative, a world is not defined either as a unity (or monistically) or as a community (or pluralistically) but as a community of differentiated unities and a unified set of differentiations.

At least one implication of this position can now be stated, namely, that Lloyd's view redefines and cuts across the traditional viewpoints of monism, dualism, and pluralism. These, as Lloyd sees them, are not descriptions of the floor plan of a universe, not accounts of a fixed structure, but epistemological devices for the explanation of anything.   Monism, pluralism, and dualism are generic characteristics of all being.   Monism connotes the oneness or unity of anything; pluralism connotes the manyness or community of anything; and dualism connotes the fact that unity and community are irreducible principles.   All three are epistemological abstractions—monism for the complete and total relationship between things which overlooks their separating uniqueness, pluralism for the disparateness and individuality of each thing which overlooks its relation with all else, and dualism for the polar activity to which a plural universe and all in it is subjected. Hence monism, pluralism, and dualism are abstractions for the various phases of a world of interrelational activity.[47] Monism is a "solvent and metaphysical peacemaker"[48] which functions to correct for an overemphasis on difference. Pluralism acts as the metaphysical Mars, shattering experience into many quarreling parts and serving to remind the philosopher that difference is as important as unity. Dualism is the metaphysical midwife bringing new definitions of monism and pluralism into existence.[49]

Lloyd feels that his functional view of these "free principles of activity" permits a more significant interpretation, and he attributes this insight to pragmatism. Pragmatism is indifferent to these traditional metaphysical rubrics for the following reason:

For pragmatism . . . neither dualism nor monism can be anything but free principles or general motives of all experience . . . both of them being always, let me not say merely present, but active in experience, and so being realities of experience in a sense that no static metaphysics could possibly imagine . . . .[50]

Pragmatism makes each of these principles real and vital in every problem in life. Each becomes functional and epistemological rather than structural and metaphysical, for pragmatism "so nearly identifies experience with reality as to render a metaphysics [static variety] gratuitous if not also unseemly."[51]

Obviously, in attempting to redefine structural concepts into functional ones, Lloyd has guaranteed that he is neither monist, dualist, nor pluralist in the usual sense of those terms. There is, however, one sense in which Lloyd appears to favor monism and to be a "metaphysical peacemaker": he exhibits a tremendous interest in the idea of a 'unification' of things.

'Unification,' however, for Lloyd, is simply another term for 'interrelation.' But unity and difference, matter and mind, reason and sense are all related for Lloyd in a way which can easily be misconstrued as an assertion of monism.[52] Lloyd constantly speaks of "one life," which seems, on the surface of things, to constitute some kind of monistic absolute. But his interest is primarily in the 'relating,' not the 'related,' in 'unifying,' not 'unity.' He is concerned with empirically verifiable verbs, not extraempirical nouns. Unity is a frame of reference—the systematization or ordering principle—of any plurality, in terms of which it must be understood. Things have a character when they *act* like unities for their parts. Plurality, on the other hand, represents the things related, systematized, and ordered. Whether or not Lloyd succeeds in remaining consistently within this view is a question upon which the significance of this analysis hardly depends.

11. *Life*

We have just described a world in abstract relational terms and must now make a transition from these to living relations. It seems to me that Lloyd accomplishes this transition via three emphases: (1) he identifies relationship with movement; (2) he identifies movement with self-movement; and (3) he identifies self-movement with living movement. Inasmuch as Lloyd can guarantee that all things are self-moving, he can meaningfully extend his vitalism to say that "all things live," and he might meaningfully call his logic of such relationship 'life-logic.'

Let us transcribe the meaning of Lloyd's world of relational activity into an outline of his metaphysical view as developed so far. The world and each thing in it has been conceived of as a dynamic, self-directing, interrelating system. All things *act* 'organically.'[53] Since a world is not only animate but self-animate in the sense that it relates and interrelates itself, "the universe lives."[54] But a problem arises. Is Lloyd bestowing life distributively or collectively to a universe? The answer depends upon what is meant by 'life.' Lloyd himself is characteristically unclear in his use of the term. He never distinguishes the senses in which he is using it. He will specifically deny that *each* thing lives, and mean what is customarily meant by 'live' rather than what he has defined as his meaning of 'life.'[55]

If we interpret the term 'life' narrowly, to mean a state characterized by such activities as locomotion, digestion, and reproduction, the answer is obvious. But if we mean by 'life' *any* kind of relational activity—relationship in general—even if we mean by that only the 'movement' involved in everything's being what it is, then Lloyd necessarily implies that all things have life distributively. To be at all is to be animate. To be at all involves relations and interrelations. Perhaps another way of putting this would be to say that each and all things live in the sense that they have a history, a place in space and time which individualizes them, relates them, and commits them to a career.

In support of the idea that each thing must live in some sense, Lloyd insists that the dichotomy between the organic and the inorganic must be demolished:

What men really mean by the inorganic . . . is [that] so much of what the world contains . . . fails to come up to an idea of the organic that is determined by certain discovered and at least partially understood forms. Simply the inorganic is not organic as certain recognized specific forms are organic. Still, even in thinking of it [the inorganic] at all, men at once relate it to the organic that is known to them, and so definitely assert a *fact or principle of organism* that is deeper and broader than any of the already recognized organic forms.[56]

In thus demolishing the distinction between man and clod, Lloyd places man firmly in a natural world and emphasizes the continuity of all existence:

. . . every individual is one of the distinguished things [in a world of infinite differentiation]. Even men are things, distinct from other men, or from animals or plants or clods of earth.

True, a man has a greater individual power over nature than an animal or a clod, but this means no more and no less than that a man is the single organized activity of a larger, more complex group of things. A man is still a relational part [like all others] of the whole. His greater power, instead of isolating him, only relates him more closely, and his activity only realizes him as an organ [one of many] of the whole.[57]

Lloyd seems to subscribe to three senses in which a thing can be said to "live." For him all things live distributively, collectively, and, under certain conditions, in a way which I shall call 'vicariously':

(1) Each thing lives in a distributive sense inasmuch as it is a small system acting to systematize its parts. In this most fundamental sense everything that exists lives, since to exist at all is to exhibit individuality, systematization, and hence character.[58] Anything that is, is already a small persistent unity of the relations between its parts. Each thing lives in the sense that it "acts" organically in persisting through change.[59]

(2) All things live in a collective sense inasmuch as they contribute to the being of other systems. Because each thing is related to any other system, it contributes to the organization and individuality of the larger, more inclusive system. This may be illustrated by an example from what is usually understood as an organic world: The cells of the brain are small systems with their own individuality and life. Hence all cells have life distributively. Since they enter into the system that is the brain, they have life collectively in its functioning. For Lloyd this applies to the 'inanimate' as well. The stone in a wall has life in a distributive sense in that it is a unity for its parts; it has life in a collective sense in the unity, organization, and individuality of the wall in which it is a part. In these two senses, each and every thing lives by virtue of its character as both part and whole.

(3) All inorganic things live insofar as they have community with the 'organic.' In this sense, stones and clods live not by means of their own nature but because all living

things use them and man knowingly uses them. Inorganic
things live vicariously, if you will, through their community
with organic things, through sharing a life with the organic.[60]
If I may look ahead of our story, when all 'organic' things use
and man knowingly uses his environment, the 'living thing'
becomes a whole for its parts by including them in its own
dynamically living operations. Although the clod, in one
sense, is no less or no differently alive than man, it is alive
in a less involved and less complex manner. When man
expresses life by planning, manipulating, and valuing his universe, the clod shares these living relations by being caught
up in man's unity to the extent that he sees it, digs it, utilizes
it for his needs. The clod, potentially or actually, lives as it
is physically, intellectually, and evaluatively enmeshed with
man's living activities. 'Inanimate' things coöperate with
the 'animate' to form one larger systematic unity, which is
physically expressed if not completely physical. "All things
live" vicariously insofar as they are utilized by living things
at all, and even more significantly insofar as they are utilized
by the knowing-valuing agent. While the first sense of life
springs from the unity of a thing, and the second from its
community, the third springs from the fact of relationship
between unity and community. Whether or not Lloyd
intends to distinguish these three senses, or is even aware of
them, they emerge nonetheless.

To return to the direction of Lloyd's view, then, organic
life means physicality imbued with a principle of organic
activity which defines and relates things, which makes them
intelligible, which gives them individuality and character.
But since they are dynamic relations, since they are self-
defining and self-relating, they are *not only intelligible* but
intelligent:[61]

. . . the deeper truth in the simple fact of the world's composition
is the fact of relationship, which makes the unity of the world
consistent with the differentiation of its parts; and because the
relationship is dynamic instead of formal, being even identical
with the world's activity instead of a passive condition, the world

of things is intelligible, and, by virtue of its inherent intelligibility, also intelligent . . . things are not mere relations; they are not merely related; they are themselves in so far as real a relating activity, which is mind.[62]

Perhaps one of the most striking aspects of Lloyd's widened conception of life which obliterates the distinction between animate and inanimate is the adaptation he makes of the Aristotelian tradition. For both Lloyd and Aristotle the defining characteristic, essence, or formal cause of a thing is what it does. Both find that function defines existence;[63] both can speak analogically of the 'psyche' of the axe, for example. Both can understand man as one link in the chain of existence; both can place man in a natural framework. But Lloyd nonetheless makes several adaptations of this basic tradition.

First, Lloyd pushes Aristotelian functionalism into vitalism, by taking the term 'soul' to mean life in an extended sense. Relational activity is, for Lloyd, very much what psyche is for Aristotle; but for Lloyd psyche includes dynamic existence as one of the functions of a thing. Hence all things live in the sense of having active systematization (and therefore relationship) as one of their functions—their minimal function. The as yet unused and unknown clod functions in a minimal sense: it is part of the relational activities of a world.

Secondly, whereas 'psyche' for Aristotle represents the defining principle of a living thing and the way it can be spoken about, for Lloyd it represents the way anything ontologically is. Whereas Aristotle seeks essences and definitions, Lloyd emphasizes life as transcending formal definition. Whereas for Aristotle language can define life, for Lloyd it cannot entirely do so.

Thirdly, biology suggests Aristotle's method of analysis, but in Lloyd it becomes part of the content of his thought. Biology not only motivates Aristotle to describe the parts of animals, but also influences his technique of definition. Biology and metaphysics become synonymous for Lloyd.

His interest in biology arises in an intellectual climate befogged by Hegel's logic, Fichte's romanticism, and Social Darwinism. The resultant position, influenced by all of these, is a metaphorical and cosmic biologism quite alien to what Aristotle would have understood the meaning and function of biology to be. Lloyd uses Aristotle to develop a type of extensive vitalism and panpsychism[64] which Aristotle would have disavowed—and which could only be developed in the neighborhood of the twentieth century.

It is indeed no wonder that Lloyd subtitles *Dynamic Idealism* "An Elementary Course in the Metaphysics of Psychology," for 'psychology' means to Lloyd what the Aristotelian tradition means by it, namely, a study of the 'soul' in the Aristotelian sense of that term. Soul, Lloyd says, is "the substantial reality, the fulfilling life of the body, or life as responsible to its incidents, or body as organic . . . ."[65] Lloyd equates movement or function with life and life with mind by maintaining that movement, life, and mind exhibit relational process on varying levels of complexity. Thus mind, in the most basic sense, means the self-directing, indwelling, self-realizing process exhibited by all things in their very existence. Mind is expressed on a more involved level by the forms of life which we ordinarily call 'animate,' and on a still more complex level by man. All entities form a chain of relation with each other, which we shall call "dimensional difference."[66] Each is a variation of the same basic principle of action called "life." While all things engage in relational functions by merely existing, animals display a dimensional variation of these by moving through and eating in a world, and man exhibits a still further dimensional variation by thinking and valuing a world. Hence, thought or mind is not only a part of man's definition, but part of the definition of a world.[67] A world not only has order, and hence mind, in its own right, but man, as part of that world, thinks it and thereby exhibits the world as thinking. Lloyd turns inward to examine man, for man provides the fullest exemplification of a world's relational activity.[68]

12. *The System of Systems*

Lloyd's view of a world composed of interlocking systems leads him to a kind of system of systems. Since each thing is a system only insofar as it relates itself to B, C, D, and so on, where are we to stop? Lloyd says that process never ends. Hence we must relate A to an entire universe. What does this "entire series" or "entire universe" or "all" or "the whole" or the "infinite whole" mean? "The whole" has been defined as an adverb, as a way of acting, as the systematic character which every term in a series exhibits. "The whole" has been stated as a *principle* within experience and hence empirically verifiable. Yet we find Lloyd saying that "we have been *assuming* what perhaps we had *no right to assume,* namely, the reality and integrity of the whole."[69] And with more methodological caution than a purely empirical statement of relationalism would seem to require, he says, "While not positively certain, then, on the evidence, even while, as some might insist, very uncertain, there still is *possible* the reality of a whole."[70] We find Lloyd distinguishing between a small whole and something which seems to be *the* whole. "Only a small whole, which can never be *the* whole, can be tyrannical over parts."[71] Polarities are spoken of as the "greater" and the "lesser."

In short, the theme of "the whole" is so pervasive in Lloyd's thought, the meaning and expression which he gives it so diverse, that not only is its explication one of the most difficult phases of an interpretation of his work, but its meaning is of primary importance in understanding his thought. On the one hand, Lloyd denounces absolutes as static, fixed, final, and outside of experience. Methodologically he repudiates them and historically he attacks them. On the other hand, his entire point of view seems to be built on an assumption of an absolute, redefined as it were, and placed squarely, if uneasily, in experience. On the one hand he asserts a universal relativism[72] and on the other he insists that "philosophy can never stop short of a theory of the universe."[73] Its duty to the whole forces it to encompass all else if it is to maintain integrity. What does Lloyd mean by "the" universe? Is he speaking empirically or mystically? Does he mean that philosophy must express a general and all-pervasive theory of system, or does he mean something more than that, or does he mean that *and* something more?

Ambiguity reigns whenever Lloyd speaks substantivally of "the whole." Granted the difficulty of speaking solely in adverbial terms, does he mean "all things" in a distributive or a collective sense, or is he introducing a third and perhaps a supposedly indefinable sense? Does "all" mean each one of many? Or all as a group? Or all as a term standing for something besides each and many? Does "the whole" refer to anything acting systematically, all together acting systematically, or some kind of system of systems? Does he mean to imply all three senses? Is he speaking empirically *and* mythically?

Let me indicate some of the variety of meanings Lloyd gives to the term; let me also show how he contradicts each of these. Then perhaps we can, in a kind of meta-language, determine what the concept means for him.

(1) "The whole" seems to refer to anything acting systematically; and this, it will be recalled, permitted Lloyd to say that a thing was "*functionally* a whole-containing part." Yet it cannot mean this alone, for Lloyd maintains that a thing cannot be a system except as it relates itself to all other systems. By virtue of such infinite relation, each thing was defined as a system.

(2) "The whole" seems to mean the largest frame of reference that can be distinguished; the *complete* whole could not exist, since it implies that process has stopped. Yet it cannot mean this alone, because Lloyd would not have us think of the whole in terms of "mere size."

(3) "The whole" seems to mean all there is in a cumulative sense, because, as will be seen later, relationship is spatially and temporally real or "actual." Yet it cannot mean merely this, since such a whole is an accumulation or "aggregation,"[74] but not a "system."

(4) "The whole" seems to mean an infinite system of all *activity*. The system of systems in this sense would have to be defined as a verb and would have to be present in any and every experience It would have to include all past, present, and future activity understood as entirely interrelated and seen *in toto*. But what could *in toto* mean when a world is described as unendingly in process, except possibly the total *potentiality* of all movement? Yet here again Lloyd would, I think, deny this, on the grounds that it implies an absolute possibility, a something outside experience.

Now let us examine from a larger point of view what these four alternatives and their explicit denials could mean. Is Lloyd *redefining* an absolute in empirical dress or is he insisting that absolutes cannot be defined? Is he in spite of himself defining a new brand of absolute better suited to a world conceived functionally rather than structurally, namely, the total possibility for movement in a world? Or is he showing by continual contradiction that an absolute cannot be defined and hence cannot exist? Were the last interpretation the correct one, we would have to abandon his theory of system understood relatively and empirically also, since our first three interpretations of his meaning of "the whole" exhibited no fewer contradictions than the last. At the very least, contradiction cannot mean denial,[75] for if it did, we could find no meaning for Lloyd's concept of "the whole."

Lloyd is apparently formulating a theory of relational system which indicates the presence, in experience, of something larger than experience. He is trying to show from a theory of relations that some kind of absolute is required to make any system of relations intelligible and, at the same time, to deny that it can be empirically described, to assert that, being "the whole," it resists delimitation. Such an absolute would have to be described poetically and mythically. In short, Lloyd would tell a true myth in order to subscribe to relativism. Were Lloyd's absolute *not* a myth, it would be subject to the same criticisms he makes of older absolutisms. Were it not a *true* myth, his ideal would be isolated from the real, body from mind, and thought from experience. Were Lloyd's system of systems *not* mythical, it would have to be meaningless; were it not a *true* myth, it would be outside of experience and be equally meaningless.

Lloyd is fully aware of these methodological difficulties, as I shall indicate in developing his theory of truth. The concept of 'the universe as a total whole' is the myth which makes any system meaningful. Let us not forget that philosophy to him is appreciative and not just descriptive; it is "speculative, even in a sense imaginative, inexact, poetic [and] not soberly literal."[76] Philosophy is the poetry which the thinker has the duty to enunciate and which, when enunciated, reaps a rich harvest of paradoxical humor, making the philosopher a comedian. As the true myth, philosophy would be applicable to all experience and science, but proved by neither. Apparently, since an absolute is not permitted Lloyd empirically, he develops it poetically. But since he grants that poetry is built from prose, philosophy from science, his theory of relational systems as an empirical, analytical enterprise is not invalidated thereby. In fact, his world could be given two equally satisfactory presentations: first, as a redefined idealism with emphasis on his monism, and, secondly, as an empirical but poetic naturalism with emphasis on pluralism. If he could be said to subscribe to an absolute in any sense, it would have to be defined as the possibility for growth inherent in any self-animate, pluralistic system, in any individual thing. Lloyd's absolute is, then, hardly identical in formulation or intent with the absolutes from which it is in revolt. It is found in things; it is a way they act and interact. If I may apply to Lloyd's work a phrase from his own conception of process, the "spirit" of the absolute may remain, but it has indeed gained "new flesh."

From within Lloyd's thought, absolutes and relatives form a polarity relationship. Neither polar term would exist isolated from the other, but together both would exist by virtue of the principle underlying the polarity.   To anticipate this account a little, such a world would have to be described as both 'relatively absolute' and 'absolutely relative.'   In these terms, how can we call Lloyd *either* relativist or absolutist, or, for that matter, either idealist or naturalist? As he puts it, "Current philosophy . . . knows not whether it is idealism or realism.   A most happy predicament!"[77] While Lloyd enjoys the comedy of the situation, let whatever reader will, ponder on whether a relatively absolute world— or an absolutely relative one—is described either idealistically or naturalistically.

13. *Will*

It should not be surprising that Lloyd's extensive vitalism harbors a basic anthropomorphic notion which he calls "will."   Since the concept is never systematically developed and since reference to it is dispersed and cryptic, it will be necessary to reconstruct and systematize its meaning.

Lloyd uses the term "will" in both a particular and a general sense.   In the general sense, it is an adverb qualifying "life," which has already been interpreted dynamically rather than substantivally.   It represents the vitality and energy by which the organism engages in all its diversified types of relational activity.   It describes a quality of relational activity.   Perhaps the general sense of the term can best be explained by pointing out that it is similar in meaning to the Latin *animus*[78] and to the Greek *horme*.   "Will" connotes the energy and force intrinsic to self-movement or living movement.

Will is neither an absolute in an idealistic tradition nor a universal in a realistic tradition, but a trait exhibited generally by a universe of particular things because it is exhibited by each particular thing.   Will is not hypostatized by Lloyd into an entity, nor does it exist apart from experience. It is not a causative agent.   It does not mechanically push the organism either externally or internally.   It is not a creative power; and it does not make the relations which it modifies.

Will is not an epistemological category and is not to be confused with either reason or emotion: "Will [is] not a passive faith nor yet a formal reason,'[but] is the primary faculty of adventure.... Faith may recall and cherish and suggest; reason is ever an excellent guide, a finder of ways and means; but will ventures and realizes."[79] Although thinking and emotive activities require movement of will, will is a broader notion. It is not to be identified with thinking, because the organism relates itself physically as well as intellectually to an environment, and will is required for all types of relationships. It is not to be confused with emotional craving, because it is the physical, intellectual, and spiritual straining and striving of the *total organism* to reach its fulfillment. Will is expressed not only emotionally and intellectually, but spatially, temporally, and physically, also. It is the total 'craving' of the entire organism to exist, to develop, and to fulfill itself, to self-relate, to interrelate, and to grow. Will, Lloyd says, is activity,[80] while "feeling and reason [are] indeed only its attendants."[81]

Let us consider the meaning of will in a particular entity, after which we can consider Lloyd's poetic generalization of the concept. Will represents the energy with which any organism engages in relating activities. Hence it is the empirical basis for the separation of this *particular collection* of relating activities from the web of its interrelations.[82] It represents each organism energetically engaged in its own expression and fulfillment. Thus, in Lloyd, any particular thing is made empirical, made self-active, and made describable by will.

Will represents the particular organism seen as a center of energy—a configuration of cross-relating energies. Will is "the power of action,"[83] Lloyd says; it makes the organism move, it is its "spirit."[84] As its spirit, will is what makes any organism not merely move as living, but move in *this particular* way. Will is particularized movement; but it is, further, *striving* particularized movement. Equally important, will is the qualitative aspect of activity. Will is the driving compulsion of an organism to relate itself internally —to become *an* individual unity—and to relate itself externally—to become part of a community. Will, then, is the immanent guiding spirit of any organic action. It is the striving of everything further to define its own individuality by greedily relating itself to more and more. It is the "vital" aspect of the organism because the organism behaves in an ever-ingesting biological fashion.

Since will gives an organism individuality and community, it makes it at once empirically real, epistemologically intelligible, and experientially immediate. As the 'lifeness' of this particular thing, as the "vital impulse" or the "impulse to self-expression,"[85] will holds each particular thing together during action and change. It preserves all the characteristics which make this thing not that one. But since a thing gains internal unity by means of the difference it bears to other things, will is essential to the preservation of organic difference. Will not only gives a thing its 'thisness' but gives all other things 'thatness' relative to it. Will represents that aspect of the life of any organism which no other can exactly duplicate. It guarantees that a universe is in process of all possible permutations and combinations of organic interrelationship. Will is the hunger for relationship by which a world is bound into interlocking systems, by which it is made systematic.

Will for Lloyd is not to be identified with the irrational as distinct from the rational; on the contrary, it serves as the *basis for* the intelligibility of things. Nor yet is will superrational in an extraempirical sense, for it is the foundation of empirical existence. Will is individualized "spontaneity" manifested by every organism in its 'eagerness' to engage in relational activity with a world of companionate things. Will is "adaptive activity that is at once conscious of its meaning and constrained by its consciousness."[86]

Will, as the relational predicate of life, is itself subject to being understood in a more generalized sense. Speaking of the vitality and hunger of all things, Lloyd somewhere describes will as "the passion of a universe!" The concept is valuable to Lloyd because for him it helps to erase the distinction between the animate and the inanimate, the organic and the mechanical. It serves to accent his conception of relations as unified and organic rather than discontinuous and formal.

It may be profitable to compare Lloyd's conception of will with certain other conceptions which naturally suggest themselves, namely, those of Schopenhauer, Trendelenburg, and the early Dewey. In one basic sense Lloyd comes close to Schopenhauer's voluntarism. For both, will has cosmic significance; for both, will exists on varying levels from the inorganic to the human. But Schopenhauer finds will a property of the universe, whereas Lloyd finds it a property of individual entities—a necessary condition of individuality. Schopenhauer's meaning most clearly emerges as distinct from Lloyd's when he identifies will with Kant's "thing-in-itself" apart from the individual expressions of it. Lloyd's generalized conception of will, which superficially seems so similar to Schopenhauer's, is actually an account of the broadest traits of a world of individual entities—not of a world in contradistinction to individual entities.

For Schopenhauer, will is impulse, emotion, desire—even instinct[87]—and as such it forms the background of his anti-intellectualistic strain. For Lloyd, will is expressed equally in any activity, whether it be emotive, cognitive, or simply "relational activity" or existence. Hence, insofar as the nature of things (organisms) is defined by will, Lloyd's conception guarantees the knowability and, in that sense, the rationality of a world. Will for Lloyd is not feeling opposed to intelligence, not irrationality opposed to rationality, but the activity of an intelligible world of relating and interrelating entities. Unlike Schopenhauer, Lloyd, more sensitive to a scientific emphasis on 'force' and 'energy,' finds it easy to discriminate energy from emotion. As a result he revises the account of will stemming from a romantic tradition into one far more in harmony with his basic Aristotelianism.

For Trendelenburg, Schopenhauer's romantic concept of will[88] as a cosmic principle is transformed into the category of activity—a technical concept serving to link human purpose to historical movement and movement in life to motion in things generally. Lloyd develops this emphasis, but broadens the concept of will by using it to unify the living and the nonliving as participants in one world, making it at the same time the defining characteristic of any and all individuality. For Trendelenburg, "The will is then first will in the full sense of the term, when it is able to act in response to the motion of thought . . . ."[89] For Lloyd, will is the active character of any and all organic relations. The stone, the tree, and the child all express will on levels which vary according to the quality of their potential interrelatedness. The better defined or more explicitly manifested the organism's relations to a world, the more will is *significantly* expressed. Trendelenburg makes a distinction between the will and the good will, the good will, according to G. S. Morris, acting "in opposition to the desires and independently of sensuous motives."[90] Lloyd could not make this distinction, nor claim the consequences of it.

Lloyd's view of will is close to that of Dewey as expressed in his early work *Psychology:* " . . . the essence of self is the self-determining activity of will."[91] Both Lloyd and Dewey find that will in some sense expresses the "unity of self"; for both it is activity. But although for Dewey will may, in this sense, be the maker of the psychological individuality of the human personality, it hardly seems to be the maker of the metaphysical individuality of any entity. Whereas, I think, Lloyd and Dewey agree in outline on the meaning of will psychologically (in fact for Dewey will is even an "objectifying activity"[92]), Lloyd both generalizes the conception and inflates it to encompass a cosmic activity of self-unity and self-relatedness. All in all, the distinctness of Lloyd's view of will from any of these others seems to be in its metaphysical rather than in its emotive, moral, or psychological character.[93]

Process

1. *"Dynamic" Relations and the Nature of Logic*

Chapter I defined an empirical world, "Reality"[1] Lloyd calls it, as a dynamic interrelating community, a self-moving system of interpenetrating systems of relations describable equally well as a community of differentiating unities or as a unity of communal differentiations. To state the conclusions structurally, the world is completely related, is an infinite "hash," as Lloyd dubs Anaxagoras' "infinite mixture,"[2] which he takes to be a primitive statement of a relational world.

In what sense does Lloyd mean that everything is related? How is a planet related to a chair, the moon to an amoeba? Lloyd does not mean that all things are directly and immediately related, but rather that they are indirectly and mediately related. To put their relationship one way, both moon and amoeba act systematically. Each is a whole for its parts; each exhibits the operation of infinity. Moon and amoeba are related because they each *analogously share in a principle of systematization.* To put the relationship in another way, both planet and chair were defined as systems by the same process which distinguished each from all other systems. Hence planet and chair are related by *belonging to one world.* To share a principle of systematization *is* to belong to one world.[3]

What is the nature of these relations?   First, Lloyd says that all things are not merely relat*ed*, but are relat*ing*.   A related world would be made up simply of component parts united by some external and arbitrary force.   But a thing, as we have pointed out, is more than a *sum* of parts.   It is a *system* of parts.   Hence, each thing unifies, organizes, and systematizes itself by being at once a system of relations for itself as whole and a relation in a larger whole.   Lloyd's world is self-relating by virtue of its individuality and differentiation.

Secondly, the relations of Lloyd's world cut across the categories of 'internal' or 'external' relations.   Internality makes a relation necessary, but not necessarily spatial or temporal.   Externality makes a relation spatial and temporal, but not necessary.   In Lloyd's world, however, relationship is both intrinsic and necessary to the things related, and spatiotemporal or "actual."[4]   Distinguishing "actual" from "formal" relations, Lloyd says:

Says some one here, and very appropriately: "There is a wide difference between saying that things are relations and that things are related.   Were they only relations, there could be no real things, no terms of relation, only pure formal relationship.   A world of mere relations must be impossible, since there must be things, definite, real, substantial, among which the formal relationship prevails.   There must be cousins as well as cousinship, legs and arms as well as the angles and other relations that enter into the determination of a chair, coins and commodities as well as prices."   But relationship is other than the mere formal external condition that the objector here has in mind.   Relationship is not formal, but dynamic.   It is, quite in and of itself, substantial.   It cannot be both real and formal.[5]

The conception of "dynamic relations" takes lessons from biology.   All relations are *active* in the same sense that parts of the body are active relations in the functioning of the body as a whole.   All relations are *self-active* in the sense that a biological organism is self-active.   All relations, as we shall see later, exhibit a permanence-change polarity in

the same sense that biological evolution takes place in time,
but is itself a spaceless, timeless principle of relationship.
All relational activity exhibits rationale and direction, which
Aristotle calls "entelechy" and which Lloyd terms "intelligence,"[6] and sometimes "consciousness."[7]   Hence, all things
are organic, and the self-activity of all organic things is their
consciousness.

Since the conception of relation takes lessons from biology, logic must take lessons from life.   Although Lloyd
never writes a systematic logic, his work makes repeated
efforts to direct logic away from formal channels, and yet
also away from traditional idealistic conceptions of an ontological superstructure which is logically prior to experience
and into which a world must fit regardless of whether
experience is mutilated by an appearance-reality dichotomy.
Lloyd finds neither view satisfactory.   Both deprive a world
of life and movement.   The first isolates language from
experience (Lloyd finds these functionally related), and the
second dichotomizes things and relations, and, in effect, the
real and the ideal.[8]   Pleading that "nothing in philosophy is
so much needed . . . as the adjustment of the science of
abstract thought to the science of organic action,"[9] Lloyd
proceeds to interpret logical judgment as a relation between
the knower and the known, a construction of reality, "a self-
conscious experience of reality."[10]   Language becomes a
translator of the environment about which we think; judgment, the "tension of adjustment"[11] between organism and
environment.   After one article on the subject,[12] Lloyd abandons direct attack, but contrast between his view and the
two other views occurs in many guises.

Lloyd's position on logic, as a third alternative to the
views of logic as ontology and logic as the theory of relations
between statements, is a particularly telling manifestation
of an idealism in transition.   As an idealist, Lloyd understands logic to be a combination of metaphysics and natural
history—metaphysics because it seeks generic traits of existence, and natural history because it is concerned with some-

thing actually unfolding. Since there is 'one life,'[13] there must be only one logic about that life. Since life is "organic," logic must not be "dead" but must describe organic relations. As an idealist, Lloyd finds the subject matter of logic to be the relations of existence and not the relations of statements. Its propositions must describe, not merely posit. And the relations between propositions must always concern necessity, never probability. The application of logic must extend to an entire universe and not merely to that part of a universe which is language in the sense of the verbal symbol.[14] Logic must unite all things into an order or system, and not treat language or any other part of a universe as an isolated phenomenon. A chair "is really no chair until through active use it is related to things beyond itself."[15] To paraphrase, thought is only thought when it is seen as one among other equally basic activities all of which have a biological origin and a natural fulfillment. Despite the fact that Lloyd's logic is metaphysically conditioned, since its major concern is the function of things and since it undertakes a rationale of self-directed biological activity it departs sharply from the epistemological logics of earlier idealisms. This, of course, is not to deny that Lloyd, both in terminology and technique of formulation, is considerably influenced by Hegelian and post-Hegelian logic.

But the contrast of Lloyd's logic with other logics must not lead us to see his logical enterprise in a false light. Lloyd's logic is "inner logic"[16] or inner process, the rationale of developing alteration in a world. Life being subject to polarity relationship, logic is therefore poetically mad and recalcitrantly contradictory: " . . . whenever the logic is, as in some measure it always must be, 'inner' instead of fully explicit and sophisticated, the resulting doctrines are bound to be figurative or poetic . . . ."[17]

2. *Polarity*

Lloyd never uses the term 'polarity.' Perhaps Hegelian habit ("negation," "antithesis") dominates him, but I believe he abstains with reason. In his terms, process understood most generically is a movement from unity to alienation to unity, from "at-one-ness with self" to "alienation from self" to "restoration to self."[18] It will be recalled that both 'unities' in the process were fictional limits necessitated by the serial character of his universe. Since neither term existed in space and time, existence was defined as all possible combinations within both limits operating as a community. This is also true of the terms composing a polarity relationship. Neither term exists in space and time; a polarity does not exist, but all possible combinations of polar relationship exist. To put this in another way, Lloyd refuses to describe a world in structural terms, preferring functional ones. He does not describe what a world is, but what it does, its 'becoming' in a Heraclitean and Hegelian sense. Although he does not reduce structure to function (because space and time are real, as we shall see later), structure is subordinate to function; it is only "the base"[19] upon which function depends, but to which it is never reducible.

Despite the fact that Lloyd does not use the term 'polarity,' his "negation process"[20] *operates* as a polarity. "Opposition is only a great although a subtle mixer,"[21] he says, and, "The things opposed, then, must truly be hopelessly involved in each other";[22] negation, instead of being a process of final separation is a way of relating and uniting.[23] Lloyd's "alienation processes" develop as a system of mutual implications fully deserving the term 'polarity,' which I shall take the liberty of using. Lloyd's own terms for polarity relational activity are confusing for two reasons. First, since he is describing a relationship that is a process, it has to "move" in some sense. Hence he is obliged to use different terms for different stages of that movement. Polarity relation must 'start' with the simple assertion of two opposed terms, which he often describes as a "dualism." When he refers to the process as continuing and becoming more interrelated, the situation is a "duality." Such terminological nuances can disconcert the reader. But, secondly, for

Lloyd, all processes are relations and all relations are processes.   Hence his terms must imply a combination of these
ideas.   The situation becomes linguistically intolerable when
Lloyd uses terminology traditionally applicable to physical
movement alone for the operations of relational process.
The result is, at times, an almost incoherent account of a
process which in some sense does not seem to move and a
relationship which in some sense does move.

Polarities, for Lloyd, are both unified and opposed, but
in the earlier stages[24] of his work the emphasis is on their
unity, whereas in the later stages,[25] except for his last article,
it is on their opposition.   In this last article, however, he
seems less sure that there is an actual gap or duality in the
polarity of the knower and his environment: ". . . reality
simply may not be . . . homogeneous or monometric . . . but
rather *would seem to be in some sense* quite dual.   *At least
it must be thought* dualistically."[26]

Lloyd's antithesis or polarities must be distinguished from
what Kant calls "antinomies" and from what Bradley calls
"contradictions."   While Kant's antinomies are evidence of
a transempirical structure superimposed on empirical knowledge, Lloyd's antitheses are indicative of the inherent recalcitrancy, humor, and paradox of an empirical world.   While
Bradley's "contradictions" are proof of the impossibility of
empirical truth, Lloyd's antitheses are proof that empirical
truth is so meaningful, so vital, and so large that it tends to
be "whole," to be unlimited by any particular definition.
While Lloyd sees Bradley as using his contradictions to prove
the phenomenality of a universe,[27] Lloyd himself uses polarities to define its reality.   While Bradley uses contradictions
to defend the justification of doubt, Lloyd uses polarities to
defend the justification of belief.

The process which in Chapter I we approached in terms
of whole and part, unity and community, may now be
approached in terms of polarity relationship.   The entity A,
as the positive term, functions to define itself, to maintain its
self-identity against all else; hence the 'thesis' is analogous

in function to what we have called a part.   And –A, or the antithesis or negative, functions to relate A to the rest of the universe by exhibiting what A is not.   Since the antithesis implies the thesis in its denial of it, it is analogous to what we have called a whole.   Lloyd's "negative term" is a name for that phase of process responsible for the specific altera- tion or direction of anything.   But this "negative term," in opposing a given A, functions as a whole or "inclusively" by assimilating A into a larger unity.   Thus, for instance, eight- eenth-century democracy is the negative term for military aristocracy, but functions as a whole for, or inclusively for, that aristocracy by assimilating the limited ideal of the divine right of kings into the larger context of the natural right of each man.[28]   Protestantism negated the limited concept of the confessional in order to include it more comprehensively in the idea of conscience.[29]   The negative term, then, is inclu- sive and accounts for movement.   It is "a very common atti- tude or motive in experience"[30] or that phase of living activity which is most immediately responsible for anything 'coming into being.'

3. *The Logic of Antithesis*

Lloyd distinguishes seven principles of polarity relation- ship.[31]   But he warns of a possible misunderstanding of these distinctions.   They yield only a "cross-section" or a "formal" and abstract account of process, for they describe relationships qua relationships as if they were not also proc- esses.   They examine process stopped at the moment of becoming and extricate the principles of activity from spatio- temporal, living relations.

The concept of antithesis or polarity relationship is cru- cial for Lloyd's intepretation of such basic matters as the meaning of mind, matter, and motion.   His article "The Logic of Antithesis" is merely a "preliminary report," a preface to later developments which draw on it as a rich source of supply.   Consider what Lloyd feels his analysis will accomplish.   First, he hopes that it will provide new meaning for the body-mind relationship (and will offer a nonreductive and yet a nondualistic basis on which a pragmatically inclined epistemology can be developed). Secondly, he expects that this new meaning will alter idealistic and empirical traditions (and fuse these into a more impregnable position). Thirdly, he expects that it may have some influence on doctrines of motion (and pave the way for a view of process which does not violate a principle of continuity and yet is consistent with emergent evolution). Hardly small hopes!

The first of Lloyd's seven principles of the relational processes involved in all antithesis is the "mutual reproduction of terms." Each term of a polarity relationship is relative to the other in the sense that "neither can be without the character of the other."[32] Each is infused with the character of the other. Lloyd does not mean that each term is *defined* in terms of the other, for terms relative by definition are not guaranteed to be ontologically related. Nor does he mean that the terms of an antithesis imply each other by contrast, since each actually shares the character of the other. To underline the point, Lloyd's first principle is that each term of an antithesis again splits into a smaller antithesis. Each term is a smaller duplication, a microcosmic and analogous illustration, of the larger antithesis of which it is only a part. In the terminology of Chapter I, the differentiated A was both whole and part by virtue of reproducing the antithesis between the undifferentiated and the overdifferentiated A.

The second principle, "duplicity of meaning," is a corollary of the first. This principle is that each term of an antithesis has two significations, or a "dual meaning," by virtue both of the mutual implication of the two terms and of their individual duplication of the entire antithesis. Hence, each term must have a meaning representative of each side of the antithesis it individually harbors. On the one hand, it must have a meaning representative of the thesis, and, on the other, a meaning representative of the antithesis. Since the thesis is analogous to a part, one meaning of each term will be local, narrow, exclusive, and one-sided. Since the antithesis is analogous to a whole, the second meaning of each term will be both-sided, big, deep,[33] free and hospitable, and will include the positive, as the negative must. Lloyd applies "the biological figure of inheritance"[34] to the negative, which inherits "the general principle, the basal, radical life or nature of the positive; if never the exact formal structure, the essential function."[35]

Let me try to indicate Lloyd's meaning by using the body-mind polarity as an illustration. "Body" would have two meanings: its exclusive, partial meaning of extension in space and a wider, inclusive meaning of certain operational characteristics which cannot be reduced to extension in space but which are dependent on it. "Mind" would have as its exclusive meaning the individual manifestations or activities of mind, and as its wider meaning the rationale in all things which includes but cannot be reduced to individual manifestations. If we carry this second polarity into a further subdivision and consider mind as a human phenomenon, then "perception" would be its narrow meaning and "conception" its broader one. The first illustration of the meaning of mind suggests that Lloyd's definition is close to the sense of the Greek *nous;* the second paves the way for empirical tendencies.

The third principle, "identity of opposites," is inaccurately named, because Lloyd does not mean 'identity,' but 'unifying activities,' of opposites. This principle is a recapitulation of the two preceding principles for the purpose of drawing the implication that they are processes as well as relationships. Since the terms in a polarity are a mutually duplicative and implicative unity, each term communally shares the function of its opposite via an infinite series of terms. A polarity in process of differentiation moves by virtue of what Lloyd calls the "tension"[36] within it. To use the language of Chapter I, the very operation which makes the part more individualized, at the same time interrelates it more intimately with everything else. Hence polarities not only do move, they must move and be self-moving.

The fourth principle, "serial mediation," asserts that A

and −A are not cataclysmically opposed, but, since each polar term contains the other, their opposition is "intensified" by an infinite series of terms which uniquely represents (mediates) every possible degree of difference between the polar pair.   The two terms of a polarity represent the infinite series "short-circuited."[37]   By rejecting the idea of cataclysmic and abrupt difference between the terms of a polarity and by substituting for it the idea of serial mediation, Lloyd maintains that the difference between the terms is more *intense* because their relationship is more binding.   "Serially mediated," the difference between each and every term in the series is not merely one of *degree* but of *kind*, not merely a difference of quantity but of quality.   To put it another way, since the difference between A and −A is *infinite*, it can never be represented quantitatively, but must be understood qualitatively.

This fourth principle provides Lloyd with the idea of infinity as a function; it is a tribute to the principle of continuity and justifies his use of analogy.   Since infinity connotes a quality exhibited by each term in its active relations with its neighbors, it becomes an adverbial conjunction in his system.   As adverb, infinity is a quality of the movement of each term, the way in which it acts in being different in kind from every other—in being, in a word, metaphysically unique.   As a conjunction, infinity is that which unites all terms into a series and in which they all share.   In a series merely without a last term, each term is quantitatively different from every other, but in a series in which *each term* acts infinitely, each is not only quantitatively but qualitatively different from any other, which fact cements all into an interrelated whole.   Since all terms are functionally related in a series, a principle of continuity is guaranteed; the operations of any term are analogous to those of any other.   To illustrate, the difference between body and mind is not merely a difference of degree, but of kind.   Neither can be reduced to the other, yet each is functionally related to the other.   The two extreme terms, body and mind, represent abstractions for an infinite series of entities all exhibiting both body and mind in varying degrees of quantity and quality. The infinite occurrence of these in combination that is a world serves to reiterate their relational differences with an intensity which isolated and abrupt difference cannot have. From this point alone it should be clear that Lloyd is hardly an idealist of the traditional stamp.

Lloyd's fifth principle, "difference in kind and degree," guarantees that each term of the series is unique, discrete, and absolutely individual. Insofar as each term is completely original, difference in degree must involve equal difference in kind if no member of the series is to duplicate any other. Since Lloyd, like Leibniz, finds the merely duplicative term unnecessary in the nature of things, difference in kind must always accompany difference in degree. Each entity in an infinite series functions as a universal; and this we pointed out in the last chapter.

The sixth principle is "dimensional difference," at other times expressed by Lloyd as "dimensional variation" and "mediative change." All change involves qualitative differences—"dimensional" differences. Thus for each quantitative difference there is a corresponding qualitative one. Quality and quantity are incommensurable but related. Lloyd sometimes pictures them as at "right angles," to suggest their irreducibility and yet their relatedness. Dimensional difference can be seen as the way in which the negative term relates to the positive. We said above that the two terms of the antithesis imply each other. But the negative term acts "inclusively"; it does not deny in the same way that the positive affirms; it provides the larger and more significant relationship which both sides share; it is a whole which is always more than the sum of its parts. In this sense, dimensional difference is the principle of *productivity* and *growth* within process. Lloyd's position really forces him into identifying mere quantitative difference and qualitative growth or alteration. For if the distinction were made, he would be taking the position that there are differences which do not represent changes. Another way of putting the matter is that for Lloyd all change is growth.

To illustrate with the polarity of life and death, life is not merely an absence of death, nor is death merely a termination of life, but natural and immanent in life, making life mean something more than either life or death alone.[38] Death, as the negative term, is witness to a larger whole shared by both life and death alike, namely, "a fulfilling, wholly conserving continuance of the life that now possesses and encompasses us [the life that is not merely the living of any *particular* thing] . . . asserting confidently that our immortality is, not is to be, and is in and of the very life we are here and now leading."[39]

The final principle, "parallelism of all difference," takes two forms. First, it means that the relations holding between all terms in an infinite series are analogous, and, secondly, it means that there is a one-to-one correspondence between the series of quantitative differences and the series of qualitative differences related to and yet incommensurable with it (at right angles to it). The first form is a statement of *lex analogiae*. Whatever principles of movement can be derived from an examination of A and B will be present in an analogous form between A and C, and so on. Hence, Lloyd justifies his search for generic traits of existence. The second form is the foundation for a functional relation between quantity and quality and serves Lloyd epistemologically as the basis of a functional interpretation of psychophysical parallelism.

Polarity relationship has just been described in fixed structural terms. Now let us consider it as a self-moving process in which the "antithetical terms actually lose themselves in each other."[40] The process 'begins' with a simple opposition of two terms, a "dualism."[41] But neither term exists: these are the mythical extremes of a series—"a hypostasis of extreme difference,"[42] "only *theoretically* possible" and hence "never found or attained, being only posited, asserted, or indicated."[43] Existence is a combination of entities already self-implicating or "in tension." The interstraining terms mutually imply and reproduce each other, at which point they pass into an interrelating "duality." No sooner has the negative begun to function than, by virtue of its acting 'wholely,' an infinite series of interrelating terms is implied. With infinity "set in operation," each term reiterates, in its own unique way, the relationship between, yet the incommensurable difference between, each term and all other terms. The series undergoes a uniform process shared by each term with increasing "intensity."[44] The process approaches 'completion' (the overdifferentiated A), in the sense that each term approaches the limit of its unity and differentiation. The operation of infinity is becoming fully or infinitely realized, or, as Lloyd puts it: ". . . the operation of infinity, must always mean transcendence of some particular base . . . some kind of projection from one plane to another or others, or, better still, translation of one form of reality [one dimension] to another form or other forms of reality."[45] The process reaches "the point of saturation."[46] A "crisis"[47] develops in the series as the tension between the terms increases in intensity and arrives at what might be called the bursting point.[48] At this catastrophic point, each term in the series undergoes a qualitative change in the relation between it and every other term, hence the relations of the entire community of terms gain a new qualitative character. In short, the series grows or develops, it unfolds. At the point of precipitation[49] the growing series has developed in that the antithesis is renewed on another and qualitatively altered level.

In the largest sense, such a crisis develops whenever any organism encounters the confining limits of its own individuality, whenever the restless hunger of an organism simply to be or to do or to know and to be related to an infinite universe meets the obstacles of finitude. In an epistemological investigation the "crisis in the series" develops when the inquirer meets the limitations of a context to which any particular inquiry is subject. Here the empirical world operates as "control" on the thinker's "spontaneity"; it besets the thinker with difficulties and paradoxes which indicate that his thought is outgrowing old categories and that new formulation is already latent.   Since the moment of crisis or growth is applicable to all things, it takes as many divergent forms as there are things to grow.

4. *Process as Polarity*

Movement cannot be a property of isolated things; otherwise the serial relations which bind all terms into an organic unity would be broken, making the world an aggregation and not an organism, a collection and not a system.   But, further, since movement is known by a comparison of one thing with another, the whole cannot be said to move, because a whole which moved would function like a part.[50] Hence, neither isolated part nor whole, but only interrelated parts, can be said to move.   Since all parts are related to all others in a system, "travel [change] is *commerce, not separation* . . . ."[51]   Using Lloyd's illustration of travel as a special application of a general principle, we may say that the traveler does not move *away* from one place *to* another, but takes the old places with him as he moves.   The change consists in a relational interaction between traveler and place. The traveler, then, "both goes to a new place and remains in the old";[52] he both moves in one sense and does not move in another.

From this point of view, motion should be spoken of more accurately as the polarity of moving-rest: ". . . motion is the manifestation, not of a composition or aggregation of isolated positions, but the interaction or the organization of always related positions."[53]   A world is defined as active relations which perform as a stable system: "The movement of the part . . . is the rest of the . . . system."[54]   While the system persists, the interrelating parts continually move with respect to one another and with respect to some stable framework within which they can be understood to move.   Change, says Lloyd, is the "perfectly continuous expression of the persistent relations of coexistences."[55]   Motion "is always expressive of the existing relations of the parts of *some* whole."[56]

It is no wonder that Lloyd chides James on his "paradox of paradoxes," the "pluralistic universe," since such a universe could be described equally well as a monistic pluralism or a pluralistic monism.   Lloyd feels he is interpreting James less narrowly in insisting that a *universe* of moving parts is evidence of a "nonmoving" whole or system which relates those parts.   More than a mere multiplicity of entities in flux, an empirical world is a nonmoving system within which change takes place.[57]

From a purely mechanical point of view (as opposed to an organic view, which includes it), a thing can be said to move only by virtue of a permanent or nonmoving basis in terms of which its movement is measured.   But this so-called permanent basis in any one context may itself be moving in another; and this is what it means to say that movement is relative.   The question of whether any particular thing operates as either the permanent whole or the moving parts depends on the context.   To put this point another way, nothing is absolutely permanent or absolutely moving, but all things exhibit activity which is a combination of moving rest or resting movement.   As Chapter I pointed out, the extremes of the series, or absolute motion and rest, cannot exist and are experientially fictitious.

In making a transition from a purely mechanical and quantitative or artificially abstract account of change to a biological or organic one, we shall find Lloyd emphasizing another aspect of the persistence-change polarity, namely, change as in some sense without loss.   Change without loss refers to the persistence of the altering organism in the sense that each thing exhibits its past in all present activities.   Change without loss means change with gain.   And change with gain is synonymous with "growth" or "development." Each growing thing is at each moment 'more' than it was before.   All things alter yet persist through alteration; all things change yet recapitulate their past; all things move yet exhibit their past experience in their present life and activities.

In a later section of this chapter I shall deal with some of the difficulties that arise out of Lloyd's general conception of change. At this point, however, it is worth while calling closer attention to certain of the formulations already quoted, and to certain other formulations, all of which suggest one type of difficulty. Notice the following statements:

[Change is the] perfectly continuous *expression* of the *persistent* relations of coexistences.[58]

... motion ... is always *expressive* of the *existing* relations of the parts of some whole.[59]

... change is the ever *fulfilling expression* of *what always is.*[60]

... in motion the *inner nature of the whole* is expressed ... .[61]

Motion . . . is the expression or *realization* of a *system of relations.*[62]

The problem I shall raise concerns the meaning of the pairs of terms I have italicized, and the effect they have on the general notion of process (see below, section 12).

5. *Space and Time as Relational Activities*

Lloyd develops his theory of space by refuting older views. He repudiates an absolutistic or Newtonian sense of space as a noun—as an empty container—on the grounds that such a view implies a structural and irreconcilable duality between existence and the conditions for existence. (Lloyd's own "dualities," as we have seen, are functional interrelations.) The view of space as a container understands it as composed of points or parts, of which Lloyd says: "Simply a space composed of points can have no reality, since either its parts will be separated by intervals, or vacua, and then in space, not space itself, or will be absolutely contiguous, and then, however numerous, without magnitude singly or collectively."[63] Hence, the view of space as a collection of points does not define space, nor does it account for motion, as Zeno demonstrated.

Lloyd then elaborates two polar positions springing from the notion of space as a containing form, both of which he rejects. The first he calls the "intuitionalistic view," which Kant holds, in which formal space is a "peculiarity of mind" —an a priori form. The intuitionalistic view understands space as an empty but subjective form which experience fills. The second, the polar opposite ("the other side of the dualism"), Lloyd calls the "sensationalist" view, which Locke holds, in which formal space is "a wholly physical or 'primary' quality, of matter."[64] Here space is an empty but objective form which an objective world of matter fills. In both views Lloyd finds the knower separated from the known, the real from the ideal, and things from each other by a breach which can never be healed.

Time can be treated as equally external and independent of events. Turning to history in a generalized sense, Lloyd points to four consequences for an account of change if time is treated as a self-existent entity which is real even when empty. First, no event could be related to any other, but each would be isolated and accidental. Hence the temporal series would be full of breaks and gaps. The child could not become a man, nor could any event be related to its causes. There could be no laws or organizing processes relating the growing organism either to its past or to its future. Secondly, were time external to events, generation and corruption would be sudden and abrupt. Things would spring out of nothing and be irrevocably annihilated. Such a view of change must find all events "the work of a brutal chance or a lawless miracle"[65] and presupposes a philosophy which is either crudely materialistic or supernaturalistic. Thirdly, since miracles require an arbitrary agency to effect them, this lawless sense of chance presupposes an external and therefore whimsical agency in the form of either a supernatural deity or a supernatural but efficient chance:

To a people, for example, subject to some absolute monarch or some infallible church, where monarch and church get their authority from a world or a nature altogether alien to this world and to human nature, time is a mere form, the present having no significance and the past and the future being unreal just because past and future. What wonder that through the middle ages, the things of time were said to be illusory and predictions of the millennium were very common and the real or the spiritual was made altogether opposed to the temporal![66]

Fourthly, Lloyd maintains that if time is made formal, it is thereby made illusory. He finds this "particularly offensive"[67] and offers a crushing methodological comment: "To find an illusion is hopelessly to unsettle the point of view from which it is found and to enforce adoption of another point of view."[68]

The new point of view necessitated by these objections Lloyd names the "essence-theory"[69] of space and time. Derived from the conception of biological evolution, the essence theory attempts to accomplish three things: (1) to relate movement or growth to the nonmoving or persistent; (2) to relate the temporal or sequential relations to the eternal or nonsequential (the now to the always) and the spatial or coexisting relations to the nonspatial (the here to the everywhere); and (3) to relate the temporal to the spatial, or sequence to coexistence, hence to relate all parts of space to all parts of time. With this accomplished via polarity relationship, Lloyd's essence theory of space and time can guarantee: (1) that motion as growth involves persisting relationships—that all things grow yet nothing is lost; (2) that spatial and temporal relations define the actuality of each thing and the connection of each thing with all things; and (3) that space and time are co-relative.

Let us consider how he works it out. First, space and time are nothing in themselves. They are relations, not things. But since all relations are processes for Lloyd, space and time are activities not substances. Relationship is real only if dynamic.[70] As relational verbs, space and time are ways in which the organism acts—ways in which the organism defines itself and by which we pronounce it 'physical' and 'material.' As relational verbs, space and time are "essential to the real" and are phases of forces "in application of which or in identification with which life consists."[71] Since a universe was described as an infinite series of actual (spatiotemporal) relationships, space and time are "intrinsic to events," "material," "concrete," and "full," and hence empirically real.[72] Reality, says Lloyd, is spatially and temporally plural.[73] Space and time are materially real "dimensions"[74] of reality.

Since things *act* spatially and temporally, space and time are "at once a *condition* and a *result,* of organic activity."[75] As a *result* of organic activity, space and time become defined as the organism manipulates and uses its environment. Hence, space is measured in "units of work" or "units of experience" and "is a force which man applies whenever he acts" (as it is for Dewey):

> The common units of measurement, furthermore, are indications that the measured space is a living force. Such units, for example, as the foot, the ell, the cubit, the fathom, the span, the pace, and the finger all give what they measure a dynamic character. Like them, too, in principle are "a stone's throw," "shouting distance," "as far as eye can reach," and so on. And a wayfarer, in reply to an inquiry as to how far he has come, says that he has come so far that his legs refuse to hold him.[76]

Answering one of his mythical objectors who asks about mathematical measurement, which is so much more abstract, Lloyd says: "When is measurement, however accurate, without an interest in the adjustment of some agent to the means and incidents of his activity? Accuracy only brings a greater freedom; it only liberates a greater force."[77] Space is the result of organic activity insofar as knowledge of space is built by a manipulation of environment and measured by that manipulation. A child runs, falls, touches, and throws until he develops a spatially ordered world in which he moves freely and effectively—the measure of his effectiveness depending on the measure of order with which his experience permits him to invest a world; the measure of order which his world exhibits depends on his effectiveness.

Space is a *condition* of organic activity in the sense that the spatiality of the environment provides the possibilities for physical action. Space and time are "projections"[78] of organism. Understood concretely, "space is the relational whole which constitutes the world's *ableness* to an *organic self* that sees and feels and moves."[79] Understood abstractly and hence apart from the interaction of organism and environment which makes them, space and time are two forms or abstractions for the unification of things;[80] they are two ways in which the relations between part and whole express or manifest themselves. To contrast Lloyd with Kant in this connection: for Lloyd space and time are *natural* conditions for *activity*, for Kant they are *formal* conditions for *knowledge*.

Space, Lloyd says, is a "living mediator."[81] As a force, it cannot be separated from the activity of the self, and, in fact, is as much a part of the self's activity as the self's activity is of it. Lloyd celebrates their interaction. Speaking of architecture, he says:

Curves and angles, however, so different for different peoples or for different times, are sure records of life's conditions, be these climatic, geologic, or economic; . . . they are the crystallized life of the people . . . . The great work of architecture is a temple whose very curves and angles speak to men of the life that they are actually living. It is, then, no mere place of worship, but itself shares in the life that the worshipper would realize; no form of life, but alive itself.[82]

If we treat space and time as mere position and mere duration, they are actually abstractions for environing conditions. Space as mere position is an abstraction for the *permanence* of organism, while time as mere duration is an abstraction for its *alteration*.[83] If one asks a physical question, space and time are measurable unities or units of measurement, but if one asks a metaphysical question, space and time are phases of a larger relational process which expresses itself (among other ways) in terms of a polarity unity

of permanence and change. Organism is defined by a combination of the spatial and temporal and the space-less and
eternal, of the here and the now, the everywhere and the
always, for "being anywhere is also being everywhere and
being ever is also being always."[84]

To further explicate the point that organic action defines
itself in terms of a polarity of permanence-change, Lloyd
reminds us that location in space is not isolation but relation.
A thing is spatially located by a description of its surroundings; it is temporally located by a description of the before
and the after. With time and space understood as active
relational forces, space operates to relate a part to a whole,
a creature to an environment, while time operates to relate
past conditions to future alterations through the medium of
the present. Hence, both spatial and temporal characteristics are applicable to every organic relationship. Space
is omnipresent in every position of space, while the parts of
time are always contemporaneous with the present.[85] Thus
Lloyd is brought to say that "a space of whose parts coexten-
sion or omnipresence is true [the whole-containing part]
and a time whose parts are contemporary [the eternal
moment] are *themselves* [a nonexistent abstraction] spaceless
and timeless . . . ."[86]

Space and time, then, are abstractions for activities which
are a working combination of the temporal and the eternal,
the spatial and the coexistent—the changing and the permanent. The organism does not live "in" time and space,
and yet is "of" them through activity. One *lives* and *uses*
time, and "a life that uses time is as eternal as it is temporal."[87] To return again to the terms of Chapter I, an
organism is spatial and temporal in the sense that its individuality distinguishes it from the rest of the universe, but
it is nonspatial and nontemporal in the sense that it is communally interrelated with a total universe. The organism
expresses both a here and a now, an always and an ever.
The "tensions" between these polar extremes define life,
or existence; therefore, for biology, "life is no local and

temporal endowment but the affair [a spatiotemporal activity] of an indivisible whole."[88]

The final consequence of Lloyd's views of space and time, which bind his world together, is already implicit in what has been said, namely, that space and time are functions of each other and are relative to each other.[89]   If we describe their relationship as a problem of relationship between coexistences and sequences,[90] time and space form a polarity which is a smaller duplication of the larger polarity of space and spacelessness, time and timelessness.   For the smaller polarity as for the larger one, each is "a truth about the other, a visible token of something hidden in the other";[91] each is a "projection" of the other.   Since each is an abstraction for a type of motion, each is measured in terms of the motion of the other; each is an interrelated phase of the total activity of organism:

. . . time and space must be truths about each other, each a witness to something in and of the other, space of contemporaneity even in time, and time of motion even in space . . . space or coexistence conserves the temporal, making it eternal, and time or sequence realizes or expresses the spatial or local, making it omnipresent.[92]

6. *Causality*

Lloyd's view of causation, like his view of change in the large, straddles two apparently contradictory ideas.   Events must have a necessary relation with their causes, yet they are not determined or predetermined.   To put it another way, events must be originally related to their causes, and yet develop; they must not violate the law of continuity, yet they must emerge or grow.

Lloyd develops his organic view of causation by distinguishing between unity and uniformity, between a "vital" and a mechanical conception of the relation of cause and effect.   Agreeing with Hume, Lloyd asserts that the world of individual events will never reveal a necessary connection between cause and effect.   The world only exhibits things acting uniformly; it never testifies that they *must* act that

way.   According to Lloyd, Hume is compelled to deny necessary relations between cause and effect because he treats a
world mechanically.   Kant, on the other hand, is guilty of
a polar but equally mechanical view.   Kant examines a
knower in isolation from his world.   The result is that while
Kant finds a necessary connection between cause and effect,
this necessary relation is empty, and hence likewise formal
and mechanical.   While Hume atomizes a world by examining *particular* causes and effects, Kant phenomenalizes a
world by finding cause and effect to be empty forms provided
by the knower.[93]

Lloyd analyzes the Kantian deduction of the categories in
general and the category of causation in particular in order to
show that Kant foreshadows later developments.   But Kant's
view, he believes, foreshadows his own because it foreshadows pragmatism, with which he has strong affinities.
Lloyd insists that it is the *principle* behind the categories
which is a priori and not the categories themselves.   What
is this principle that Lloyd sees?   It is "mind's having, as
it were, a native hold on novelty and real, not just formal,
difference, on mind's being born to get, to grow, to outdo,
and even outlive [through action] its *formal* structure at any
time . . . ."[94]   Kant's empty categories prove to Lloyd that
when a knower is acting in a world, experience is not merely
routine and duplicative, but developing and growing.   To
put it another way, Kant's empty categories prove that the
activity of a knower can find infinite, internal, and necessary
relatedness in a world of causes and effects.

Lloyd's conclusion, then, is that a necessary relation
between cause and effect cannot be found in a world of
discrete events, nor yet in a world of cognitive forms, but
only insofar as an organism "translates"[95] (interacts with) its
environment.   The meaning of causality stems from the
meaning of related events in Lloyd's conception of relational
or organic activity.   Causal connection implies a vital,
dynamic unity, not an objective, mechanical uniformity or
a subjective, but empty, unity.   On this basis, cause and

effect constitute a relational situation such that all events must have an entire universe of causes, but such that no particular event is ever necessarily related to any other particular event.   Since all events are necessarily connected with an entire world, Lloyd has preserved continuity in a world of causes and effects.   There is no causal relation, and hence no necessary connection, between individual events. As an isolated situation, any particular cause-and-effect relationship would be repetitious, mechanical, and fixed, and could leave no room for growth.   As a relational situation, in which each part or entity is relating itself to an entire universe through action, no particular cause-and-effect relationship can ever be exhausted.   Each new event is qualitatively incommensurable with ("dimensionally different from") the world of causes which produced it and yet is a realization or fulfillment of some of the infinite possibility of relationship latent in its cause.   Hence, Lloyd has preserved the evolutionary and developmental character of his world.   The causal relation is not "individualistic";[96] it cannot be understood as isolated from or "irresponsible" to an organic whole. It is a consistent, developmental expression of organic relations.   The relationship is neither arbitrary, determined, nor predetermined, but "free," since empirical events *in toto* represent the working out of a "free principle" not a "narrow programme."[97]

So far we have been discussing causal relationships as active.   We may treat them as mechanical, however; we may understand causes apart from effects for purposes of analysis.   In this sense the relation between any particular cause and particular effect is repetitious and routine.   Scientific truth, then, though true, is only part of the truth, the rest of which is metaphysical or broader truth.   Scientific law describes the mechanical and uniform.   The mechanical expresses that which occurs irrespective of historical or temporal divisions, and hence is a "contemporizing agency."[98] But unlike action, its counterpart, it only *formally* contemporizes or unites the past and the future to the present, whereas action *actually* contemporizes them. While scientific law gains the right to disregard temporal divisions, it is penalized by operating as a *formal* rather than a *vital* unifier.[99]

7. *Change as "Mediation"*

"Mediation" is Lloyd's term for process interpreted as self-directing, conserving growth.[100]   He distinguishes it from three other theories of change, which he calls "theological," "spontaneous," and "mechanical."[101]   Contrasting mediative change with "theological" or "absolute" change, Lloyd repudiates the latter on the grounds that the created thing lacks necessary relations with its causes and hence need not have any causes.   Lloyd feels that "production *ex nihilo*" requires a supernaturalistic framework which substitutes miracle for explanation.   Mediative change, on the other hand, neither asks favors of an empirical world nor bridges experimental evidence.   Change, as Lloyd would define it, must always imply a set of causes or previous conditions to provide a context for alteration.   Since the altered can never be without predecessors, his first prerequisite for a theory of causation is that an empirical world be defined as a never-beginning, never-ending chain of cause-effect relationships. At the very least, events have causes.

But Lloyd is not content with this purely empirical observation.   If activity is equated with growth and development, all events *must* have causes productive of that growth. Hence, while "spontaneous" change makes the relation between cause and effect only *accidental, arbitrary,* and *sporadic,* mediative change requires that the relationship be *original, continuous,* and *necessary.*   Necessary causal relationships provide the basis for Lloyd's assertion that all events must have direction.   The concept of mediative change not only furnishes Lloyd with a theoretical basis for empirical activity understood as growth, but it underlines his insistence on a principle of continuity relating past and future to the present.

The contrast between the concept of mediative change and the concept of what Lloyd calls "mechanical" change makes explicit the remaining characteristics of the former. While mechanical change means *uniform* variation or identical result under identical conditions, mediative change provides for *emergent* variation, whereby each event is unique, new, and developmental. While the "routine" of mechanical change deprives a world of life, novelty, and individuality, mediative change insures them. While mechanical change is only quantitatively or mathematically measurable, mediative change must be described qualitatively as well as quantitatively. While mechanical change implies alteration occurring by means of the action of one force on another, and is therefore external and accidental, mediative change implies alteration as internal and self-directed.

Mediative change is then defined as organic or living activity, in contrast to mechanical motion. As organic or living activity, mediative change equates motion with *physis*, career, or development. As growth, it has two aspects: (1) It is self-moving and internally directed change, and hence supplies the rationale or meaning of the organism. (2) It implies that the method of alteration is necessary while the content moved is neither determined nor predetermined; hence it means the fulfillment of "persistent relationships" or laws in new ways. It means that the past and the future maintain a necessary chain of continuity through the medium of the present, yet the present is not completely bound or restricted by them. It involves alteration in the sense of empirical change in and of things, yet this alteration does not violate the metaphysical persistence and permanence of relations. Since the real is "immanent in the relative,"

Reality is necessarily active or dynamic . . . it is a tension of differences [polarities] . . . at once developmental and conserving or counteractive, giving movement at the same time they insure poise. This tension of differences, moreover, involves constant change [which is] . . . the persistence of reality, the maintenance of what is.[102]

Mediative change is "mediative" in that each thing exhibits or mediates an eternal possibility[103] or relational principle in its own unique way and translates it into its individual tongue; it is mediative in that each part is responsible to the whole, since each part is a microcosm and hence mediates or exhibits the same change or growth taking place in all the parts.

8. *Dimensional Difference*

The new growth, the new variation of past relations, the new "dimension" represents change by accretion without loss. Its minimal trait is that all the relational characteristics of the varied are maintained in the variant. The variant is not simply a collection of past relationships *plus* something more, but past relationships with new adverbial qualities. To put this in terms of polarity relationship, the new dimension is always negative and hence always relative to and contextual with the positive to which it is in opposition. The new dimension preserves the past. But inasmuch as it is negative, it functions inclusively and is *more* than an accumulation of difference from that against which it is a protest. Hence the new dimension *includes* the positive and yet is qualitatively different from it and incommensurable with it; it is analogous to "ratio" over against "mass."[104]

From a physical point of view, then, the new variant seems to 'emerge' from the old, but from a metaphysical point of view, the old is qualitatively altered. The 'emergence' is a qualitative variation of persisting relations. As Lloyd puts it, "Indeed the relation more than anything else is what evolves."[105] Struggling to express what he means by change which is yet not simply change, Lloyd, as we have seen, sometimes refers to dimensional alteration as a growth in intensity[106] between persistent relations.

Incidentally, Lloyd's categories are insistently mathematical, yet he does not give or intend to give a mathematical interpretation of a world. Despite his persistent use of such terminology as "mass," "ratio," and "infinity," mathematicism suggests to him a crude and physicalistic materialism which he neglects no opportunity to repudiate. Philosophy, he says, "can ill afford to lose itself even in the special phenomenalism of so general a discipline as mathematics."[107]   Lloyd uses mathematical terms as metaphors, and does so frequently, apparently because he feels that mathematics is less encumbered by contextual limitation than any other discipline.   It seems to Lloyd to offer a freer, broader, and more fundamental language in which to express the generic traits of existence.   But we find him using biological language to refer to logical relations as well as mathematical language to describe living processes.

Lloyd applies his dimensional interpretation of alteration to a vast range of subject matters.   For example, a dimensional interpretation of sociological development understands the individual as a social unity developing from a "soldier," or an externally controlled agent, to a "mechanic," or an internally controlled one, the latter being a dimensional variation of the former.[108]   The history of philosophy exhibits dimensional variation, Lloyd feels, by moving from supernaturalism to pragmatism,[109] or from an environment viewed as apart from and hostile to man to an environment viewed as intimately related to and coöperative with man.   Chapters V and VI will indicate how Lloyd's dimensional interpretation of events gives sustenance to political liberalism, social democracy, and religious humanism.

9. *Process Conceived in Valuational Terms: the "Principle of Use"*[110]

A description of the meaning of what Lloyd calls the "typical process" can hardly be more than impressionistic. Perhaps the broadest meaning that can be given the concept is that each event is a partial, distinguishable, determinable thing, is "used" as a means for the development of some more inclusive whole.   Each thing contributes its present 'life' to a further growth of a more general life of which it is a part. It contributes its individual growth to communal growth. What Lloyd wants to call attention to in the "principle of use"[111] is exhibited whenever a "living" and "vital" organism becomes lifeless, meaningless, and "a formal letter," whenever an organization of parts is in some sense *re*organized. The determination of the onset or the completion of life is arbitrary, for change, as a continuous, indivisible process, can only be artificially divided into parts and only inaccurately given a beginning or an end.

Every organism, then, either actually or metaphorically "dies." How can we define 'die' broadly enough to cover all of the 'wholes' to which Lloyd intends it to apply? Let us say simply that a thing no longer functions as it did; it no longer acts like the same living organism. It ceases to have the characteristics it formerly had; it loses its individuality. Its mere death or alteration, however, cannot mean annihilation; otherwise the principle of continuity would be violated and the polarities of generation and corruption would not be self-implicating and would not *together* define the activity of a thing. Hence the "dead" organism is only relatively dead, and for the same reason that when it was alive it was only relatively "alive." The organism dies in the sense that it is no longer an end in itself but a means to a more inclusive end,[112] no longer an organism but a "mechanism" providing the raw material for future growth. No living thing or "institute," then, is destroyed (Lloyd's universe is self-conserving); instead it becomes an "instrument"[113] for continuing growth, a part of a continuously and universally developing life. Reaching metaphorical heights, Lloyd calls death as he understands it the motive of "sacrifice" in experience.[114] He says:

The letter passes; the spirit comes in its power and license; and the spirit gradually recalls the letter, reviving it, transfiguring all its lines, as fuller meaning always transfigures recalled fact. Growth certainly implies outgrowth, but man never has outgrown anything fully until he has grown back into it or has brought it up into the reality of his new life, finding that what his new life is he really meant before and so that his old ways must, after all, be capable of present translation and *use*.[115]

The process from generation to corruption to regeneration is so fundamental to Lloyd's account of a world and so universal of application that he gives it a variety of divergent but analogical expressions. Several articles are devoted to it, and *Dynamic Idealism* boasts an appendix titled "A Theory of Immortality in Outline." Corruption involves "the mortality of the letter" and the consequent "assertion of spirit"[116]: "The visible ways of life and thought, the codes and the creeds and the institutions, the prevailing doctrines and rites of all sorts, which at any time constitute the letter"[117] must pass; they must lose their sanctity and intrinsic worth for a society and be rejected. But the "spirit," the life, the principle, the previous end, survives or persists through change and is revived in a dimensional variation of itself, a more inclusive formulation of itself. To suggest the mortality of all things in the interest of something else, Lloyd speaks of "the principle of use." He sees a connection between use as a cosmic principle and the pragmatic conception of meaning and truth (see Chapter IV).[118]

The "spirit" becoming the "letter" can be equivalently described as the "vital" becoming "formal." For example, the ideas and the values which any culture finds meaningful become meaningless and ineffectual. The concept of an unknown and transempirical realm, which influenced the course of civilization during the Middle Ages, passed and became meaningless for the culture attendant upon the rise of modern science. But since the principle or life of the meaningless form must survive, an age of science revived the idea as an empirical yet-to-be-known that is present in all inquiry. In this regenerated sense, the principle of the unknown has gained a new dress. It is no longer understood as apart from a world or as isolated or aloof from experience. The idea of mystery as that which we could never know except with God's knowledge died to give place to the idea of mystery understood as the unknown but knowable in nature. The idea of the supernatural died to be redefined as the possibility of growth and development in every experience.[119]

Lloyd describes the matter in still other ways. The organism seems to become a mechanism or tool, the "institute becomes an instrument"[120] in behalf of new developments. Biologically speaking, the cells of a living body die to insure the continuance of total biological function—they become the mechanism for the continuance of organism. Personally, the human individual uses a physical world (including his own physicality as part of that world) as an instrument for the expression of any type of value, whether that value be mere existence or pursuit of further goals which are dimensional variations of sheer unqualified life. Intellectually, the knower uses a physical world for intellectual and technological development.

Lloyd's own philosophic activity, consciously or unconsciously, duplicates the pattern of the "principle of use," which he sees as a kind of putting of new values on old things.[121] Not only does he "put new values" on old terminology with a free hand, not only does he conceive of his own work as related to the past and supported by historical precedent, but he also devotes part of his work to defining the heritage that older issues, ideas, and figures have bequeathed to the present. A really living presentation of classical figures and issues in the history of philosophy has long been recognized as a pedagogical service, but Lloyd gives this enterprise metaphysical support. Refusing to permit ideas to be outdated or issues to die, he shows their influence on modern controversy.   Since there are no sharp breaks in his dimensionally related world, the present really "fulfills"[122] the past. He satirically alters his customary terminology on the grounds that "it may be outdated."[123] He frequently struggles to interpret sympathetically thinkers with whom he has little community. Perhaps his conviction that nothing is ever lost did much to make him the penetrating historian he was; perhaps it set the stage for a type of analysis which must be fruitful because it offers a theoretical basis for and a justification of a continual review of the past; but, in any case, the success of a dimensional interpretation of history is independent of the metaphysical foundations from which it springs.

10. *Freedom as Organic Necessity*

For Lloyd a concept of freedom can never involve action which has in any sense extricated itself from cause-and-effect sequences. Like the self-determinists, Lloyd understands freedom to be related in some sense to environmental determination. Freedom is not freedom *"from"* a world but freedom *"in"* it.[124] Furthermore, freedom is in some sense *self*-determination, for life "induces its own determinations. It is free . . . because the necessities are its own necessities."[125] In this sense life is "law-free."[126] However, the intellectual climate of Lloyd's other ideas forces him into some special qualifications which make him discontented with the definitions offered by others. Unlike Spinoza, he is dissatisfied with the solution that understanding makes men free. Freedom must be larger and more pervasive than freedom grounded in understanding alone; it must, then, be defined within a different framework. Describing freedom in a generalized way and emphasizing freedom as dependent on use, Lloyd says that what freedom involves is *conscious doing* and therefore being a *party to the doing*.[127] Hence, although understanding in the sense of wider perspective does bring one kind of freedom, thought alone is insufficient to bring freedom *in* a determined world. Only understanding as *used* thought, as thought eventuating in successful action, satisfies Lloyd's requirements. Thus man is not free because mind can have infinite ideas, or because it can soar to contain all substance and see *sub specie aeternitatis;* rather, man is free in that he can *infinitely use* both things and ideas. Man is free in that he can knowingly act, and hence successfully *interact* with or use a world. Man is determined, on the other hand, in that he is presented with *this* environment and no other, in terms of which he must knowingly act and in terms of which he must carve out his freedom if he would.

Torn between his view of a world ontologically predisposed to move and the idea that human freedom must not interfere with ontological necessity, Lloyd solves the problem by insisting that although the method of dimensional altera- tion is determined, the specific content of what is altered is not prescribed. Thus all is intelligible according to some *discoverable plan,* but not a *specific* one: ". . . no limits can ever be set to possibility."[128] To be free is not to be prede- termined, indetermined, or mechanistically determined, but to be internally self-determining. Hence the dimensional process is described as not exhausted by "accumulation or routine."[129] As Lloyd puts it elsewhere: "An indwelling possible is always so much larger than a possible that is defined and assertively isolated and hypostatized. Nature contains so much more than Heaven. Heaven is, but nature grows."[130] Nothing is completely determined except the fact of growth itself. While all things *must* grow, the particular kind of growth that occurs results from free choice. Yet choice is made within a specific, determined context. "The past is perhaps the law, the necessity; the future is the motive or impulse or freedom,"[131] Lloyd says. Present choice fixes the limitations by which a future context is to be defined; it is partly self-determining and partly self-determined.

11. *Progress*

Does evolutionism commit Lloyd, as it does so many other thinkers, to a theory of inevitable progress imposed, if not on each thing, nor yet on a whole, then on the relations between all things? Does not his view of dimensional varia- tion require that some kind of progress be involved in every process? If one means by 'progress' simply growth in the sense of cumulative development, the answer is affirmative. In this sense progress really means pro-gress.[132] But assert- ing that all things grow, even that all things must grow, is far from saying either that all things grow toward some goal or that the goal is in some sense morally better than the start- ing point and hence that each movement of growth is better than the previous one.

As with so many other problems, Lloyd's pronouncements on progress are bewilderingly diverse. He will, for instance, with characteristic obscurity, define progress as follows: "Progress is the timeless because defining and contemporizing law of the past, whether as thought or as environment, becoming the motive, which is only the defined and contemporized future, of the present."[133] Or he will, in the same breath, say, with disarming simplicity, "Progress is history."[134]

Although Lloyd asserts that growth is ontologically necessary, he denies that the necessity is imposed from without and finds it intrinsic to the nature of organism. He also denies that growth involves a goal or fixed static end. Process so defined ontologically could not be conceived of as completed, still less as approaching an overall completion. The idea of progress does not necessitate a distant goal of perfection toward which "imperfect humanity is making its slow, so very slow, and uncertain, so very uncertain, pilgrimage."[135] Since the principles of relationship are constant, Lloyd finds the idea of progress as a movement out of or away from one thing and toward another particularly repulsive.[136] Development is in and through the indefinite possible relationships that nature presents.

But while Lloyd's moving relational world permits no end to process, it has a direction. Each new discernible phase of process may be described as dimensionally or functionally superior[137] to the preceding one. The past is in some sense "fulfilled." Lloyd speaks of relations growing to a "higher level"[138] and becoming "more intense."[139] He tries to give directional process a meaning without asserting that relational activity grows morally better. Generally speaking, growth means a *freer and more facile* expression of existing relationships,[140] which have in some sense become "more complex" thereby. Lloyd seems to mean by "more complex" that the sheer number of possible interrelations increases—that a greater variety of qualitative variations of the permanent principles of relationship becomes actual, explicit, and "worked out." But he tries not to express growth *solely* in terms of numerical increase, saying that each new variation represents an old relationship grown "more intense." Aside from the question, which we shall omit for the present, of whether or not he can really reconcile permanence and change, it should be clear that his concept of the "dimensionally superior" attempts to describe growth as greater relational involvement without necessarily ascribing moral betterment to the situation.

Having understood all things organically, having extended the connotation of organism to sticks and stones, we are obliged to interpret what Lloyd means by greater "facility" of operation when the agents are what we normally consider 'inanimate.' How, for example, can a stick's operations be said to grow 'more facile'? Lloyd insists that the relationships between man and his environment are co-relative. As man becomes more operationally effective, more skilled, ever more capable of manipulating and using his environment, the environment, as a co-relative polar term, becomes more useful and more technically developed. The stick, for instance, functions more effectively, more usefully, and in more complex ways. Progress, then, is defined as the development of technical skill, increased efficiency, and augmented understanding. In giving a general account of the direction of progress, Lloyd speaks of the greater adaptation or naturalization of man in his environment[141] and of the increased dependence on rational methods and technical instruments[142] to effect a freer, more successful, and more diverse community between man and his world. Progress involves a clearer consciousness of the conditions of activity, a wider, deeper, and broader partnership between an organism and its co-relative environment.[143]

Though Lloyd's evolutionism and his insistence on necessary growth and development do not commit him to a theory of moral progress, the "objectors" to whom he so often refers make a significant point when they accuse him of "an optimistic passion for progress"[144] and seem to mean moral prog-

gress thereby.   Refute them as he would, Lloyd does entertain a kind of moral optimism.   It is not so much his evolutionism, however, but his general theory of polar relationship which is the culprit.   Moral relations imply the polarity
of good and evil.   Good and evil, as polar, are equally necessary and equally serve growth.   Whatever grows in the
moral world is always as good as it is evil—but also, of course,
as evil as it is good.   Thus Lloyd is often reduced to stating
a kind of faith or emotional preference with respect to
whether there is or is not moral progress.   Each crisis offers
"as much a possibility of progress as danger of decline,"[145]
but in the last analysis, "the best kind or value always wins
and winning raises the plane of future struggles."[146]   If we
move forward despite appearances of backwardness,[147] evil
must then be an illusion.   If evil is an illusion, so is good.
Lloyd must choose between either good and evil as illusory
or good and evil as real.   He avoids the first choice by asserting with methodological perspicacity that philosophies
of illusion cast their real in jeopardy.[148]   But unfortunately,
since both must then be real and, if real, equally contributory
to growth, his ontology has brought him to the pass of asserting the pathetic Leibnizian tragicomedy that whatever is, is
for the best.[149]   His theory of polar relationship has brought
him near to asserting so much as to risk asserting nothing.[150]

12. *Problems in Lloyd's View of Change*

(1) The first problem in Lloyd's conception of change
arises from his definition of change as the expression of relations that already exist, and this problem theoretically besets
him at every point and takes a variety of forms.   If change
is an expression of relations that already exist, what, in these
terms, is meant by generation and corruption?   How can
the brute facts of physical change be understood?   Is not the
term "expression" begging the question?   What test can we
apply to ascertain whether all change *is* an expression of
relations that already exist?   Granted that change is a qualitative development of relationship, development is *alteration*

in some sense. To put it another way, something *happens* when institute becomes instrument; something happens in any kind of growth. Granted that growth cannot ever be adequately measured quantitatively, regardless of possible new techniques to that end, yet generation and corruption cannot be denied on that account. Despite the fact that one can agree with Lloyd that things are not generated from nothing or totally annihilated, still, generation creates something that has not occurred in just this form before and corruption in some sense destroys a previous condition.

Lloyd employs his metaphor of "focussing"[151] to solve the problem. The organism as a set of relational activities does not come into being; it is not generated, but is simply a spatiotemporal focussing of relational possibility. A set of relational activities is "focussed" in that it exists here and now; it is unique and induplicable. The focussed relationship individualizes stable relational patterns at this particular time and in this particular place, making them by definition at once physical, finite, and constantly changing. "Focussed relational activity" is, at every moment in its alteration, an individualized configuration of abiding relations, which Whitehead would call an "event" and which Leibniz, speaking more substantivally, would call a "monad." Relationship is then defined as continuously focussed and refocussed and never unfocussed or disfocussed. But unfortunately, we must still account for the difference between focussed and refocussed if more than a verbal solution is to be achieved.

(2) The second problem, the problem of novelty, is one that would arise even if the problem of how change occurs were resolved. Lloyd wants to affirm novelty in the concept of mediative change or dimensional variation that expresses his theory of process. Yet his theory will not allow change to be other than unique versions of persisting relations. His universe, in a sense, exhibits not growth but rearrangement; and in this, at least, he is not so very distant from Spencer.

(3) The third problem concerns the meaning of the term

"permanence" in Lloyd's thought. (*a*) What does he mean by saying that any particular movement implies something permanent? And (*b*) what does he mean by saying that the laws of movement are permanent? As concerns *a*, Lloyd has called our attention to the fact that all movement involves a stable context in terms of which it is recognized and defined. The movement of the parts presumed the rest of "*some whole.*"[152] Hence, we understand and measure movement against a framework which is permanent *relative to it*. He has further pointed out that what is permanent in one context is moving in another, larger, more inclusive context. The question is whether Lloyd pushes this principle into some kind of absolute permanence against which (or total context within which) all movement in the universe is measured. In other words, is Lloyd absolutizing a relativistic account of movement in the same sense that he seems to have absolutized a relativistic account of system? As for *b*, to put the question in terms of the laws of movement, what are Lloyd's permanent relational principles which all things exhibit? What is the status, for example, of the principles of antithesis? Are they the stable ways in which things *do* act? Or are they the ultimate laws of growth *according to which* all things *must* act? And would the former constitute a relative permanence or relative context, and the latter an absolute permanence or absolute context?

(4) The fourth problem lies in the paradox of a world in which everything changes except the laws of change. Is Lloyd really maintaining that while things expressing laws of change alter, and while our formulations of the laws of change alter, the laws of change do not? If he is, and I believe he is, Lloyd is false to his own evolutionism. It seems to me that the view that some aspect of an empirical world never can change is a carry-over from seventeenth-century rationalism in which a universe is conceived as an unchanging rational order. While evolutionism should have routed this view by exhibiting a world as continually in process, there are some evolutionists who, like Lloyd, seem

to feel that the laws of evolutionary change are themselves exempt from process. It also seems to me that a view in which the laws of change are necessarily changeless, in which the "permanent" is an absolute rather than a relative term, expresses a dual sense of existence characteristic of idealists. The confusion in Lloyd of the possible meanings of "permanence" causes an interpreter much difficulty. Often he shows some of the traits of abstract idealists which he repudiates. Must Lloyd not choose between a world in which nothing can change and one in which everything can change, including the relational principles or laws of change? Does he, in the last analysis, fall into the very appearance-reality dilemma which he tries so hard to avoid?

(5) The fifth problem is the problem of whether any manifestations of change could maintain their peculiar character in the face of Lloyd's thoroughgoing relationalism. Since Lloyd relates all types of change to the one generic process of relational activity, has not his relationalism become so general that it deprives specific types of change of their individuality? Although it is true that Lloyd accepts the difference between a falling body and a growing thing, although he grants meaning and significance to mechanical change as described by science, yet his view implies that from a larger, or philosophic, point of view the falling body, too, exhibits process. This not only means that its falling is a kind of growth, not only that its falling represents part of the continual process of its relations with a world, but that its falling is in some sense part of a larger growth. While the first sense is partly true, it nonetheless tends to subordinate the characteristics of mechanical change to organic change and thereby to broaden the meaning of the latter to such an extent that it, too, loses its individual character. To put it methodologically, does not Lloyd's dynamic idealism, which conducts a lifelong attack on reductivism, actually reap the same harvest by a reverse method? While Lloyd's view combats nothing-but-ism, does it not actually result in the same thing?

Lloyd equates all movement with process and all process with growth.   If he means by "growth" merely that every moment in a process differs from the last, then, I suppose, all movement could be called growth.   If he means by growth that all movement in process contributes to a cumulative development in which no moment is lost and in which every moment is part of a system of moments leading to some kind of fulfillment of the system, it is rather difficult to understand what could be meant, for example, by the growth of a falling body except possibly something like the Aristotelian actualization of its potentiality for falling.

(6) A sixth and final problem arises with respect to Lloyd's analysis of polarity relationship.   It will be recalled that the negative term was inclusive of the principle exhibited by the other.   That being so, the negative term was important as being the most immediate cause of growth or dimensional variation.   The question then is, how does Lloyd decide which is the negative term in such polarity relationships as hot and cold, person and faction, body and mind?   The question is to all intents and purposes unimportant for the first of these pairs.   But the third set is not only most important for understanding his entire outlook, it is the one in which his decision is most unclear.   According to Lloyd's view, mind is a way in which physicality acts, but again, in his own terms, body is one of the ways in which mind acts. The organism "projects" itself on space and time.[153]   While the implications of Lloyd's view suggest that mind is the negative term, it is difficult to see from a methodological point of view how he came to that decision apart from obvious preference for his own tradition.

Lloyd's categories for his theory of change are more felicitous when applied to history (in the usual sense of the term) than when applied to changes of other kinds.   In other words, they seem better adapted to the interpretations of relations between institutions or relations between concepts than to relations between moving bodies.   Lloyd's historical insights may sound more convincing than his metaphysics of process. But, on the other hand, it must be realized that without this metaphysics the historical insights might not have been possible. Lloyd's students and colleagues seem most impressed with him as a historian of ideas and an interpreter of cultural trends. In this respect their vision of him is just, but it would be an error to suppose that his historical insights are unconnected with the larger metaphysical context, or that this context does not contribute to their significance.

13. *"Biologic" vs. "Biologistic" Evolutionism*

From time to time Lloyd suggests the debt that his views in general and particularly his conceptions of "will," of the principle of dimensionality, and of continuity owe to Darwin. Finding the new biology "not a mere partial and phenomenalistic theory but a real insight into the character of the universe as a whole,"[154] Lloyd regards evolutionism as of equal significance with theology and mechanism as explanations of the universe. All three give different meanings to unity, adjustment, and eternality. Thus Lloyd suggests that while theology finds unity an extraempirical content and mechanism finds it an empirical collection or aggregation of parts, biology understands unity as a functional relation between parts. While theology finds adjustment supernaturally governed, and mechanism finds it accidental and random, biology finds it necessary and natural. For theology, eternality is a property of a mysterious extraempirical sphere of being, for mechanism it is nonending time, while for biology it is a timeless and eternal function of all things in life as well as after death.

Lloyd is aware of the influence biology has upon him. He says in one place that he speaks "as a biologist"[155] and urges in many others that philosophers take biology more seriously. But Lloyd has his own biologic view in mind. He selects the biologism of Spencer as the principal target of attack and as that version of evolutionism from which he is most anxious to differentiate his own. Making a distinction

between a "biologistic" and a "biologic" theory[156]—analogous
to his distinction between a world as *an* organism and a
world functioning organically—Lloyd indicates the crux of
his dissatisfaction with Spencer. Spencer's philosophy of
organism is "biologistic" or crudely mechanical. In direct
line with seventeenth- and eighteenth-century mechanicalism, Spencer's views are too spatially conceived. Although
Spencer's *interest* is biological, Lloyd finds his *method*
mechanical: "Spencer, like many others, although he passes
as an evolutionist, is not enough of an evolutionist to identify
human life with the nature from which it is supposed to have
sprung,"[157] he says.

What does Lloyd find to be the test of mechanicalism in
evolutionary theory? A "biologistic" philosophy treats of
organism*s* rather than of relational complexes. It atomizes
organic activity; it takes the organism to be a discrete, separate, unrelated unit and therefore describes it in terms of
physical boundaries. The physically conceived organism is
then understood merely to be composed of parts in space.

Lloyd's criticism really asks what kind of unity a physically conceived organism can possess. If a thing is composed
of isolated parts, on what grounds can we locate its boundaries? What is the connection between parts which confines
them to this particular thing? Since spatial contiguity of
parts can never distinguish one organism from another, do
we not make such a separation through prejudice that these
particular parts somehow 'belong' to this organism? How
can atomic parts be said to operate as a unity, and how can
an organism composed of them be said to interact with an
environment? Such an organism would indeed have to
adjust. And its environment, being alien and static, would
tenaciously resist that adjustment.[158]

To put this criticism another way, Lloyd maintains that
in a biologistic philosophy the physically conceived organism
is understood to "have" consciousness or life as a localized
faculty. As a result, the life of each organism is isolated

from the lives of others.   Hence, Lloyd maintains, Spencer
attributed life to the individual but was forced to deny it to a
society just because the latter was not an organism at all.[159]
According to Lloyd's definition, if life is understood to be on
the "endowment plan,"[160] then both individual and society
are thereby made inorganic.

To speak of adaptation of an organism to an environment
suggests to Lloyd that any particular act of adjustment can
only be understood in three equally unsatisfactory ways: as
a simple tautological statement and therefore as descriptive
not of an empirical situation but of linguistic agreement; as
the supernatural effect of a miracle; or as coming about "mechanically" and hence ultimately by chance, in the sense of
random and accidental action.

In the first interpretation, the term 'adaptation' would
only simulate explanation.   It would substitute a term for
an explanation.   Such a substitution would be as ineffectual
and contribute as little to our knowledge as the explanation
of the action of opium in terms of a dormitive power.

In the second interpretation, Lloyd denies that organism
can adapt to a nonliving environment without aid.   Since
the organism and its environment would be external and
foreign to one another, they would necessarily function as
two of Leibniz's monads 'without windows.'   Whatever
adaptation did occur would have to be attributed to and reg-
ulated by a force outside both, an 'occasionalistic' *deus ex
machina* who would serve to sustain every instance of adaptation at every point.   An environment which was never
shared and unified by the life of an organism urgently maintaining its individuality could never be a favorable climate
for adaptation and would indeed be inimical to self-adapta-
tion by the organism.   Swimming in alien otherness, lacking
companionship of the environment, the organism would be
forever condemned to isolation and loneliness.

In the third interpretation, adaptation would have to be
attributed to random action and would hardly be worthy of

the name.   In fact, Lloyd dubs activity in an alien environment "puttering,"[161] to distinguish it from his conception of
activity as genuinely basic adjustment.   When adjustment
involves puttering, it merely *happens* to take place; an organism might or might not repeat the performance in the same
way under the same conditions.   Lloyd feels that this sense
of the term implies a mechanical force operative on the
organism.   It excludes original movement and self-movement.   An alien force need only operate once in a while and
at random; the organism would ever find the environment
uncoöperative in sustaining adaptation.   But, further, our
sciences, springing from our adaptations to the world, would
be subject to the same random action.   If adaptation be
random, the repetitive basis of scientific law collapses.

Lloyd insists that when adaptation implies a relationship
between a living thing and a lifeless one, the living thing also
becomes lifeless and mechanical.   Plants, animals, and men
would then be an afterthought of a physical environment and
would inherit its physicality without ability to rise above it
with new dimensions of life, thought, and value.   A thing
on foreign soil could not manifest the dynamic movement
and drive ("will") which transforms a mechanical collection
of accretions into a unified and living organism.   It could
not ingest the coöperating environment.   The "organism"
amid alien corn would of necessity be a hungerless and lust-
less collection of parts continually falling apart from lack of
appetite.   This hunger or "will" functions to distinguish an
organic universe from a mechanical one.

In general, the conception of adaptation of an organism
to its environment suggests that life is ontologically subsequent to a physical environment rather than ontologically
contemporaneous with it.   It necessitates a temporally conceived evolution, overliteral in its understanding of "emergence."   If mind emerges *from* matter, matter becomes temporally prior to mind.[162]   This last objection may seem to
indicate an idealistic predisposition to give mind more value
than matter, but that is not what Lloyd means to convey.

Although he insists that the physical world is not ontologically prior to mind, yet he would not make mind ontologically or temporally prior to the physical world, either. A completely leveling democracy of mind and matter is the fruit of Lloyd's consistent relationalism.

Spencer understands an organism to have a greater complexity of parts than an inorganic entity. Lloyd rebels, because neither size nor complexity distinguishes the organism for him. Maintaining that Spencer's meaning is "flagrantly superficial,"[163] Lloyd defines organism by function and not by appearance. An organism, as a relator, whether large or small, simple or complex, always *acts* like one. Apparently Lloyd is suggesting that "complexity" is a prejudice based ultimately on spatial expanse.

Spencer's mechanicalistic organism is immortal in the sense that the whole lives on despite the death of its parts. Lloyd finds this conception particularly crude—"a sort of rationalistic distillation and objectification of the orthodox scheme of salvation"[164] bearing the stamp of medievalism. He attacks it because his conception of the timeless aspect of relational activity makes it unnecessary, because the existence of an organism and its particular parts are interdependent, and because he feels his conception of immortality does not necessitate this physicalistic interpretation.

Spencer's position apparently suggests to Lloyd that immortality consists in some kind of extension in time of the organism's life and therefore functions as a disguise for the idea that a merely extended temporal duration guarantees infinity.[165] It would seem that Lloyd is making the often-made distinction between the 'eternal' and the 'everlasting.' Since living relationship as eternal, timeless, constant is the basis of temporal duration and not vice versa, the temporally longer life, even the temporally endless one, makes no life at all. Since time is empirically real, temporal existence and duration are characteristic of the organism, but life as the fulfillment of permanent relations is eternal not because it is temporally endless, but because it has a qualitative attribute which cannot be reduced to duration and to which time is not applicable. Thus, in Lloyd's sense, life is eternal in death because it is eternal in life, since eternality is not understood as duration in time but as constancy of relationship.

For Lloyd, birth and death are *functions*, not *states of being*. Since nothing is created or destroyed in any ontological sense, immortality is experienced here and now. Since death is a principle of rebirth and rearrangement incident to every expression of life,[166] all things are continually dying, for continual death is a sign of continuing life. Lloyd's sense of individuality serves as a negative force from within to necessitate death and consequent rearrangement.

Spencer's position that the organism lives on while the parts die[167] offends Lloyd's nominalism, and overlooks the individuality and particularity of an organism, upon which Lloyd insists. A particular thisness exists only by virtue of its particular parts; individuality defines the existence of a thing. Thus, the organism which is a unity of no particular empirical parts but only for parts in general is not an empirical reality. Spencer's unity in general for parts in general cannot die because it never lived. Deprived of a significant sense of life, the organism loses even the significance of death.

It is on the basis of these objections that Lloyd develops what he conceives to be a newer and more meaningful biologism in distinction to Spencer's "imprisoned biologism."[168] Burying the ashes of early mechanicalism, Lloyd would now see philosophy describe living things and not pseudoliving ones. "Biology," he maintains, "has fallen into the error of a pure lifeless abstraction for the living and organic."[169] Thus, according to Lloyd, both organism and environment move, change, and grow, but they move together and change simultaneously. Although he would admit that the activity of an organism in its relations to its coöperating environment does 'develop' in some sense, such development could best be understood as a change in the *quality* of the relationship between the two and not as an activity of either of the terms, not as an adjustment of one side to the other.   When we say that an organism adapts to its environment, we are describing a *qualitatively changed relation between them* and not solely the organism.

Lloyd's new biologism, so pregnant with naturalistic assertion, yet so influenced by idealistic formulation, is carried by analogy into his entire philosophy, developing particularly in his views on practice.   Devoted as Lloyd is to the definition of a more successful organicism built on relationalism, he recognizes that even a philosophy of organism can be taken too literally and abstractly and criticizes Spencer on these grounds.   The word 'organism,' he says, is "a new fetishism . . . in possession of us."[170]   Again, he warns, ". . . 'organism' is getting to be used as a key to all the mysteries."[171]   But beneath these assertions both in favor of a redefined organicism and against Spencer's version lies a purpose which, although only suggested, throws considerable light on the entire endeavor and indicates the larger meaning of his position.   Organicism, Lloyd says, is "the forerunner perhaps of a thoroughly enlightened worship."[172]   Thus, since worship is naturalistically identified with worthily fulfilling practice, Lloyd's purpose in redefining organicism is really to develop a metaphysical framework for a humanistic naturalism explanatory of the meaning of practice.   But regardless of his metaphysical efforts, the purpose is attained, as we shall later see, by his accounts of religious, ethical, and political experience.

14. *The New Psychologism*

As the new biologism develops in Lloyd's thought, it becomes more akin to "psychologism."   Lloyd submits to the tendency to depict the movements of organism in terms of activities with which we are most familiar, namely, our own.   Vitalistic philosophers of every stamp have always been anthropomorphic, and Lloyd is no exception.   Perhaps attempts to deal with reality in terms of our own experience always represent a revolt against mechanicalism and reflect

experience turned inward to find a complexity which defies
a mechanical approach.

Lloyd exhibits psychologistic tendencies by his use of
such terms as "will," "motive," "impulse," "tension," or "compulsion" to characterize organic activity.   Even in his earliest work Lloyd not only refers to himself as speaking "as a
biologist,"[173] but emphasizes biology's contribution to metaphysics.   Later, however, he finds that "philosophy's present-day psychologism as shown in pragmatism, experimental
idealism, the many types of realism—radical, scientific, critical, 'new,' what you please—has quite outdone biology in its
intimations of the unity of man and nature . . . ."[174]   In discussing philosophy's relation to the various sciences, he
asserts that philosophy served biology in the nineteenth
century and that more recently it has served anthropology
and psychology.[175]   If Lloyd's thought could be said to alter
its emphasis and to be differently colored at the end than it
was at the beginning, it is on this score of his growing interest
in, and his felt reliance on, psychology.

As Lloyd becomes more openly psychologistic, there is a
gradual alteration of emphasis from biology to psychology in
actual doctrine.   He becomes more aware that the basis of
this change rests on his notion of the primacy of the self as a
metaphysical category and on the expression of "will" as
the "passion of a universe."   Life being equated with self-
expression, metaphysics soon becomes identified with psychology, and Lloyd becomes more vocal about the change.
Examining the history of metaphysical ideas, Lloyd says that
he is taking a "psychological interest" in philosophy's isms.[176]
And he remarks humorously but meaningfully that "while
art is all *eye* and religion is all *aye* [implying an untestable
hypothesis upon which he feels any credal expression must
rest], philosophy is also all *I*."[177]   Giving more technical
expression to what had now become a conviction, Lloyd
asserts, "The psychologist's study of experience is formally
different from the philosopher's or historian's, but, after all,
only as individual and genus are different."[178]

Were Lloyd to hold up his own intellectual development as a mirror for the last two phases which he sees as characteristic of the history of ideas, there would be a fair likeness. In describing the progress of philosophic ideas, Lloyd understands the primitive attitude, psychologically if not temporally, to be supernaturalism and supernaturalistic explanation. As development always takes place in terms of polarity activity, supernaturalism's counterpart, an equally crude and physically conceived mechanistic materialism, develops. The polar action of these leads to a new dimensional view, based equally on both but not on an eclectic combination of them and therefore not reducible to them. The new dimensional variation Lloyd describes as "biologism" since it takes its temper, if not its doctrine, from the study of biology. But biologism, also, through the activity of polarities alters its nature. At first, Lloyd finds it heavily mechanical, as exemplified by Spencer's account, but, later, it becomes more thoroughly relational and vitalistic.[179] This new, more vitalistic position to which Lloyd refers and which he calls "psychologism" (perhaps with his mind's eye on his teacher, James) is actually pragmatism. It, too, is derived from but not reducible to the views that preceded it. It is no accident that Lloyd welcomes pragmatism,[180] since he finds in it the "newer psychologism," manifesting, to his mind, the onward movement of ideas. Lloyd conceives of pragmatism as a combination of realism and psychologism. Thus, pragmatism "as empiricism, as pluralism or as realism . . . may be idealism also; being heroically idealistic or idealistic without being doctrinaire . . . ."[181] When examining the development of thought he points out, "Subject to theology and the church, philosophy had little opportunity of self-expression; subject to psychology . . . it has had little to restrain it."[182]

But it is clear that Lloyd's meaning of "psychology" is far removed from the content, method, and spirit of the discipline that goes by that name today, or, for that matter, did so then. The mere physical presence of his articles in the *Psychological Review* makes this painfully evident. For instance, a thoroughly metaphysical and metaphorical article by Lloyd on the relations of organism to environment, incidentally deriving a theory of knowledge, is sandwiched between rat-in-a-maze articles and masses of statistics. If Lloyd's so-called psychological articles were misplaced, it is because psychology was disowning metaphysics, rather than taking it to its bosom as Lloyd was doing.

In a reference to Noah Porter's probable shock at the progress of psychology into psychiatry[183] and its development from the study of the faculties of knowledge to the study not only of animal behavior but of the restless violence and hunger of organic life, Lloyd says, "How the excellent Noah Porter . . . would scurry to the bank of the pond of science and frantically call on psychology to come back to dry land and spiritual safety."[184]   It is no wonder that Lloyd felt that the entrance of his "new psychology" would have distressed Porter.   Now, according to Lloyd, psychology is no longer the study of sense and conception, or even of animal behavior, but the study of all relationship that anything bears to anything else. It is no longer limited to human psychology, but must encompass the entire inorganic world as well, insofar as that world becomes part of our own life.   Lloyd feels that psychology must now consider not merely *knowledge of* an environment, but *action in and with* an environment; not merely men interacting with an environment, but men absorbing it, digesting it, and growing big with its life; not merely the mind of man becoming furnished with ideas, but man becoming more intimate with and more at home in his surroundings.   As man finds the soil his natural home, psychology must describe man's relation to his environment "stripped . . . of its protective clothing, exposing what lies beneath the forms and arts of civilization . . . the battle of the nude, [which is] . . . what is here meant by any realism . . . ."[185]

The Process of Knowledge

1. *Revolt against Older Categories*

Knowledge is, for Lloyd, a specific manifestation of relational activity. His epistemology, in marked revolt against older views, is developed from his conceptions of the nature of unity and community and of polarity relationship. It is the product of a metaphysics and does not aim to lay the foundation for a metaphysics.

First, Lloyd rebels equally against mechanism whether the knower is treated reductively as he is in traditional materialism or whether the environment is abused as it is in what Lloyd likes to term, with some contempt, "abstract or formal idealism."[1] In traditional materialism the knower is deprived of his function of expressing the relational wholeness of life, which, as we shall see, is his special metaphysical characteristic. In "abstract idealism" the environment is deprived of its function, which is the physical expression of values. In both, the complexity of a world is overlooked. In both, action is defined merely as reaction—either of the knower to the initiatory action of the world or of the initiatory action of the knower to the world. In both, one side of the knower-known relation is deprived of activity and therefore, in Lloyd's terms, deprived of life. Lloyd feels obliged to put "mechanism" to rout, *whether* it is expressed in an idealistic guise or with the candor of materialism.

107

Secondly, Lloyd's awareness of the irreducible elements composing a world revolts against the injustice of the metaphysical reduction of mind to body; but it revolts equally, and perhaps more vehemently,[2] against the reduction of body to mind. With these rejections, the way is open for a position which both grants the complexity of a universe and unifies its many elements. Lloyd's refusal to fall prey to easy reductions produces numerous consequences in his philosophy which are unusual for an idealist of any stamp. For example, mind is no longer primary, reason is no more epistemologically significant than sense, unity is no more significant or 'real' than plurality, mind is no more significant than matter. "Matter and mind are related contemporaries . . . . Each is, in fact, but an abstraction for something in the other."[3]

Thirdly, Lloyd's view of the interrelatedness of things rejects atomism in all forms. Atomism deprives things of their community with other things and is itself a mark of materialism and a result of overnaïve realism. The knower and the known form a polarity relationship, and have the same traits which all polarities exhibit. Each side of a polarity reproduces the polarity in itself.[4] Hence Lloyd interrelates not only the knower and the known, but the parts of the knower on the one hand and the parts of the known on the other.

2. *The Unity of the Knower*

For purposes of analysis, let us divide the functional unity of the knower-known polarity and examine the status of the knower. Lloyd finds the knower internally related in two ways. First, the senses are related to each other, and, secondly, the senses are related to conception. But both sensation and conception are also individually related to a world as sensed and a world as thought, according to the principles of polarity relationship.

The knower, like our differentiated A of Chapter I, is an animate system of actual relations. His body is an "instrument of adjustment"[5] to itself as well as to a world of 'other' things, while the fact of its adjustment—its 'will' to adjustment—is precisely what Lloyd means by "consciousness."[6] Some of the implications of this position are: (1) the functions of the various parts of the body are, within limits, interchangeable; (2) no organ acts in isolation; and (3) sensation is not confined to special organs but is a function of the entire organism.[7]

In these terms, Lloyd refuses to separate absolutely any one sense from any other. In the first place, the knowing organism *is* sensuous and does not 'contain' senses, much less, a set number of them. In the second place, were those senses isolated from each other or from the other functions of the organism, they could not be understood as fused in one knower. In the third place, since the senses are interrelated and since Lloyd's organism is conscious at every point, Lloyd refuses to delimit the function of any particular sensation.[8] Not only does each sensation share the activity of the others, but all share in the activity of the organism as a whole:[9]

That none of man's organs act in isolation is one of the things commonly recognized but seldom very seriously applied. The Whole . . . is active in every part. So true is this that scientifically one is forced to say that walking is not only with the legs but also with the hands, or that seeing is not only with the eyes but also with the fingers.[10]

Lloyd seriously applies this. First, he denies that there is a specific number of senses, and, secondly, he insists that any kind of sensation is conditioned by and altered by all other kinds. Lloyd draws a moral for relationalism from the apparent need of the psychology of his day to extend the number of senses to include such new faculties as a special faculty for judging heat and cold, a music sense, and even a pleasure and pain sense:

So . . . whatever may be said of the particular terms in which this multiplication of the organs of sense is expressed, it must eventually have the effect of turning consciousness [not a faculty, but adjusting activities] into something that belongs vitally, not formally, to the organism.   It must make consciousness more than a mere being aware of something outside or external [entirely unrelated]; it must make consciousness [interest, will, drive to adjustment] inherent in the self's expression of an *existing* relation to something.[11]

Again attacking atomism, Lloyd relates the sensory complex of the knower to his concepts.   We learn about a world by sensory contact with it: a child learns about space and solidity, for instance, by bumping its head.[12]   Although this aspect of relationalism is a familiar and conventional theme for realists and empiricists, I cite it to indicate how far Lloyd's view is from a distrust of the senses which might seem to belong to his type of idealism.   Perception and conception, though distinguishable, are interdependent for Lloyd, while knowledge is a result of their interpenetration. Some idealists permit an influence of sense on conception, but Lloyd insists on their reciprocity.

3. *The Unity of Knowledge*

Each thing is a unity which, in turn, relates it as part to other entities.   And the knower contributes his own living unity to the situation.   The knower is in company with a world of related things to which an indefinite number of predicates can be given.   It is within such a framework that Lloyd organizes his approach to the nature of knowledge, causality, and human freedom, and, in fact, to all major philosophic questions.   One of the outstanding consequences of Lloyd's concern with the unity of a known world is reflected in his concern with the unity of all knowledge. All branches of knowledge are "wont to adopt the same general method."[13]   Furthermore, he maintains, there are striking analogies in doctrine among particular branches of knowledge at any particular time:

Atomism in physics is contemporary with individualism [in social theory] . . . a monarchical politics with an anthropomorphic creationalist theology and a heliocentric astronomy; and a Newtonian astronomy . . . [is contemporary] with democracy or constitutionalism and inductive instead of deductive logic and naturalistic theology . . . .[14]

Both educational theory and scientific methodology today subscribe to an interconnection of various intellectual disciplines on the basis of successful practice. Lloyd deduces the interconnection from the nature of being. We have always honored the idea that the well-developed thinker must find nothing alien, that he must be a citizen of the universe. Lloyd tries to guarantee this ontologically.

The aspect of the unity of all knowledge which most interests Lloyd is the interconnection of the special sciences. He usually takes for granted the interpenetration of the areas of operation of the physical sciences,[15] and he considers this negatively in *The Will to Doubt* (1907) by exploring the contradictions existing in each if regarded as isolated. For Lloyd such interpenetration is a truism. What he especially wishes to point up is the relationship between "the sciences of the mind," or psychology, and the physical sciences.[16] Should he succeed in showing the dependence of one on the other, Lloyd feels that he would have established his functional psychophysical parallelism:

Thinking of either one, of physical or of psychical science, and of its long and persistent abstraction [from the other], I seem to see a man standing with his back to a mirror and so unable to recognize himself, his own back, in the reflected image behind him. If only he would become less abstracted and turn around fairly and squarely; if only psychology and physical science would once for all face each other![17]

The "doors in the panelling"[18] which let either science into the basic presuppositions of the other open the way for such later developments as psychosomatic medicine and other sciences in which the physical and the mental overlap. In the interpenetration of knowledge, for Lloyd, philosophy alone must be excluded. Philosophy stands by itself among all other disciplines; it functions as the great unifier, the one apart which must resist partisanship. Consequently, Lloyd distinguishes philosophic truth, method, and license (if you will) from the truth, the method, and the license of all other intellectual activities.[19]

4. *The Unity of the Knowing Process*

Lloyd's most general thesis with respect to the knowledge process is what he calls the "unity" of the subject and the object, or "identity of motive and stimulus."[20] Perhaps the concept can best be explained by indicating what Lloyd does *not* mean by "unity": (1) Lloyd's subject and object are not unified by means of some preëstablished harmony. Such unity would offend his sense of the intimate, *natural* relation they bear to one another and would rely on an external and supernatural agency to bestow the gift of knowledge on the knower. (2) Lloyd's unity is not functional in the sense of obtaining only when the knower knows a world, for this would offend Lloyd's sense of that unity as *continual, constant,* and *perpetual,* and as holding whether the knower is engaged in inquiry or is asleep. (3) Lloyd's unity is not accomplished because the knower is epistemologically part of a larger knower, for this would violate his sense of the *unity of bodies as well as of minds* and would make mind in some sense superior to body, which he cannot allow. (4) Lloyd's unity does not occur because each side is a part of a larger whole—two attributes of a nameless substance—for this would violate Lloyd's sense of unity as *empirical.*

Yet if each of these rejected answers be redefined and qualified, it would be true of Lloyd's meaning. Lloyd's unity *is* 'preëstablished' *if* that means ontologically original and rooted in the nature of things. It is naturally possible, not supernaturally necessary, and is not accomplished by the aid of a *deus ex machina* either at every point or at any point (as it is for the occasionalists and the supernaturalists). It *is* the functional unity of inquiry, *if* that is understood as only a more effectively expressed version of the broader relational unity obtaining at all times. Lloyd's unity *is* accomplished by means of a larger knower if this "larger self"[21] is understood not merely as a unified collection of ideas but as a collection of bodies as well, *if* it is understood as a world shared in common. Lloyd's unity can also be understood as implying two attributes of a more inclusive substance *if* that concept is taken to mean a wider relational context, a broader empirical frame of reference.

The point of contact between Lloyd and Royce on the question of the "larger self" seems to be Lloyd's anthropomorphic insistence that the environment "lives" and "thinks." Such contact is superficial, however, since, it will be remembered, Lloyd means two things by a "living universe." First, he means that all things maintain self-identity and interrelationship. In this sense, Lloyd is giving life distributively to all things, but he really intends no more by it than that a universe is individuated. Secondly, he means that all things live and think in that they are potentially parts of the knowledge situation. Here life is given collectively to all things, by which Lloyd intends no more than that a universe is fully intelligible,[22] that all things live and think by virtue of their togetherness with a knower, and that, in being known, they share the thought and life of the knower.[23]

It would seem that, idealist-fashion, Lloyd is bestowing added dignity upon the self or knower by making him the unifier who relates objects by fulfilling his function of cognitively acting. It might even seem that Lloyd's knower brings living relatedness to a world much in the fashion in which Kant's knower brought the categories to the knowledge situation. In Kant, however, the knower gave form to the formless—order to nameless chaos—whereas in Lloyd the knower only more "effectively" relates the already related. The knower adds only a larger and more meaningful relatedness of cognitive activity and manipulatory use, of which neither inorganic nor lower organic forms are capable. Lloyd's knower invests the already related environment with a new dimension of its life: valuable, manipulatory use.

Lloyd's unity of subject and object in knowledge is not only a functional unity, but one which has infinite possible expressions. Unification in inquiry develops in and through action. For Lloyd ary inquiry empirically necessitates a frame of reference beyond the questioner. The difference between questioner and environment is resolved by means of action. The very putting of a question sets a dualism which must be "resolved in some action or at least in some pragmatic attitude."[24] Knowledge, says Lloyd, ends in a part-for-part correspondence between subject and object *being worked out.*[25] While Spinoza has only *one* unifying substance, Lloyd has an infinite possible number. Each action exemplifies unity in a unique situation. Hence Lloyd's unity of subject and object is directly and immediately experienced in all action, and particularly in the action of knowing.

Knowledge, then, is only *one* manifestation of relatedness in an infinite possibility of relationship. To act in a world,[26] to walk through it, to push it, to grow in it, to bump it are all incidents of relatedness. Lloyd resists the temptation of idealists to maintain the transcendental superiority of man over his environment by virtue of his knowledge of it. Therefore, the importance that knowledge receives in Lloyd's work is greatly diminished. First, knowledge is now only part of self-expression. Secondly, knowledge is not an end in itself, but only a means to self-expression and to further doing. In addition, the data of knowledge can never be merely "abstract ideas," and certainly not if man is to be a significant unifier of his environment and his own life. The thinker who merely *thinks* cannot be quite clear even to himself; he can be so only when he *enacts* and *applies* rather than merely *knows* ideas. Lloyd says:

In a universe, however, of alien or abstract ideas—such as the sensations and the conceptions of the still current psychological theory—there can be no thinkers, only gymnasts.

Schopenhauer . . . was unable to discover in human life any other hope than that of doing mere deeds and knowing mere knowledge, and he drew at once the conclusion that the thinker,

as if a duck condemned to live out of water, could have no more
ideal act of will than suicide . . . his philosophy is on the whole a
very profound comment upon abstract idealism.[27]

Furthermore, *used* knowledge is *valued* activity.   The acting
knower brings values to the universal life of the whole.   As
Lloyd puts it:

. . . formal reason, as the great genius of efficiency, caused just
that divorce of human values and effective activities . . . .   [It
is the] Holy Rational Empire of our time, with its dependence
on pure, reason-organized efficiency . . . [which is] by no means
holy, only soullessly rational, and impossibly imperial.[28]

If, for Lloyd, the knowledge process does not differ in
genus from other types of relational activity, it may seem
that so thoroughgoing a relationalism is forced into a reductionism which it repudiates.   Having related knowledge-
getting to bumping and pushing a world, Lloyd is now
pressed to distinguish cognitive activity from physical activity.   In order to do so, he turns to his idealism to save him.
The knower acts as a whole not only for his own parts but
potentially for an entire universe.   Ultimately, nothing else
can operate in this manner.   The clod may act as a unity for
its parts, but only the knower values, manipulates, and has
ideas about a world—unifies it in a dimensionally different
way.   Two senses of "acting infinitely"[29] thus develop—that
applicable to the clod and that applicable to man.

Lloyd avoids reductionism and at the same time avoids
an honorific role for knowledge by relating it to the simplest
form of living activity.   He strikes a balance between the
demand to treat the knowing organism as native to a world
of clods and amoebae on the one hand and the demand to
raise him above his natural background on the other.   While
the first aspect of the stress leads Lloyd in a naturalistic direction, the seconds leads him into anthropomorphic and anthro-
pocentric categories.

Lloyd's thought is somewhat like Spinoza's in the correlation of thought and extension, as two aspects of a cosmic

order. This order for Lloyd, however, is the pervasive, biological drive of all life. In Lloyd's universe, as the preceding chapters have implied, "mind" and "matter" are coextensive. Lloyd particularly objects to certain implications of the conceptions of "emergence" and emergent evolution that he encounters in his later contemporaries. Mind and the knower do not "emerge" from an alien environment. Matter is not the source from which life arises in due course through fortuitous combinations under satisfactory conditions and from which "mind" emerges as life progresses. Mind and life are equally original in both an ontological and a temporal sense. A thing "lives" in that it has individuality at all, and "thinks" in that it maintains relations thereby with all other things. And life and mind have the same temporal and ontological status as matter.[30] Lloyd also attacks emergent evolution on the ground that it implies mystical beginnings for life and mind. He feels that it would be impossible to understand how the spontaneously developed thing should come to be, in the first place, and have relations with a world, in the second. How, he asks, could such a mind know a world?

Lloyd redefines the concept of emergence for metaphysical accuracy. Newer and more significant forms of matter and mind develop, but the new forms are generically related to the previously existing "life." They are 'new' only in that they are qualitative variants or dimensions of life in the more general sense; they depend upon earlier life but are not reducible to it. Thus greater "freedom" and particularity develop in a world, for more specific and divergent variations of "life" are always in process.

5. *Analysis of the Knowing Process: Sensation*

The unity of subject and object is a process or a developing movement. As process, it cannot be divided into stages, points, or positions without atomizing that which is whole and arbitrarily delimiting a continuous movement. Stages imply a past, present, and future which are always in

flux and which slip into one another.[31]   Hence, the process
of knowledge must be continuous as well as unitary if Lloyd
is not to be as embarrassed as Zeno was either to get it started
or to keep it going.[32]

Yet for purposes of analysis Lloyd divides the knowing
process into four "stages"[33]—sensation, perception, conception, and intuition.   It turns out, however, that only two of
these (perception and conception) are philosophically meaningful, and these can hardly be called "stages," even in the
ordinary sense of the term.   "Sensation" is analogous to
what we called 'A as an undifferentiated unity' in Chapter I.
"Perception" is analogous to the 'differentiated A' in the first
aspect of its dual movement, namely, that of relating its parts
to itself.   "Conception" is analogous to the 'differentiated A'
in the second aspect of its dual movement, namely, that of
relating itself to a whole world.   And "intuition" is analogous
to the 'overdifferentiated A.'   It should be evident that
"sensation" and "intuition" are not empirical parts of the
knowledge process, but function only as limiting terms,
while "perception" and "conception" act as polar terms and
are descriptive of A in the activity of knowledge.

Lloyd objects to some earlier theories of sensation which
separate the subject from the object.   First, he opposes a
view of sensation as a process by which some kind of external
stimulus operates *on* the knower, who passively receives
it.   Secondly, he objects to sensation understood as the
internal possibility for sensation on the part of the knower.
Both views presuppose a duality between the knower and the
known which runs counter to Lloyd's position on the original
and continual unity of the two; both views atomize sensations; and neither view is a hypothesis supported by experience, for experience exhibits the sensed and the sensory agent
in combination.   In both views the definition is "formal,"
describing what is *logically antecedent* to knowledge as part
of knowledge.   Both views, to put it in my terms, are
attempts to give the undifferentiated A predicates.   They
assume a duality of 'self' and 'other' which develops only as a

result of the tension of experience and which thereby attributes the same conditions to unconsciousness as to consciousness.   Sensation as internal possibility really presupposes a
completely   undifferentiated   continuum—a   consciousness
which is actually unconsciousness.   Sensation as external
stimulus is equally abstract, and presupposes that the stimu-
lus-sense combination will or can produce a sensation which
is not, in part, determined by what one has sensed in the
past—a 'pure' sensation, as it were, given by the stimulus, in
which the sensory agent plays only the role of a registrar of
data and not of a partial determinant of them.   Consequently, to describe what sensation is without admitting a
necessary unity between subject and object is merely to
describe illicitly the indescribable.

Sensation, then, functions as a limiting condition in an
abstract account of knowledge.   A limit, Lloyd says, "sets
the law" and "deepens the reality of each member of the
series by making the series itself an organized whole."[34]   It is
only "the epistemologist's indirection, or apology, for something deeper than mere knowledge and its stages."[35]   The
"deeper thing" for which the limiting notion stands and
which it indirectly indicates is what Lloyd calls the "vital
impulse" or the "impulse to self-expression [will]," which
here is the dual necessity of both subject and object to be
interrelated in infinite ways, the spontaneous need for the
knower to find a world spread out before him as well as the
need (even more anthropomorphically described) for the
known to be the experience of the knower.   According to
Lloyd, "Psychology . . . is more than epistemology; it is biology also."[36]

Sensation so illicitly understood is an indication of the
necessity which A has to be individuated and yet related to
an entire world.   But Lloyd sees this necessity as both logical and biological.   He understands logical necessity as the
drive of the organism and therefore as its "life" or "will."
Hence, 'logical necessity' becomes continuous with 'biological need.'   Biological necessity in turn unites external stimulus and internal motive in a two-sided relational process.

6. *Analysis of the Knowing Process: Intuition*

"Intuition," for Lloyd, is an expression of what we have called the 'overdifferentiated A'—the A infinitely differentiated and therefore incapable of empirical existence. This "last stage" of knowledge is a "limit," as was sensation. It cannot be a content of consciousness. Consequently, actual knowledge is composed solely of perception and conception. The double set of terms provides Lloyd with a polarity without which knowledge could not be considered an action or process.

Epistemologically, "intuition" means "the perfect freedom of using language, or of adaptation to environment"[37]— the individual fully adapted to his environment. It is the entelechy or culminating limit of knowledge as a biological activity. Metaphysically, it means the knower becoming entirely "one" and completely unified or infinitely related to his environment. As Lloyd puts it: ". . . language and thought arc one."[38] Intuition implies a knower finished knowing because he knows and does all—the knower become an all-effective god, as it were. It thus connotes the mythical completion of the process of knowledge, which is endless, abiding, and never actually completed. It is a "limit"[39] and hence only a fiction. (Lloyd holds the view that it is unwise to be too wise about the unknowable.) But any question resulting in successful inquiry reflects the *operation* of "intuition" functioning as an infinite limit to, or the law of, a series. Thus Lloyd says, "Intuition . . . is but an epistemological disguise for the ripened act,"[40] for with it, "consciousness ripens into fluent action; with it, thought is set free."[41]

What Lloyd calls "sensation" and "intuition," though they are not empirical acts of cognition, are not to be confused with what he calls the "unknowable." Lloyd examines the historical development of the idea of the "unknowable," which plays such a major role in epistemological theory.[42] This examination takes the form of a distinction between five types of "agnosticism." First is "absolute agnosticism," or the view that reality (existence) is outside of all knowledge and hence completely and essentially unknowable. Second is Berkeley's "transcendent agnosticism," which, based upon reductionist idealism, finds reality itself knowable only to God's mind.   Berkeley is then disposed to treat sensation as "internal possibility," which to Lloyd is utterly unsatisfactory. Third is Kant's "transcendental agnosticism," which Lloyd regards as based on idealism that is no longer reductivistic in that it distinguishes two spheres of knowledge.   In this type, the unknowable has been partly removed from its transcendent realm in that it at least forms the mysterious grounds in which experience is rooted.   In Kant Lloyd sees the unknowable brought closer to experience, but still treated as a thing—a content apart.   Fourth is what Lloyd calls "scientific agnosticism," which brings the unknowable still closer to experience, understanding it as the "yet to be known." Although empirical, this type of unknowable is still not a part of the content of knowledge; a sharp dichotomy still exists between it and the knowable.   As soon as something *not* known becomes known, the unknowable loses its character and, at least in any specific case of knowledge, ceases to exist. Fifth is the "agnosticism of radical empiricism," the type to which Lloyd feels that he subscribes.   Here the unknowable represents the living immediacy which is an aspect of all knowledge, whether perception or conception.   The unknowable enters into *perception* as the uncapturable immediacy of any relational situation.   Nor is this immediacy what other philosophers have regarded as the felt quality of sense data; it is, rather, the felt quality of *the unity between knower and known*.   The unknowable enters into *conception* as the residuum of interrelatedness implied by all conception but never exhausted by it.   This idea will be expanded later.[43]

7. *Analysis of the Knowing Process: Perception and Conception*

Perception and conception constitute the polarity by means of which the knowledge process actually moves.   The process of cognition is governed by the same principles of movement as were outlined in the general analysis of relational activity. In the process of knowledge the knower differentiates internally into parts which are now describable as perceptive and conceptive, and, at the same time, he differentiates himself from the outside world and is subject for its object. In turn, the outside world differentiates itself into an infinite plurality. This state of internal and external differentiation illustrated in both knower and known is repeated in the relations between them. To recall the general account of movement, an "alienation process" develops (1) between the knower and the known, or the subject and the object; (2) between the parts of the known—or a plural universe including both A and –A; and (3) between the parts of the knower —perception and conception.

Lloyd warns philosophers that when perception is understood as isolated from conception, "sensation" is falsely interpreted to be either internal possibility *for* sensation or external stimulus *for* sensation.[44] In both cases a limiting condition of the knowledge process is illicitly given predicates. In both cases the undifferentiated A is treated as though it were differentiated.

Similarly, when conception is understood as isolated from perception, a view of "intuition" develops which interprets it as capable of producing either universally valid truths about experience or some kind of absolute truth which transcends empirical verifiability. Again, in both cases, a limiting condition of the knowledge process is given predicates—the over-differentiated A is taken literally.

Perception and conception, then, represent two contemporary "stages" contributing to one process. They are a polarity in terms of which knowledge is a growth and a development, and are analogous to the two phases of the activity of the differentiated A.[45]

8. *Consciousness as Tension; Impulse and Control*

Lloyd characterizes the knowledge process in terms of "tension."[46] Apparently he chooses the term because it suggests the moving-rest polarity in terms of which all process must be defined. Tension as rest suggests the permanence of the relationship. Tension as movement suggests action which relationship implies and necessitates. Further, the term indicates the conjunction of subject with object, the subject and object understood with reference to one another and in communal relation, which Lloyd calls "consciousness." "Tension" in Lloyd corresponds to Dewey's "*inter*action." Like Dewey's term, it implies a 'situation' containing two interrelated factors. The term seems to Lloyd particularly suitable because it implies that the relation between subject and object is not merely one of knowing, but one of *doing* as well: "Consciousness is never epiphenomenal, but, even like the ideas belonging to it, always mediative; never merely ornamental, but always useful."[47]

Lloyd often equates the terms "consciousness" and "tension."[48] Since tension implies both movement and rest, consciousness, like movement, is conceived as a relational unity of coexistences and a continuity of sequences.[49] Since tension implies spatial action, the organism is no longer conscious when no longer active.[50] Suggesting self-movement, consciousness is, significantly enough, described by Lloyd as "interest"[51]—a native and fascinating community of subject and object which internally excites an organism to be receptive and externally excites a world to present its infinite diversity. Thus Lloyd's definition of consciousness as interest (which, incidentally, plays an important part in his pragmatic philosophy of education) is another way of stating the earlier contention that the organism does not *have* sensations, that sensations are induced neither by the outer world nor by the mind, but rather that "the consciousness of an organism *is* sensuous."[52] In this relational theory "consciousness" is the name for an organism's sensory and cognitive activities, continuous with all activity and essential to the character of its life: ". . . consciousness is an interactive function or product, involving all parts."[53]

Tension differentiates perception from conception and

subject from object, and itself exhibits a double aspect, as must all things. It is subject to polarity and therefore to a dual interpretation of its meaning. The dual aspect of the moving-rest polarity implied by tension Lloyd calls "impulse and control"[54] and, again, the "centrifugal" and "centripe-tal"[55] motion implicit in organism. These term sets repre-sent two aspects of the knowing process. They suggest, on the one hand, the forward push, the desire and the need of the organism to relate to all beyond its boundaries, and, on the other, the restricting conditions put upon each organism by its own individuality. "Impulse," which Lloyd some-times calls "spontaneity" connotes the dissatisfaction of the whole-containing part with its partness. It represents the part 'wanting to be' *actually* whole-containing and not only potentially so. This forward push of organism is as true for any activity as it is for the knowing activity. It is as true for walking, pushing, and breathing as for thinking. By "impulse" Lloyd is attempting to point up what he sees to be the primary characteristic of relational complexes. The very activity which underlies individuality forces each thing to grow, develop, and digest the whole world. It is what drives A by nature and necessity to relate itself to every-thing else. It means not only that the thinker hungrily hunts knowledge, but that the walker rushingly covers distance and the appreciator avidly enjoys.

"Control," on the other hand, is that aspect of the moving-rest polarity of relational activity which forces A back into its own boundaries. It connotes individuality, uniqueness, and discreteness, to which A is subject and from which bounds it would forever escape. It represents in Lloyd's thought the fact that the knower's individuality colors his world, that the walker tires, and that the appreciator becomes overfull and nauseated.

9. *Matter as "Translator"*

In Lloyd "matter" is not defined as a thing or a stuff out of which anything is made, but is the name for a *general func-*

tion, the 'mattering' of a world, I suppose we may call it. Although matter *is* empirically real, we cannot describe it without at the same time describing our own characteristics. We cannot predicate of it without hopelessly admixing it with ourselves and literally stumbling over our own feet. *What* matter is cannot be determined; its characteristics can be anything that the subject's education, talents, and place in history make it.   Consequently, a thing must be described in terms of *what it does.*   However, we are brought to ask what it *is* because the tension between perception and conception gives a kind of stable character to our impression of it.   Psychologically, at least, percepts are more readily understood as objects than as acts or related functions.

Once again Lloyd follows a consistent functionalism. Matter is the bridge or "medium of exchange" which renders exchangeable what he calls man's "life to himself"[56] and processes in the environment.   Matter "mediates" objectivity to subject and vice versa.   It is the nature of the object to display itself as otherness to the subject.   Matter is a general "function"[57] in that its substantial otherness must be described functionally; it is "general" in the sense that it is "capable of as many applications or expressions as there are relations in experience."[58]   Thus matter serves as the sea of solidarity, the medium of otherness, in which any and all relationship must take place.   Matter is a function in the sense that it can "mediate"[59] (manifest) all that the subject wishes to express.   It is able to "translate"[60] into objectivity all that the activities of the subject require.   It "mediates" ideas in the sense that it permits bridges as imagined by engineers to be translated into actual bridges; it permits values to be translated into books and music.

Thus Lloyd describes the subject and its environment as intimately and originally related.   The environment never fails to *fill* the needs of the subject with matter.   All that man requires in order to express values is furnished him by the environment, which co-operates with him.   It not only gives him his own body, but a world of infinite bodies into which to translate these values. Hence, ". . . civilization seems to have depended on both a set medium, or staging, like environment, and a freed medium, like language . . . . Man's so-called natural environment is only his reading to self, or his life at large to self, vicariously maintained."[61]

The notion of "mediation of the environment" (its translation of values, sensations, and ideas into material form) has a number of consequences. In the first place, it supplies man with a material basis for values and gives him the necessary "material wings" (Santayana) strong enough to carry him as high as he would fly. Man is placed in a natural world which co-operates with his spiritual as well as physical needs rather than in one which acts as the obstacle to them.[62]

But Lloyd's conception of matter as whatever the subject makes it is not a return to a kind of Berkeleianism. Lloyd avoids reduction of matter to ideas. He does not put the subject in what, for Berkeley, would be God's place. He is saying, on the contrary, that the be-mattered environment is reflecting the qualitative character of the knower who knows it. He is insisting that the world is qualitatively different for a child than for an adult, that it is empirically a different world today in the age of machinery and technology than it was in the Renaissance. In fact, he is stating a truism, namely, that the environment grows and changes with the people who change, and change it. Thus the environment is not created by the knower, but it is qualitatively varied by him. Lloyd contends that the state of the environment never outruns or lags behind men, but, with cosmic justice, always keeps equal step. The natural world has the character it has relative to the attainments of men. It was mechanical, "erratic, given to extremes, dependent on chance or miracle"[63] when men were. The external world has never taken unfair advantage. "It has confronted man, so to speak, in like size and kind,"[64] for man and his world are "creatures of one life, twin-born and . . . twin-growing."[65]

Further, the environment as mediator for the individual translates and crystallizes in matter what he is, and thus offers it for all others to share.   The environment functions as the communicator between ourselves, and is thus the core of sociality.   We can have a society, a language, a common science only because we share the same environment, which is then collectively a crystallization of our total character, thought, and activity.   The environment functions much as does Dewey's "funded experience," only here the funding is objectified and preserved in material form.   By such crystallization our thought, activity, and values are made available to our contemporaries, as well as to future generations who will inherit our world and our activities.   Our progeny will face a world which serves as a monument[66] to our own past activities and values.   Lloyd's notion of translation shows his divergence from Berkeleian idealism by its insistence on the solidarity and empirical reality of matter.   Not only is matter real, but it provides the bond which joins men together in community rather than acts as the obstacle which separates them.   Matter is a messenger from the past and a harbinger of the future.   Matter gives constant tacit evidence of past as well as present thought, activity, and value whether we be conscious of its testimony or not.   Matter, however, is only one of the two great mediators between ourselves and our neighbors and between ourselves and all things 'other,' for it shares this function with language.   Lloyd's theory of language is so uniquely suggestive that I will consider it separately (see section 10, below).

Because Lloyd's interest in activity understands matter as a function, his interest in relationality must view that function as reciprocal.   Change in a relational world, we said, finds activity in a *complex of relations* rather than in a *particular agent;* hence not only is the environment a function of the self, but the self is equally a function of the environment, albeit the bringer of a new dimension.   Thus the *environment environs*[67] me as I act in it.   Here Lloyd pushes his sense of the interaction between agent and environment into a relationalism perhaps even more thoroughgoing than that of Dewey.   For Lloyd the agent does not manipulate the environment any more than it 'manipulates' him. The environment, as a verb, acts on the agent as well as the agent acts on it. The bird flies through the air, but the air 'flies' the bird as well. To recall our general analysis of change, "Travel is a commerce, not a separation." By travel, the agent is as much an expression of environmental relations between places as they are of him. Thus I, as warm, react "on myself as a function of the room," while "the thermometer does but show nature, as it were, measuring herself, reacting upon herself . . . ." To open the window is "only one of the many motions in which the heat of the room has found expression."[68]

The environment is a verb to our verbs, an activity to our activities. We function in terms of its activities in the same way that it functions in terms of our activities upon it. Lloyd concludes that "the room changes its own temperature"[69] as much as we change it, since we are part of the environment from a larger point of view. Consequently, the environment 'lives.' It is so intimately a function of us and we of it that it shares our life. As it holds up to us in solid form the picture of what we ourselves are and of what the history of the race has been, as it permits us to translate into it new qualitative types of expression (dimensions) that we bring to it, as it shares in the wholeness that we bring to it, the environment lives our life with us and is a material counterpart of that life.

The idea that the environment lives is productive of further interesting consequences. The environment is so closely related to the subject that a history of the environment is an accurate mirror of the history or the state of man's development. For this reason, Lloyd in various places examines the "inner logic" of an environment: the types of rulers, the principal occupations of the people, the character of the laborers are what determine the state of development of the people in it. The intellectual climate and its physical equipment always grow with us; our very questions, our intellectual controversy, and the state of our sciences will tell us what we are.   The outer world "is our whole history, nay, our whole evolution, our past and our present and our future, made contemporaneous, or all the existing incidents of our being active as one.   And what are we as conscious and animate but intimate functions of that which encompasses us?"[70]

Insofar as the environment "lives," it is "spiritual" (or value-holding) in two senses.   First, it is spiritual in the sense that it shares our organic valuing life with us and gains spirit by proximity to us.   In other words, the physical world is "spiritual" by virtue of our companionship.   Secondly, the environment is spiritual in the sense that in its own nature as an infinite function it can reflect, crystallize, and materialize our values for us.   It is fully capable of translating values.[71] The living environment reflects the self, the knower of it. The interpenetration of all intellectual disciplines reflects our own unity, our own unity reflects the interpenetration of the physical and psychical sciences, and each reflects the unity of the self and the environment.   Science itself, Lloyd says, is "self-consciousness of self" or self finding its own meaning in that which superficially seems alien.   As we have pointed out, Lloyd maintains that every question implies a distinction between ourselves and a world which ends in a one-to-one correspondence between subject and object being worked out.   With the putting of a question, "the inquirer enters upon a process which involves finding himself, such finding constituting the meaning sought—in the thing inquired about or relating all the specific details of the thing, as they are analyzed out, to answering factors discovered in his own nature . . . ."[72]

Thus, by virtue of the mediation of a material world, the knower and the environment exchange gifts.   The self, a knower and therefore a relator and a bringer of unity, enriches the environment with its own larger fulfillment. The knower unifies the physical world and gives it new life. He expresses ideas, acts, and values by means of it and therefore "fulfills" it; he makes it a recipient of values and therefore a type of thing it would not be in his absence.   The knower brings wholeness and completeness and therefore "truth." Being unique and capable of infinite expressions via the environment, he brings genius and originality to a world of matter. By virtue of his ability to know, he brings new dimensions of action to his world, causing it to grow, progress, and move in endless new ways.

The environment in turn equally honors us. It will be recalled that like scientific law, the environment is a "contemporizing agency"; it holds the past and the future in the present. By present-ing the past and the incipient future, the environment permits us to speak, act, and predict. By becoming all that we have been, it permits our very racial memories to be present to us.[73] It solidifies the knower's activities and values, which, in turn, may serve as material for further cultural development. As a permanent record of the knower's valued activities, the environment serves as a "mediator" between generations.

Both Lloyd and Dewey maintain that the organism cannot be understood apart from its functions. On the other hand, its functions maintain no existence separate from the organism's action. Thus the organism and its activity must be understood with reference to each other. It is to connote this "organism-acting-in-environment" relationship, which Dewey calls "interaction," that Lloyd employs the term "translation." "Translation" means the interaction of a *particular* self with a *particular* environment, and the term not only takes the place of what has been so similarly called "transaction" in Dewey's sense, but, in addition, points up Lloyd's further emphasis on the *individuality* of any organism-environment transaction. Thus, for Lloyd each organism *translates* its particular transaction in its own distinctive tongue; it enters into a uniquely trans-lated trans-action, if you will.

10. *Language as "Mediator"*

For Lloyd men can communicate verbally only because they communicate in a broader sense. Language, Lloyd says, is a "mediator,"[74] and a "two-faced"[75] one at that. Language "mediates" in providing the means by which the gap between polarities is bridged.   This would be a commonplace if you and I were the polarities involved.   But you and I are not polarities at all;[76] we are merely different from one another. Lloyd insists that our discourse is only possible because of a larger community which we both share and which serves as the basis of our talk.   What is this larger community, this broader discourse, which makes verbal discourse meaningful?   Unlike Royce's community, it is not ideal, but physical. Verbal communication is one form of a broader, logically prior communication with a physical world.   Words and sentences depend upon and are responsible to this broader communication.

The term 'language,' then, does not mean merely verbal symbol, but is extended to include parts of the environment as symbols.   Furthermore, 'environment' is not merely the immediate physical surroundings of any organism, but the entire outer world, the total other-than-self.   While the written and spoken word provides a means of communication between man and man, the used environment provides a means of communication between man and animals, and in fact between all parts of an organically related world: "The outer world is essentially linguistic.   It is the language through which all the manifold forms in the hierarchy of organisms have intelligible communication, and are so enabled to lead at once a single and an indefinitely differentiated life."[77]

The use of language, then, is a phase of all organic life, not just a phase of the life of human beings.   Both spoken sentence and used environment serve to relate parts into one whole and systematize a set of relations.   While a sentence relates words into an idea, an act relates man to a universe. Both sentence and act are units for their parts.   As Lloyd puts it, language consists of the "parts of fluent activity in general instead of merely [the] parts of speech,"[78] and again, language is not the "medium of the exchange of abstract thought, but the basis of an organized life."[79]

Language plays the role of the 'one' to the 'many.' The used sentence is the one for the *dis*embodied many, or words, while the used environment is the one for the embodied many, or things. Language is therefore analogous to what we may call the "spiritual" activity of the person, or activity which in some sense modifies the whole. Insofar as the "spacial or physical objectivity is spiritual also, or the same as worth,"[80] things as well as words have gained wings.

Communication for Lloyd is really effect*ed* community—community happening or in process. A universe and an unspoken language are potentially language. Environment used and language spoken actually become languages. While both the environment and the spoken word are parallel in their function, the environment is much broader in that it is available to all parts of organic life and not merely to men.

Language in both its broad and its narrow sense is not only a condition but a result of activity; perhaps the term 'token' of activity would be truer to Lloyd's temper. The fact that we find an environment physical is a mark of our using it—of walking, sitting, writing, and bumping. The fact that we find our thought conceptual is a mark of our intellectual use of environment—of ideationally planning action in it. As language *is* used, it defines the conditions of activity. The use of language is a pause in activity, a "cessation of self-expression,"[81] a withdrawal or "hesitation"[82] preliminary to what Lloyd calls "activity to self."[83] The pause before speech defines the conditions of activity in exactly the same way in which a pause in action defines the conditions of future activity. To enunciate a situation is more clearly to understand it. To use a world is to be more effective in later use of it. Without understanding we could not have spoken at all, but, having spoken, we understand more fully. Without having used a world, we could not have acted at all, but, having acted, we act more successfully. Lloyd gives some significant examples of language in operation or "activity to self" in both the broad and the narrow sense of language, and points out their analogous relationship:

The day laborer who would deal the second blow more accurately than the first, pauses [the symbol develops as the laborer conceptually defines the medium] that the involved relations may define themselves, but the first had given him the interest in accuracy for the second. Reading, too, is not psychologically different from the laborer's reflection. The presented page, we usually say, in its symbols awakens a very highly complex imagery, in the form of reminiscences of all sorts and suggestions and fancies, but it all stands for a life that the reader has come to live to himself [the double language the reader has come to use and hence know]. It is his past, which as he reads returns, but in the form of an object, in which the unity of the present is symbolized, and through which a more accurate blow at life is in preparation.[84]

Language, then, operating as a mediator to effect community between the knower and his world, really involves a withdrawal from action, at which point the relationships between them are symbolized. It will be recalled that the knower-and-known polarity splits into a smaller polarity of perception and conception on the side of the knower. While the act represents a nonlinguistic symbolization of an environment, the word represents a verbal symbolization of it. Spoken language is the environment made "portable." To put it another way, as the gap between knower and known is spanned by the knower's manipulation of a physical world, the chasm between perception and conception is bridged by written and spoken symbols. As a result, the physical world ceases to be 'other' or solely physical, while words are no longer bubbles of syllables but expressive of meaningful action. As environment and word become symbols, each defines previous acts and used words. As symbols, the defined word and act are more utilizable for further action and talk. The physicality of the environment is now "spiritual," being big with the knower's valuable action; and at the same time words, analogously, are big with his thought.

Communication with a physical world is one side of Lloyd's notion of a double-faced language. The other side is the interpenetration of conception and perception which produces verbal symbols. From the first springs the act, from the second, the verbal symbol. While the physicality of a world, as it were, "translates"[85] the knower to his environment and the environment to the knower, verbal symbols translate ideas to sense and sense to ideas. Only on the basis of these communications within ourselves and between ourselves and a physical world can social communication by means of verbal symbols take place. All communication ultimately rests on the possibility of symbolizing either in word or in act.

What, for Lloyd, is a symbol and how does it arise? Using a metaphorical term borrowed from psychology to describe the process of symbolization, Lloyd calls the symbol an "after-image"[86] of experience. Begging that the term be taken in a broad sense, he maintains that the symbol as an after-image has the most basic characteristics of a name. When the laborer paused to review the situation that had just occurred, when he hesitated before the next hammer blow, he was caught in a situation of "tension"[87] between his spontaneous urge for action and action as controlled and premediated. He was poised between overt expression and rehearsal of the past. During this time he "named" what had occurred; he rehearsed the past act and redefined the conditions for a more successful future one. During the moment of pause perception faded into conception. In accordance with Lloyd's general "principle of use,"[88] the merely perceived image loses its immediacy and becomes a symbolized conception. The perceived image becomes an idea. The idea will, in its turn, "set activity free." At the point of symbolization "ideal experimentation" (Peirce) takes place by means of the fluid and adaptable symbol. Symbolization, then, is both a condition for action and a mark of a controlled act. Lloyd says that "in an image or object or symbol . . . [undergoing ideal experimentation], the self is set free. No symbol is mere symbol that is not proved so by some action in use of it . . . ."[89] As ideal manipulation takes

place, a verbal language develops which results in a more
facile and effective act—in an act in which the agent's past
experience is more successfully adjusted to present problems.
Lloyd asks, ". . . what is language, if not a complex of 'dying
metaphors' or 'material associations,' or 'passing reminiscences,' dying or associated or passing in the interest of
organization or adjustment or fluency?"[90]   Language, then,
is the symbolization of experience for the purposes of ideal
experimentation which ends in action.   Perception gives
way to conception, and "thought sooner or later dies in a
fulfilling conduct; naming is succeeded by doing; the self,
only for a time identified with its isolating thought-organs,
abandons the rehearsing and the after-imagery, returning to
its world,—entering the World of Acts, passing from appearance to reality."[91]

Language is a "medium of exchange."[92]   In a particularly
optimistic vein Lloyd asserts that language is in some sense a
"standard"[93] measurement.   In fact, the physical environment appears to function for Lloyd as does standard currency.   What he seems to mean is that the physical environment provides exchange between physical goods on the one
hand and the unifying services of the knower on the other.
Lloyd does not commit himself on just how far verbal language can be honored as standard currency—particularly
when spoken by philosophers.   In any event, the implication
is that the verbal symbol can be relatively standard *provided*
it *takes cognizance of prior conversations with the environment,* provided that words are defined in terms of experiential activities, provided, if you will, that words are defined
'pragmatically' in an experimentalist sense!   (I might add, in
passing, that however "standard" and reliable Lloyd's conversations with his environment may have been, his verbal
conversations with his fellow man never reflected this re-
liability!)

Lloyd's conception of the "mediation of environment" as
standard currency of physical and intellectual exchange is
another of his own provocative ways of expressing the foun-

dations of what Dewey calls "transaction." It is his formulation of the nature of and justification for pragmatic definition. As is true of all his other terms, Lloyd chooses it
because of its overtones. Not only does "mediate" suggest
"transaction" between a knower and the known, but it suggests adverbs of versatility, fluidity, and ease of manipulation to modify that transaction.

Speaking specifically of language as used symbol, Lloyd
gives it three functions. It is (1) "objectively descriptive,"
(2) "individually redemptive," and (3) "socially or organically
mediative."[94] Some suggestive meanings develop. Descriptive symbols permit withdrawal from immediate action and
thereby stimulate ideal rehearsal or experimentation. They
bring interpretation to the impulse expressed and clarifica-
tion for the knower in that they make him conscious of what
he had not fully understood before verbalization.[95]

As "individually redemptive," language provides the
possibility for individual self-expression and therefore freedom in a social group. Along with its more obvious celebration of the relation between human fulfillment and freedom
of speech, this seems to suggest that environment as language
crystallizes values of all kinds and renders these values
exchangeable. It not only supports the naturalistic contention that all values have a physical basis, but it also emphasizes the social interchange of such values. By developing
organs for functioning "to" oneself,[96] language provides intellectual activity with techniques and methods by means of
which the individual participates in group life.

As "socially mediative," language is the basis of organized
life. It not only offers a physical environment symbolized to
provide the basis for communal thought, but it presents a
stage upon which communal activities of a broader sort can
take place. Language not only "mediates" between men
who otherwise would be internally isolated, but it also
"redeems" them from estrangement from lower forms of life
and a world of inanimate things.

As itself a developing activity, used language has a history. Lloyd distinguishes two historical interpretations of the nature of language, which he contrasts with respect to adequacy: first, a "creationalistic"[97] interpretation, and, secondly, a "naturalistic" one. In periods when language was viewed creationalistically, or as Heaven-sent, men felt that they were special creatures because they were language users. They thought of inspiration as verbal, indulged in prophecy, and considered 'the word' and 'the book' sacred. But when language is regarded naturalistically, it is "no longer [understood as] the repository of a fixed truth or the seat of any mysterious power"[98] which sets men on a divine level, but as the "medium only of a thought that lives in and with the whole life of mankind."[99] The "naturalistic" view, which Lloyd accepts, understands language as a developing phase of animal existence, as conventional, and as contextual and extended to all animals: "All conscious creatures,[100] low or high, are addicted to what is language essentially."[101]

11. "Idea" Defined

Having examined the environment and the mediating bridges that link it to the knower, we can now explain the function of ideas. Lloyd's view in this respect is perhaps one of the most significant results of his relationalism. Since truth is found in the relations between things, the only kind of predication available for a description of an object concerns its relating movements or functional activity.[102]

It is an easy transition from a functional view of things to a functional view of ideas, from things as forces to ideas as forces. If ideas apprehend the movement and action of things, they *must* take their character from the things they are ideas about. Consequently, "ideas [are] not forms but forces,"[103] says Lloyd. In fact, "consciousness is always a planning."[104] If Lloyd is to maintain an epistemological realism, if ideas are "forces," they are forces of an agent who uses them, forceful "plans of action"—'forceful' when they instigate successful inquiry, 'plans' because they are ideational manipulations of an environment by a subject described as a "planner" and an "organizer." The transition is now complete. Relationalistic organicism has become pragmatism.

But Lloyd's pragmatism is only half of a larger metaphysical story. On the one hand, ideas are forces and plans of action for successful manipulation of a world; but on the other hand, as such they are, as well, real agents relating the polar terms of knower and known into one metaphysical unity. On the one hand, knowledge is a process, a set of verifying activities in an empirical world; on the other, it is a supratemporal, as well as a temporal, set of relations. On the one hand, mind is no longer the transcendental bringer of order to a world, for unity and order are equally referable "either to the outer life [environment] or to the inner [mind]";[105] but on the other hand, mind permits the knower to be a "whole-containing" part. On the one hand, questions are answered not by a priori speculation but by action in a world; but on the other, Lloyd's metaphysical resolution of dualism has equal importance with his assertions of the crux of pragmatism. Thought is the "use of consciousness for some act of adjustment,"[106] but it will be noticed that Lloyd uses the term "consciousness" to connote "mind." And, finally, the end of knowledge is successful practice, but for Lloyd this ultimately means that the end of knowledge is a one-to-one correlation between subject and object being worked out. It is evident that the metaphysical unity of subject and object shares honors with, and sometimes almost obfuscates, the lurking pragmatic methodology.

12. The Process of the Process of Knowledge

The final outcome of the knowledge process is that Lloyd makes the process itself undergo process. In examining the history of epistemological thought from the Middle Ages to the present, he reviews three types of metaphysical presuppositions which gave rise to three types of epistemological theory.

The process, as he sees it, is one from metaphysical dualism to epistemological dualism to a disavowal of metaphysics altogether—or pragmatism.[107]   Lloyd finds that epistemological thought of the Middle Ages offers a "metaphysical dualism." Allegiance was given to a complete separation of mind from body, spirit from matter. Truth-seeking was consequently understood to mean a search for the *structure* of things, or an account of the nature of *things* as *discrete* entities. This became inadequate and a new type of approach to the problem of knowledge developed. The earlier metaphysical dualism became an instrument, a tool for something new and qualitatively different, namely, "epistemological dualism," which puts to use the former static, inactive, and structural type. With epistemological dualism, truth is understood to mean a description of the acts of things, of relationships; but the relationships are still understood to be epistemologically (if not metaphysically) separate from the knower. Finally, in contemporary philosophy, epistemological dualism ceases to be an institute or a framework in terms of which all is understood, and it, too, becomes a tool for a new type of "dualism," offered by pragmatism. Here truth is no longer found in *descriptions* of relations but in the *actual relating activities* of man using a world. With pragmatism, truth comes to mean 'relatingly doing.' Consequently, Lloyd heralds pragmatism as an "including negative," an "irrationalism"[108] denying the earlier rationalism and thus offering a new dimension to philosophic thought: "The substantial progress of thought, except for somehow persistent and discouraging idealistic lapses, has been a gradually preparing triumph of so-called natural realism."[109]

Like all other processes, epistemological theory illustrates the "principle of use" and moves "from institute to instrument." Each phase of the process utilizes the previous phase, but develops from the use of it a new dimension or new perspective which is born of and related to the previous phases, but which is "dimensionally different" from and not reducible to any or all of them. Lloyd takes his own view to be using the first two stages and exemplifying the last.

Lloyd further supports the sequential development of epistemological theory by an examination of analogous and interrelated historical developments. Guided by the conviction that the method of knowledge-seeking, the character of the knowledge gained, and the evaluation of the results are "social studies," he examines man's interpenetrative intellectual surroundings for the light these will throw on the changing views of the nature of knowledge.[110] He traces, as we have seen, the conception of the idea of the unknowable, distinguishing five types of agnosticism.[111] The same development is analogously displayed in his distinction of the number of ultimates that have been found in a metaphysics,[112] in the tests for truth,[113] and in the conceptions of the nature of God.[114]

It is significant to observe that for Lloyd the process of the process of knowledge, which is here presented as an account of the intellectual history of the race, is at the same time an account of the process of individual inquiry. The presence of a problem for an inquirer is analogous to the stage of "metaphysical dualism"; the interplay between fact and idea which Dewey has stressed is analogous to the stage of "epistemological dualism"; and the solution of the problem is analogous to the stage of "pragmatism."

As Lloyd's "experimental idealist,"[115] armed with a pragmatic epistemology, spiritually returns to his world at last, Lloyd sees the ultimate goal of society to be a unification of the human and the natural, the "liberation of the soul and the spiritual realization of the body,"[116] "the life of the free soul and the natural body."[117] Confidence in natural processes will gain mankind freedom not *from* but *in* nature in that his will need no longer oppose his natural environment; instead he can rejoice in saying, ". . . I will that nature's processes do the work."[118] Like Santayana in expressing "ultimate religion," Lloyd finds lusty[119] participation in nature's activity the antidote for fear and dejection in being its victim. Thus:

The creative will [creative utilization of necessity] can belong only to a soul that has given up all spiritual abstraction [psychological isolation] and aloofness [epistemological isolation]; that also, though comfortably established on earth, refuses to be put to sleep by an orderly routine and system; and that . . . applies the very life and force of nature to making the world different.[120]

Lloyd defines his "near" or "naturalistic idealism"[121] as a "moving principle," a "way of life," not a fixed creed or body of doctrine. Thought and act interpenetrate and reaffirm man's powers. Although this process of interpenetration always exhibited itself in the same manner, even among his animal ancestors, man now *understands the process* as his natural reception into a natural world.

13. *Lloyd and Pragmatism*

Lloyd believes pragmatism to be the solution to the traditional knowledge problems. In action, a knower makes intimate contact with a world; he interpenetrates his diversified self with a diversified environment. Knowledge is relative to the inquirer and revelatory of him to himself; it is no longer "objective" or apart from the inquirer. Action is not *in* a world or *through* a world but *of* a world, by means of a world.

Lloyd finds in pragmatism an assertion of the importance of the self irrespective of whether that assertion be lawless and self-willed (as James's version has a tendency to be) or whether that self be the creator not of truth but of the tentative hypothesis (as in Dewey's and Peirce's version).

Taking cognizance of the different types of pragmatism of his day and yet suggesting their similar stresses on self, Lloyd maintains that pragmatism can furnish "loose and dangerous tests," but also responsible and "vital" ones.[122] Despite the subjectivist tendencies of certain kinds of pragmatism, Lloyd sees pragmatism guaranteeing the importance of the individual inquirer without destroying epistemological realism and without becoming solipsistic. He finds James's pragmatism asserting self by giving will an important place.

The subject as strivingly alive—as vitally rather than mechanically knowing—invests the object with meaning. Whatever depends on will and not necessity (being organic rather than mechanical action) "is not merely real, but both real and ideal."[123]   Since the negative polar term includes its positive in a larger whole, Lloyd sees even James's pragmatism affirming reason by denying the conception given in earlier idealisms. 'Reason,' for James, means the intelligibility (or, in this case, the believability) of the world at large and not either a special faculty or a superempirical entity.

The second aspect of pragmatism which attracts Lloyd is its implications for the unity of subject and object, since it prescribes action and experimentation rather than debate of the truth a priori. Pragmatism finds the older metaphysical questions concerning *how* the knower *can* know a world irrelevant; it assumes and guarantees knowledge by the fact of action.   Without unnecessary display, pragmatism adopts a relationalistic metaphysics by assuming that things are both knowable by and intelligible to an acting knower. Pragmatism has "eaten" its metaphysics: ". . . in pragmatism the metaphysical cake has been absorbed."[124]   And again, pragmatism is "certainly not a metaphysics, but [is] metaphysical at every pore."[125]   Thus Lloyd finds pragmatism a living exemplification of his own emphatically metaphysical position, despite obviously differing starting points.   Pragmatism acts out, as it were, what he would say.   In pragmatism's infinite possibilities for resolving problems Lloyd finds the subject and the object related at every point.   Pragmatism understands experience "as always moving to the resolution of some dualism, of some distinction between formally incongruous things, of some real problem or conflict . . . ."[126]   Relationalistic idealism greets realistic pragmatism as the savior of the day.

Finally, Lloyd feels that pragmatism is asserting the significance of reason by relying on it in practice instead of merely writing its praise and insisting on its transcendentally aristocratic heritage.   The new conception of adventure suggested by the pragmatic experimentalist, implying a willingness to submit to the results of experiment, Lloyd takes as an indication of trust in the larger life within which we live. Pragmatism trusts reason rather than merely declaring trust in it.   The knower struggling with a continually problematic world manifests the outward and forward plunging of the will.   Lloyd's "spontaneity and control" parallel Dewey's interplay of idea and fact.   According to Lloyd, pragmatism's test for truth shows tacit conviction that reason is to be trusted, that action will truly reveal existence, and that experiment is truly the touchstone of reality.

Emphasis on the self as a major category Lloyd would find to be the principal criterion of any idealism.   Emphasis on reason as pervasive of all things—as the bearer of intelligibility in things and not merely as a special faculty of men—Lloyd would find to be the proper consequence of any *modern* idealism.   Action as demonstrating a unity or admixture of subject and object Lloyd would find to be the major characteristic of his *newer* idealism.   Indeed, he finds in pragmatism the very essence and core of "realistic and experimental idealism"[127] as he is defining it.

14. *Lloyd and Hegel*

It is undeniably true that Lloyd owes a great debt to Hegel.   Perhaps this influence is most significantly represented by Lloyd's concept of polarity relationship and his method of analysis explicating it.   But C. M. Perry goes far indeed when he speaks of Lloyd as follows:

Granted the universality of Lloyd's principle [of dimensional variation], did he do more than give a new expression of the principle of dialectic?   Did he not say in effect only that the thesis is one dimension, the antithesis a second, and the synthesis a third? . . .   If such is the case would it not have been better to retain the dialectical terms and explain space and time in them as Hegel did in his philosophy of nature and thus avoid the danger of spatializing all the qualitative characters in the universe?[128]

It is true that both Lloyd and Hegel find negation or antithesis to be the inner ontological secret of existence. Both agree that negation is, in some sense, responsible for process. Both agree that reality is characterized by contradiction, and yet is "relational," or, at least, not illogical; Lloyd, particularly, devotes much energy to insisting that the world is reasonable and intelligible. Both agree that philosophy is an expression of a theory of development. Both agree that nature and spirit are essentially one. Both come ultimately to an optimistic view of human development (although Lloyd attempts to escape this result). Finally, Lloyd makes frequent use of a rationalistically tempered method.

Lloyd seems, for the most part, unconscious of his debt to Hegel, repudiating him the few times he does mention him. Speaking of his own analysis of the relations between antitheses he says somewhat grudgingly that it has a "possible suspicion of Hegelianism."[129] But besides the many elements which may have contributed toward his desire to free himself from Hegelian influence, Lloyd is *justified* in declaring himself removed from German philosophy. Not only does he sharply diverge from it at many points, but, most important of all, both the motivation and the outcome of his thought are pragmatically and naturalistically colored and hardly to be identified with the thought of Hegel.

Lloyd's conception of polarity relationship, which, more than any other aspect of his thought, reveals Hegelian influence, is certainly not a mere duplication of Hegel. Though it is true that both Lloyd and Hegel are bent upon exhibiting that all things are intimately connected in a great totality, yet Hegel does this by means of a dialectic of objective mind, while Lloyd does it by an examination of the defining characteristics of organism. Lloyd's polarity relationship is dyadic, not triadic. While Lloyd's polarities are mutually implicative, they are never resolved in a synthesis. Each new positive at once implies a new incommensurable negative. Hence development, according to Lloyd's position, is an alteration of the relationship *between* polarities on an ever-differing qualitative level. For Lloyd the negative can never be reduced to a denial of the positive. The negative is incommensurable with its positive. Development takes place not only by means of a synthesis of negative and positive but also by means of an inclusion of the positive by the negative on a new dimensional level. Change, for Lloyd, is a qualitative alteration of the ever-present, never-resolved polarity relationships.

Both Lloyd and Hegel interpret a world process, but Lloyd interprets a developing nature while Hegel is concerned with an Absolute Idea. For Hegel thesis or antithesis represents only one side of the *truth*, while for Lloyd it represents only one side of an entity. For Hegel each synthesis comes progressively closer to the Whole Truth or the Absolute Idea, while for Lloyd the activities of polarities only make explicit what is already implicit in nature. Lloyd's polarities advance toward no final goal, much less an intellectual and disembodied goal. For Hegel "The Whole" is outside all possible experience; for Lloyd "wholeness" is an aspect of any experience. Lloyd's polar terms are not opposites swimming in an extraempirical absolute, but are related in and through the functional activity of organism.

On innumerable other grounds Lloyd's views are considerably removed from Hegel's. The natural sciences are unimportant to Hegel; for Lloyd they are the basis of philosophy, which interprets and "fulfills" them. Hegel is concerned with thought, Lloyd, with action; Hegel, with *the* truth, Lloyd, with "only something like the truth." For Hegel the real is the rational; for Lloyd the real is the relative. While for Hegel being is thought realized, for Lloyd being is the realization of the possibilities of action and growth. While in Hegel, in support of the so-called intellectualist thesis, nature is subordinate to spirit, in Lloyd spirit is life and life is nature. For Hegel art, religion, and philosophy are life forms of Absolute Spirit; for Lloyd these, among other types of valuable human activity, exhibit valuational levels in the relation between the human organism and its environment. Hegel is a monist; Lloyd finds both monism and pluralism functional principles of explanation.

All in all, Lloyd's adaptation of Hegel is far more removed in spirit than even this enumeration of differences would indicate, for Lloyd is irrevocably colored by the twentieth century. Lloyd's purpose in philosophizing is not to reach The Truth, but to illuminate practice. Lloyd's constantly altering dyad undergoing dimensional variation is directed toward a most un-Hegelian end, namely, a closer and more fulfilling relationship between the human organism and its environment, a more successful doing in a more developed and diversified world.

15. Lloyd and Kant

From casual references in an article or two it appears that Lloyd found some who considered him a Neo-Kantian of some sort.[130] Strangely enough, though Lloyd disparages Hegel, his view is more directly related to that of Hegel than to that of Kant, whose penetration he frequently lauds. When Lloyd asserts that "Kantian formalism, in spite of—or because of?—its present aridity, strikes me as most excellent fuel for us pragmatists and our particular conflagration,"[131] his metaphor is more apt than he realizes. His reaction from Kant is deep and thoroughgoing.

Not only does Kant's terminology develop in Lloyd a passion for terms found in everyday experience, not only is Kant's separation of the phenomenal from the noumenal contrary to Lloyd's identification of them,[132] not only does Kant's concern for the knowing process stimulate Lloyd into a devaluation of knowledge as subordinate, in one sense, to action, but Lloyd is also pushed into realism as a reaction to Kant's transcendental aesthetic, and into pragmatism as a reaction to Kant's transcendental dialectic.

In Kant the categories of knowledge are transcendental, while in Lloyd the acting agent functions transcendentally.[133]

In Kant the categories are universals; in Lloyd universality is a characteristic of the agent's action. In Kant the categories are broader and deeper than any experience, while in Lloyd the agent is broader than any specific experience, rising above the differentiation of the world by collecting it into a unity in action.

Poetry, Comedy, and Duty

1. *The Problem of Truth*

If any concept in Lloyd is elliptical and inexact, if any merits the term 'vague,' it is the concept of truth. Lloyd's views on the subject are implicit in all his writings and explicit in none. On the one hand, truth seems to have definable characteristics. Lloyd defines it as constantly altering, relative to some point of view. Yet, on the other hand, truth seems to be indefinable. The difficulties can be partly resolved by exhibiting some of the senses in which Lloyd uses the term. There appear to be at least four, and they are all so interrelated and so interdependent that to discriminate them seems counter to Lloyd's intention. Yet we must do so in order to understand his position.

First of all, we can speak of scientific truth—prose about a world which refuses to be entirely prosaic. Scientific truth is never absolute truth and is always relative to a point of view which is particularly narrow, exclusive, and special-istic, describing only a part of a world. Scientific truth is limited by conventional and artificial boundaries. Next, we can speak of philosophic truth which takes an analytic form. Philosophic analytic truth is the prose which would be wider than any particular science, which would exhibit the inter-connections between the sciences, which would generalize from scientific statement, and which would formulate uni-

versal principles about existence. Thirdly, there is philosophic speculative truth, which describes a world from a
more inclusive standpoint, from a point of view so wide,
broad, and deep that it violates the language of current
philosophical formulations. The task of expressing wider
categories demands that the speculative philosopher have
"courage and vision" to abandon the "formal consistency"
of the limited, specialistic, partisan intellectual climate that
gave him birth. While the language of speculative philosophy is paradoxical, inexact, "free and speculative, not scientific; poetic and visionary, not sober; often cryptic or . . .
apocalyptic, not normal and intelligible,"[1] it is really so only
relative to the categories which it would broaden and from
which it is in revolt.[2] Speculative philosophy, as Lloyd
understands it, is assertion of truth from the broadest possible frame of reference—truth which includes more than
one context and hence borders on truth from all contexts
(or no context) and, accordingly, is never to be taken literally
but always poetically. Finally, there is a fourth sense of
truth, a "principle of truth," which emerges from Lloyd's
views, and it underlies, unifies, and binds together the three
preceding senses. The "principle of truth"—the poem that
is life—represents an absolute, if we may call it that, on
which rests the burden of Lloyd's entire view. This sense
of truth is unnamable, indescribable, and not found in any
one formulation, since it is found in all. This is the truth
that is "Reality": "Reality is not knowable face to face; it is
beyond the reach of positive [scientific and philosophic]
knowledge; though dwelling in, and informing all knowledge, it can never come to the surface of knowledge; for so,
to its own betrayal, it would take sides and get a habitation
and a name."[3] This is the truth that is "life." This is the
truth of "the whole."

2. Truth, Life, and Statement

What are the most general characteristics of truth in a
world of relational activity? Truth, Lloyd maintains, is

found in the relations between things. The relations between things he describes functionally and dynamically. Accordingly, Lloyd pays his debt to evolution, making movement the source of truth.   Truth is primarily a property of life or action, not of statements.   It is found in the action and interaction of things, in growth and development.   It is found in polar activity, particularly in the history of the development of ideas.   Truth as a property of action rather than of propositions motivates Lloyd's battle with formal logic. And *because* truth is a property of action, Lloyd infers that the tests of truth are no longer either conformity or consistency; these are only "formal" tests relating to the use of language.   The copy theory of truth Lloyd associates with medieval dualism and creationalism; it is the

. . . outcome of ecclesiastical assertiveness and isolation, [making] man live with reference to what was at once outside and alien. Being himself of two separate and exclusive parts and natures, [man] was put in this situation: his physical nature had to adapt itself to an external spiritual life, and his spiritual nature, returning the courtesy, had to adapt itself to an external physical life.[4]

Since dualism implied two isolated natures,

. . . each must be in itself identical and consistent and the two with respect to any possible relation between them must, if positively related, literally conform, and, if negatively, absolutely non-conform. Dualism, honest with itself, can allow no middle course . . . the two tests . . . necessarily interfere with each other, and knowledge, accordingly, each test in some measure compromising the other, may be made "phenomenal," as Kant, in fact, found it . . . if two things are dualistically different and exclusive, neither can really assume any positive relation to the other . . . without compromising its own identity and consistency . . . .[5]

If truth is a property of life and is found in the interaction of things, the tests of conformity and consistency must be seen in a new light.   Truth must be conceived of in terms of manipulation and use, and the test of truth is successful solution of a problem of adjustment.[6]   Conformity and con-

sistency, Lloyd maintains, are only tools for plotting successful action.   There are no final tests for truth for the reason
that there is no final truth.[7]   Associating final tests with
"perfectionism, medievalism and static structure," Lloyd
holds that the tests for truth are now *infinite* in number and
occur wherever action yields "adaptation."   In this fashion
Lloyd's truth that is Reality supports a pragmatic theory of
truth!   Lloyd would deny validity to a logic of propositions
in order to be a pragmatist!   He would annihilate formal
logic in order to affirm his logic of life.   But perhaps even
more important is the fact that along the way Lloyd has
interpreted the status of conformity and consistency so that
they are "no longer institutes, but instruments; no longer
ends, but means":[8]

Man has become, thanks to his past, not a mere creature, but a
freed agent . . . with instruments [and tools] . . . a skilled mechanic
. . . .   [He is no longer] a soldier or no longer a creature of some
external will or power . . . "going" or "working" can mean nothing
more and nothing less than skillful action, the at once capable
and effective use of some highly developed instrument . . . the
medieval tests, conformity and consistency, still hold . . . [but] in
their new role of testing the means or instruments of action they
really have a larger significance than that which first belonged
to them.[9]

   But Lloyd is not content solely to redefine the older tests;
by a suggestive analysis he traces the lineal descent of
pragmatism from Zeno through Kant.   In defense of his
own pragmatic version of what can be said to be "true," he
adds, "It is, again, a conscious act in time rather than any
present idea that is true.   A present idea can be said only
to mediate [put in a form which renders it communicable
and hence exchangeable between men and between each
man and his world] a true act."[10]   Statements *about* a
world, Lloyd insists, are instruments by which we communally report to each other the interaction and interrelationship of things and by which we mutually describe our
conversations with a world of things!   Our statements tacitly

record our relative success in "adaptive activity" or our relational adjustment with an environment.

Since truth lies in the dynamic relations between things, it becomes, by means of ideas, a "force, not a form."[11] Truth as a force is the proper companion of ideas as "plans" of action.[12] As the product of a desiring and valuing planner, such truth must be "relevant or usable truth,"[13] for ideas are only "stepping stones"[14] to a successful relationship between man and his world. The desiring agent plans the solution of a problem.

As a result of this position, all statements about a world are, for Lloyd, only relatively true. They are relative to each other, relative to a specific context (scientific truth), and relative to a larger context (philosophic truth). Statements are relative because they imitate a moving world and attempt to duplicate its processes in a static medium. They are relative because they describe structures and not processes. They are relative to the question asked, to the way it is formulated, and to the context within which they gain meaning: "Not all questions are put with the same care and elaboration of a laboratory experiment; some are very inexact and inarticulate indeed; but all live in human experience only as their answers are developed with their putting."[15] But our statements are relative to something more, namely, to a kind of largest context or "spirit" of truth which is present in every statement. As Lloyd says, "All things are 'relative,' but only because reality is at once free from anything, and yet inclusive of all things."[16]

Statements are not only relative, but also contextual. Since each statement delimits only a part of an infinite possibility for action and interaction, it defines only a part of the movement of a life which is "whole"—a life in which each movement is related to and involves all else. Our statements are always from a point of view because they are only *means* to truth, tools for the description and appreciation of some particular activity and never for the exhibition of all activity for all time. Our statements are only the expressible, partial account of a life that is present in every action but totally describable in none.   Were any particular statement or point of view *the* truth, fixed and absolute, all others would be illusion.   But as Lloyd frequently insists, philosophies of illusion put their real in jeopardy.   Were any particular statement *the* truth, it would describe a world whose processes had stopped; it would describe "the whole" as if it were a part; it would take actuality for potentiality. Hence, with truth located in life and action, with statements described as relative and contextual, "truth became . . . in want of a better word, a spirit; reality was a life; perfection was a power."[17]

What then is this fourth sense of truth—this truth from a largest context—upon which all depends?   Are we not asking the same question that was asked in Chapter I, namely, what is the system of systems?   Lloyd's absolute, if such it may be called, has played a part in every discussion, yet it seems to be explicit nowhere.   It appeared, when we discussed process, as the "function of infinity."   It appeared, when we discussed knowledge, as "the unknowable."   Now it appears as "the Truth—a spirit."

In order to understand what it means for Lloyd to call truth in this fourth sense "a spirit," "the whole," "life," "reality," let us return to the concept of "acting infinitely." Each thing exhibits systematic action.   System is an adverb applicable to every term in a series, inasmuch as everything is relating to everything else.   It is the bond, the adverbial conjunction, that *each* term expressed dynamically.   In every relating situation there is inexhaustible relatedness.   Any statement about a situation isolates a part of this relatedness from some point of view.   For this reason the endless richness and possibility of relatedness cannot be represented by any statement or any number of points of view.   "The whole," therefore, is this inexhaustible relatedness.   Nor should it be confused with the sum total of all relationship, for it is not a quantitative conception, any more than the term "infinite" was: "Always in anything, empirically, there must be a residuum of the unrelated [one can never exhaust the relations of anything], which Kant . . . [is] too strongly disposed to hypostatize [into the thing-in-itself] . . . ."[18] As we saw in Chapter I, relations were active, dynamic. As we saw in Chapter II, activity was identified with growth. Hence "the whole" is the indefinite possibility of growth or development in any and every situation. It is what I have called the 'system of systems'[19] and what might be called 'the context of contexts' because it is life, which is the ultimate framework for all possible predication. Every statement is relative to some context within "the whole."

Now if no statement can ever do justice to "the whole," or "the truth," if any statement is partial, then the truth is found only in movement, in the relations between things, in life. Lloyd's "absolute," then, is that which can never be fully represented by propositions. It is found in experience, in action. It can be lived but never completely stated. We come into closest contact with it in immediate experience. The very fact of immediate experience proves an indefinitely differentiated world. Lloyd inclines to think of a redefined absolute as the immediate, indescribable quality of action, for in action the interrelation of things is best exemplified. When identifying his position with an "idealistic pragmatism" he says, "Pragmatism has not slain the Absolute absolutely; it has only provided a *successor* to the throne and *changed the ruler's prerogative.*"[20] To point up the fact that "the whole" must belong to any and every relating situation he says, "If you don't place unity in a concrete thing, then it must be *the* unity . . . we have unity at the expense of concreteness."[21] The terms we have been using, like "the whole" and 'the context of contexts,' are to be understood adverbially and not substantively: "Truth hath neither visible form nor body; it is without habitation or name; like the Son of Man it hath not where to lay its head."[22]

If statements are always relative and contextual, they ought to be called meaningful rather than true. Statements, as I have pointed out, are "instruments for effecting the adjustment" of the human organism to its environment. What does Lloyd mean by "meaning"? He makes a distinction similar to that sometimes set up between psychological and logical meaning. Thus, statements have "inwardly personal" meaning and "outwardly pertinent" meaning.[23] Lloyd repudiates James's subjectivistic interpretation of pragmatism. Though feeling and emotion always accompany ideas, though ideas always arouse extralogical overtones, the meaningful statement is not defined by these emotions and overtones. For Lloyd, as for Peirce and Dewey, a meaningful idea is a plan of action that can be tested in experience. The meaningful idea may have psychological value, but it is made significant by virtue of its "adaptive" value. To carry Lloyd's concept further, the new test for truth includes the old ones; the new test measures the effectiveness of the adaptive unity between man and his world, while the old ones measured only a section of the unity of experience. Hence, the new test is parallel to the nature of the person, who acts as "a whole" for the faction "as part." To make what Lloyd would call a "philosopher's sum," the new test is to the old ones as the function of the person is to the function of the faction in the life of society.[24] For this reason Lloyd asks, "Is it to be wondered that those who have insisted on this test have been charged with individualism, subjectivism, even solipsism?"[25] From Lloyd's point of view this charge is unjust because it involves forgetting that class life promotes personal efficiency in the use of an instrument. Interpreting the matter in this way, Lloyd finds that the test of 'working' still involves individualism, but hardly subjectivism or solipsism:

There may indeed be a certain liberation of the individual from the slavery of the class [by the new test] . . . but, as he uses the instrument given to him by that [social] life, he becomes, not less, but more a social being than ever, for, leaving the companionship and the loyalty of uniformity and routine, he enters into the richer fellowship of unity and creative life.[26]

If Lloyd's concept of "the meaningful" is not to be confused with the psychologically satisfactory, it is not to be confused with the empirically unverifiable either. The meaningful idea, for Lloyd as for Dewey, springs from the need of an inquirer which wells forth in a question. As answer to a question, the meaningful idea is meaningful by virtue of the conditions under which it has been formulated. Lloyd prefers to ascribe "meaning" rather than "truth" to ideas because he relates the category of "truth" to action rather than to description. Further, he wishes to include 'psychological meaning' in the total conditions which eventuate in action. He wishes to relate facts and values, description and appreciation, but not to reduce one to the other.

Since our statements are only relative and contextual, both scientific and philosophic assertions are not the truth but something like the truth. Both are constructions of reality. No statement is to be taken literally, lest it be taken absolutely. All are imaginative constructs for the purpose of illumination. All enhance the worth of experience. Lloyd justifies his own work on the grounds that it may make experience more meaningful by its imaginative account of life. The good philosopher must take his readers beyond the familiar—both in language and in doctrine—he must seek "adventure" and offer "vision."[27] Philosophy requires the courage to propose something new and depends on the imagination: "There must be in all effective life, in all real travel [activity], some generosity, some abandon, some candor towards difference; in short, some vision of the incommensurable."[28]

Ultimately, of course, the reason for this position is that no statement or no collection of statements is "the truth" because "the truth" is a system, not an eclectic aggregation. The result, however, is that "facts" are to be taken less factually. Facts, according to Lloyd, spring from a point of view. They are constructs within the framework of a particular universe of discourse and hence are only "true" to a degree of probability determined by practice. When Lloyd terms facts "imaginative constructs" of reality, he does not intend this to be a statement implying universal phenomenality. Lloyd repudiates Bradley for such a conclusion. On every hand Lloyd insists that all things are relative. He calls himself a "realistic idealist"[29] and contends that nothing is made "unreal" by his view. If Lloyd sets about developing a theory of perspectives, it is not in spite of but because of his 'absolute.' As a preface to what we today call 'objective relativism,' he asserts that the medieval conceptualist saw that "God's natural philosophy would be Realism, while man, talking and writing . . . has no choice but Nominalism."[30]

3. *Lloyd's Quarrel with Formal Logic*

Truth being a property of life, Lloyd conducts a continual and, in one sense, unnecessary battle with formal logic. Because truth is found in the relationship between things, he denies that it is a property of statements. The reasons for the conflict are primarily terminological. Were the term 'validity' instead of 'truth' used for formal relations, perhaps Lloyd could have been more cordial to formal logic.

Primarily, Lloyd's hostility seems to spring from the fact that formal logic resides outside of his "one life" and lacks community with the other sciences.[31] Unlike any of the others, it devotes itself to an account not of a world but of language,[32] and hence its enterprise cannot be subsumed under the general enterprise of science as Lloyd defines that term. Secondly, formal logic is powerless to guarantee Lloyd's metaphysics; it is unable to do the tasks Lloyd sets for logic. Thirdly, formal logic is conceived by Lloyd to rest upon the three principles of classification, identity, and contradiction toward which he expresses violent antipathy, because he is convinced that his metaphysics must and does contravene them. In the last analysis, perhaps, Lloyd here tilts with windmills. He fails to see the consistency of the first two of these principles with his own view and largely misinterprets the meaning of the third. This is clear if we examine his attitude toward each of these principles in turn.

(1) Lloyd's attack on the principle of classification is based on his view that each thing has an absolutely induplicable position in an infinite series. To classify would be to violate the metaphysical uniqueness which everything has. Each quality of each thing is precisely what it is only in companionship with all the other qualities of that particular thing. "Are no two things alike?" Lloyd asks, and then answers, "If they were, they could not be known as two."[33] Each quality is unique by virtue of its place in *this* system and no other. Hence qualities described as "common" are not identical metaphysically, for nothing is describable in the same way as anything else:

Most surely a red rose is not red as anything else is red. The redness of a rose is peculiar, because the rose itself is peculiar. No quality of anything can be independent of any of all its other qualities; and to assume an independence is to make the quality an altogether external mark, and then not a quality.[34]

To look at this objection from another vantage point, a class is not an aggregation of similar properties, but a system of terms related to one function. Logical classification groups things structurally, and hence arbitrarily and externally unites them. It absolutely and arbitrarily separates completely interrelated qualities, and hence breaks the bonds of continuity. Thus the principle of classification may be a logical device, but from Lloyd's metaphysical viewpoint, it is an inaccurate, inept abstraction.

Associating classification as it is "usually understood" with unfairness to real individuality, Lloyd embarks on a hard-hitting account of the sociological consequences of taking it too literally and absolutely:

The mediaeval doctrine of the genus, the doctrine of the immutability of species or persistence or disappearance of types, the Deductive Logic, the doctrine of inheritance of acquired traits, the nativistic or intuitional theories of morals and religion, all the monarchical institutions of society, all systems of caste, are distinctly hostile to any real individuality, since they assume that individuals can be . . . herded under some common arbitrary head . . . .[35]

To avoid a conception of unity as external to the things unified, Lloyd redefines the meaning of classification to provide for both individuality and difference. He is not saying that a world of things does not exhibit community, but is maintaining that community consists in intrinsic functional relationship rather than in structural similarity. Things are dynamically related by being parts of an activity toward some end to which all are means.

Lloyd does not deny that the special sciences do and must use the principle of classification; but the special sciences do not attempt to give a metaphysically adequate account of a world. The net result of his position is, first, that his objections serve to deny fixed or so-called 'natural' classes, and, secondly, that they point out that all classification is from a point of view, serving some special interest or question.

(2) Lloyd's attack on the principle of identity[36] (that "bugaboo of the hypostatical thinker"[37]) springs, I take it, from his analysis of system—from his meaning of individuality.   The entity A is not just A, but is A only with respect to the rest of the world; it is defined in terms of its relations with everything else. As will be recalled from Chapter I, A is functionally a microcosm.   To define A is not to isolate it, but to relate it to everything else.   Hence Lloyd feels that the principle of identity holds for statements but not for things.   Despite the metaphysical presuppositions involved, does this not affirm, in a backhanded way, the very same conclusion implied in formal logic, namely, that 'two plus two equals four' is a tautology, but that 'two eggs plus two eggs equals four eggs' is not?   It seems to me that Lloyd describes the properties of formal logic very well indeed when he tells us that its principles do not talk about a world of things!   Lloyd's quarrel with formal logic is a serious one only when he urges that one logic of one life should supersede the more modest logics of statements.

(3) Lloyd's violent attack on the principle of contradiction obviously springs from his confusing polarities with

logical contradictions.   Lloyd, I take it, thinks that the law of contradiction denies and abolishes polarity relationship as meaningful.[38]   Lloyd's polarities are not logical contradictions.   In his own terms, the negative does not deny in the same sense in which the positive affirms.   Polar terms are defined as mutually implicative—as parts of one system—and not as mutually exclusive.   Lloyd asserts that the negative and the positive are "incommensurable," that the negative denies only the particular *form* of the positive and hence "includes" the meaning of the positive in a new guise.[39]   Lloyd's polarities, far from exhausting the possibilities of a situation, imply an inexhaustible set of variations.

As a corollary, Lloyd feels that the principle of excluded middle violates his "principle of wholeness" in a universe. Since Lloyd's principle of wholeness must include A and −A at the same time, he cannot accept a principle which necessitates that a thing be *either* A *or* −A, but not both.   He takes the presence of both to mean the violence and contradiction which are the work of the spirit that can know no law (like that of excluded middle).[40]   "Contradiction" represents to Lloyd reality "refusing to be bound" to either-or.

But once more Lloyd misstates his own position.   His world is not A plus −A.   "The whole," he has insisted, is not a mere aggregation of all things plus their contradictions, but is different in kind from this sum.   Lloyd's "total" universe is not comparable with its parts.   How, in any event, can a "total whole" comply with a principle applicable to parts?

Lloyd does not deny the validity of the law of contradiction in the special disciplines.   As has often been pointed out, the law of contradiction cannot be denied without the assumption of it in the argument for its denial.   Lloyd's own philosophy, where analytic rather than poetic, freely uses it as a test of error.   Lloyd's thought as a system necessitates its use.   Were he really to violate the law of contradiction, there would be breaks in the interrelatedness of his ideas which would destroy their systematic character.

Finally, since the law of contradiction is abrogated only for the context of contexts, for life, for the universe "as a whole," Lloyd's thought, whether he would have it or not, is here actually, perhaps unwittingly, invoking a theory of perspectives. If we recall that the context of contexts is not an overall content or some largest framework, but is a quality of interrelatedness present in every context, we shall see that Lloyd is really implying that the properties ascribed to a particular thing in one context may contradict those ascribed to it in another. Since "life" contains all points of view, Lloyd is simply saying that the fact of perspectival contradiction does not necessitate that we consider either one view *or* the other untrue. Granted that the law of contradiction holds within every particular context (the special sciences and so on), Lloyd's battle with it rests on the grounds that it is abrogated by contradictory assertions in varying contexts both of which may be true. It seems to me that Lloyd is really wrestling with a perspectival view which he erroneously construes to be fatal to the law of contradiction.

4. *Paradox*

Two aspects of Lloyd's thought bear on the problem of contradiction—first, his concept of paradox, and, secondly, the demands of his relationalism.

(1) Lloyd understands paradox as the verbal manifestation of the presence of polarities. And he appeals to polarities in arguing against the law of contradiction. Though, as we have pointed out, this last conclusion is erroneously drawn, it nonetheless leads Lloyd to point to paradox as proof of the violation of the law of contradiction. Lloyd admits that paradox represents a violation of *conventional* language. Paradox marks the thinker pouring new ideas into old categories,[41] broadening and extending a point of view.

But Lloyd confuses the psychologically unfamiliar with the logically unintelligible—he confuses the uprooting of traditional dogma with the routing of formal logic. He says, for example, that the good philosopher must have "the courage of seeming abnormal, irrational, speculative and unintelligible,"[42] because philosophy does "violence to ordinary words of standard meanings—suggesting Mrs. Malaprop . . . ."[43] "Seeing beyond accepted forms and standards it has always brought the freedom from these, the license, the unbending, of which laughter is such an excellent expression . . . ."[44] It brings "the humor of old names for new things,"[45] and, at least in one stage of the philosopher's insight, "paradox has always seemed the only adequate and candid way of expressing what has been seen."[46] The "candid" paradox, then, "is irregular; it does not belong in well-ordered society and conversation; it violates logical conventions horribly . . . ."[47] Further, it is the business of philosophy "to be at least reasonably unintelligible" because its vision can count for nothing if it does not "imply something radically different from what prevails,"[48] and men find only what prevails "intelligible." Lloyd remarks that philosophy is profanity. Recalling that a book entitled *A Cursory History of Swearing* once appeared in the philosophy section of the University of Michigan library, he maintains that it had found its rightful place, for, if a new view is significant it is also really profane in that it violates the conventions of language and challenges its audience.[49] The humor of old names for new things "is as near to being the philosopher's stone as anything I know . . . ."[50]

Paradox, then, is a humorous and challenging exhibition of philosophic growth. It represents the need for new categories, expressing that need in terms of psychological shock. It represents a new, broader view in the language of the old. In short, paradox represents the impact of philosophic growth on old language.

(2) Lloyd's relationalism is such that he is not content to say that all statements are from a point of view and leave us with a multiplicity of contexts. In the last analysis, he is content only when each particular point of view implies

every other.   This means that paradox is not only representative of the psychologically unfamiliar, but is also evidence of "thought conserving its universe."[51]   Since all
thinking is partial, one-sided, and from a point of view,
paradox, as the linguistic exhibition of polarity action, indicates the impartiality of truth bringing opposites together.[52]
Hence, paradox developing *within* a particular point of view
represents other contexts creeping in by way of what we
have previously referred to as "the doors in the panelling."
But to say that paradox develops within a point of view is
not to say that the law of contradiction is violated, as I
have pointed out; it simply indicates that the point of view is
growing, and that, in growing, it becomes larger in the sense
that it becomes more inclusive.

5. *Positivistic Science and Metaphysical Myth*

The outcome of Lloyd's views on the nature of truth is his
distinction between philosophy and science and his analysis
of the nature and the function of each.   Lloyd makes this
distinction in part because of the general inadequacies of
the scientific enterprise and in part because of the specific
inadequacies of the positivistic science of his day.   However,
the inadequacies of both reinforce the demands of his point
of view, which would see life "whole."

The special sciences in general, Lloyd holds, are subject
to certain ailments of perspective.   They have a tendency to
interpret their results as unalterable fact in a too naïvely
realistic way.   Scientific judgment, like every other, is a
tentative and altering imaginative construct of reality—an
interpretation of experience and not an absolutely complete
and final transcript of things.   Scientists take their results
too seriously.   In an effort to show that scientific 'fact' is
itself interpretation, is not literally descriptive, but a means
to answer a question, Lloyd says:

True science . . . is synthetic as well as analytic, being interested
in something more than a decomposable object.   It is activity,
not mere passive receptivity; it is invention, not mere discovery.

. . . True science . . . is no mere knowledge of an outer world; it is invention, the invention of a tool, the making of a great machine, with use of which human life is to become more vital or more effective . . . [it is an] instrument of adaptation to environment.[53]

As a tool for more effective "adaptation to environment," scientific knowledge is changing, not final. Its answers cannot be understood apart from the needs of both the questioner and his enterprise and cannot be considered independent of the culture and intellectual climate which gave need, questioner, and science birth; for the nature of truth is a sociological issue, must be sociologically understood.[54] Indulging in satire, Lloyd offers some sociological observations on the scientist who believes his science isolated from life, and says that such science is buried in the "deep grave of technique."[55] Encompassing in his criticism many things that make science "pure mechanicalism," he says:

Scientists have their etiquette about preempted problems or fields of research, their notions about originality as dependent on working in a new field—hence the preemption to prevent transgression or theft of originality, their conceits about bibliographical information, linguistic proficiency and technical phraseology, their satisfaction over "publication" . . . "production" and even "research," and a very humble deference of each to each among the different branches of scientific inquiry . . . . Physicians . . . suffer from a professional ritual and etiquette, but they are far from being alone in their misery. Scientists are a close second . . . . Technique is one of the enabling conditions of science, but science that gets no further, that is only "pure" and "objective" and "inductive," is not true science . . . .[56]

The heart of the objection rests on the fact that

A purely objective science can at best only give a new material content to existing and time-worn forms of thought; it cannot do that in which progress must always consist, namely, develop and adopt new forms of thought, new categories; it cannot do this without betraying its objectivism.[57]

Scientific knowledge, as a product of a question, implies

value.   Since value binds all meaningful questions together, Lloyd finds—as does Dewey—continuity between all types of inquiry.   The processes of inference and verification in common experience are generically identical with the more refined processes of inference and verification in the laboratory.   Far from eliminating personal, volitional, and value experiences, all inquiry, refined or unrefined, guarantees them.   In a burst of psychologism reflecting also his views on the function of the environment,[58] Lloyd maintains that science is the self seen through the mirror of the not self,[59] which reflects and materializes that which the self values.[60] In short, while "life without science is lifeless," yet "science without life is meaningless."[61]   Both science and philosophy are interpretations of the views of ordinary life which enhance their worth.   Lloyd holds that learning and culture must recognize and assimilate not some but all things human.[62]

Lloyd is particularly annoyed that an objective and mechanicalistic science should presume to pronounce upon and condemn his vitalistic organicism.   He asks, with irony, "Are mind and matter, cause and effect, purpose, society, brain-process and consciousness such well-established conceptions, as if independent constants in the scientist's formulae, that mere external question of fact can be asked about them?"[63]   Lloyd then goes on to point out that we deny social purpose to lower organisms as a result of looking at them through a microscope, but that such an examination of man would hardly certify that he expresses social purpose either.   "Let science recognize these things," he continues, "and it will promptly exchange its external objective question of fact for direct internal questions of meaning."[64]

Insisting on what he calls intellectual "candor," Lloyd feels that we should not ask whether something is real, but, rather, should ask what is true about it.   Science must accept and interpret experience, and not phenomenalistically question its reality.   But, apparently, lack of candor was the order of the day.   Positivistic science, pronouncing on

the meaningful, would obviously outlaw the entire enterprise in which Lloyd was engaged. I suspect that this
unmentioned consideration was largely responsible for the
dissatisfaction Lloyd often feels with the sciences in general.
He frequently complains that the scientist rejoices in the
literal and the prosaic, lacking both poetry and humor, which
Lloyd considers the most important qualities of the philosopher. But it is the positivist, in particular, who would
reduce philosophic truth to a collection of the most general
statements of science, who would deprive philosophy of
system, and who would reduce the poem to the fact, appreciation to description; and it seems clear that it is positivism
which Lloyd feels to be his real opponent.

Still another qualification of the scientific enterprise
emerges. Lloyd is distressed because the special sciences
not only take their content as fixed, objective, independent
of the valuing thinker, and descriptive of reality, but also
take their method as absolute. Lloyd widens his use of
the term "science." It is a content, a method or tool, but
it is sometimes "only an atmosphere or point of view, [or]
a habit of mind."[65] In all cases, however, it is a changing,
cumulative instrument for effecting organic development.
Lloyd, as a speculative philosopher, refuses to do obeisance
to the scientific method. Philosophy must use the scientific
method, but must not be in bondage to it, must not consider
it unalterable or infallible, for science, as we shall see, "is
for philosophy, not philosophy for science."[66]

Finally, the special sciences are overspecial. Each conceives of itself as independent of the others and isolated from
all other intellectual endeavors. Hence each presents a
one-sided account of a many-sided reality, as if there were
no contenders. Lloyd, in many articles, takes occasion to
defend the thesis that the sciences are interrelated, and
only contextually separate; he says, for instance: ". . . the
different sciences are but so many different views of one
reality. Their different fields are but different related
aspects of a universe . . . sensitive to each other's contentions

and to each other's changes."[67] Of particular concern in this connection are the paradoxes which Lloyd finds latent in scientific assertion. These he takes to be repudiations of a totally physicalistic account of a world and indications of ("indirections for") the fact that life cannot be defined so narrowly. Such notions as a "conserved matter" or an undulatory theory of motion[68] indicate the thinker being a traitor to his standpoint and violating his own conception of a merely physical universe. But the physical sciences are not alone in their narrowness. Atomism in psychological theory gives equal testimony to the breakdown of a purely psychical interpretation of a world. Lloyd, as I have pointed out, resists reduction either of mind to matter or of matter to mind. The purely special science cannot be consistently aloof, but lets in all the rest of the universe, as is evidenced by the hidden paradox in its formulations. "Tennyson's 'flower in the crannied wall' is nothing in its all-inclusiveness when compared with a well-developed special science,"[69] Lloyd says.   The working hypotheses of each special science, those "doors" which unwittingly produce so many paradoxes, reveal "the principle of conserving thought"[70] or wholeness which permits it to have "the rich experience of discovering itself in the others."[71]   The stricter and more limited the formulations of each science would be, the more Lloyd's "Hibernian"[72] universe exhibits its interrelating wholeness.

Despite the fact that Lloyd holds these vices of science to be also its virtues, namely, those characteristics which make it an effective tool, science must always be abstract and concerned with knowledge for its own sake. Philosophy alone is devoted to knowledge for the sake of human action. Philosophy alone can properly unify, interpret, and vitalize scientific ideas. Only philosophy can close the gaps which isolate the members of a pluralistic universe. Philosophy as analysis is duty-bound to provide a more inclusive, less partisan, less conventional, less formal, and less special truth. The philosopher must bind a universe together by exhibiting the laws of movement and growth applicable everywhere. He must speak from a broader context unencumbered by special interest and partisan concern.   The philosopher must recognize that meaning and appreciation are as much a part of the world as fact and description: "Though it [philosophy] offer only organized scientific method, yet it must inevitably inspire an interpretation of those notions for the appreciation of life . . . ."[73]   The philosopher must not report, but must enlarge and interpret.   He must not be content with inadequate categories, but must have the courage to adopt new ones if necessary.   He must not concern himself with a world as 'thought' or 'understood,' or yet as 'felt,' but with "the world as experienced and as immediately interesting at any time."[74]   Analytic philosophy must, then, be a broader, coördinating, interrelating, and synthesizing truth. But where can it stop in its effort to encompass wider perspectives?   As analytic philosophy extends in breadth, it fuses with speculative philosophy, for all philosophic endeavor must inevitably develop a theory of the universe.

A problem arises.   Can the philosopher speak about the *whole?*   Can his assertions be *all*-inclusive?   Can he be really nonpartisan and untroubled by special interests? Can he exhibit a world from a largest point of view and yet use language?   Can he escape contextual limitations and yet speak?   Does not his very speech reveal him a partisan and committed to *a* point of view, however large?

Lloyd's solution to the problem is to assert that philosophy in its broadest function must not be taken literally. If the philosopher's ultimate duty is so to overreach himself as to describe experientially that which is present in every experience but broader than all, if he is to formulate a particular kind of imaginative construction which exhibits cosmic system, his assertions can have meaning only if they are taken metaphorically rather than prosaically, if they are understood as poetry and not description, appreciation and not fact.   Philosophy, even more than science, is interpretative and "only something like the truth," for it attempts a poetic, analogical, nonliteral synthesis of experience, which, in the last analysis, Lloyd feels must imply, if not state, the foundations and enabling conditions of experience.[75]   Hence the metaphysician is a poet, pointing at, if not speaking about, the indications in any experience that reveal it as broader than all, pointing at the experiential facts of interrelatedness as implying a quality that can be communicated only by poetic expression.   Philosophic truth has a function analogous to what we have called the "function of infinity" and is simply another manifestation of that adverb modifying systematic action.   Its function is to make explicit the implications for system present in every situation of knowing. It would cement all views into a whole and yet articulate its all-inclusive view.   It would be poetry about process.

Since, then, the ultimate duty of the philosopher is to show a world coördinated into a poetic synthesis, Lloyd is in a position whereby he can guarantee the philosopher the right to liberties, if not license, with language.   Unlike science,

. . . philosophy . . . must always be concerned, whether quietly or assertively, with the universe, not just with some special field or point of view.   Generalization is her very life and purpose and, although it may be what makes her restless and unconventional, it is her opportunity for a vital service . . . .   Her interest, too, must be vital and appreciative, not just "objective," not just descriptive and explanatory, not under constraint of too precise instruments and too accurate measurements; concerned, then, with values, not merely with facts.[76]

Having freed philosophy from "accurate measurement," Lloyd revels in (and takes full advantage of) its liberation. Now the philosopher cannot only describe a world poetically unified, but, by doing so, he can exhibit the inadequacy of current points of view.   He can show the narrowness of accepted categories, and, in short, is a harbinger of new, broader, deeper philosophic outlooks.   Philosophy as a bringer of new perspectives, as an agent of intellectual growth, is not merely traditional; it must go beyond the

familiar.   It requires "poetic vision" and freedom of feeling
and imagination;[77] it can accept no literal repetition of past
'truth.'   "The prosaic mind," Lloyd says, "the conservatively
accurate and calculating mind, treating all things as commensurable, as like in kind [when new incommensurable
developments are at stake], may help in organization . . .
but can not suffice for final and progressive action [growth]."[78]

Lloyd turns to the history of philosophy to point out the
definitions philosophers have given their occupation and
uses these as proof that they have always understood their
function to be that of new-dimension bearers, creative
thinkers, organizers, and synthesizers.   What "unbridled ex-
travagance," what "splendid absurdity," he exclaims, "the
superlativism of nearly every one!"[79]   And he adds his own
definition to the others, namely, that philosophy is the highest
comedy, with religion the divine comedy, its only rival.
Part of the gusty humor which Lloyd sees implicit in the
thought of the creative thinker who would violate conventional language is present in those very paradoxes which
give linguistic evidence that the current language and standpoint is too exclusive and narrow, and that philosophic ideas
are in the process of growth.

Let us return at this point to Lloyd's account of paradox.
Previous reference to paradox may have suggested that
Lloyd uses it as a kind of anti-intellectualistic weapon available to the philosopher, that it is a celebration of the
logically opaque and hence psychologically disturbing.   But
Lloyd means to suggest neither of these things.   Far from
being an expression of the "irrational" or "illogical," paradox
actually means simply a violation of conventional language
and traditional categories; far from being verbal gymnastics,
it represents a "demand for wholeness" or a "desire for completeness"[80] to which all things are by nature committed.
Far from being a retreat into verbal obscurantism, the paradox represents the fact of necessary growth continuously
imposed on the thinker, and this gives tacit and humorous
evidence that life will not submit to a particular and hence

one-sided formulation of its habits. Far from obfuscating or denying knowledge, the paradox suggests the direction in which thought is developing.[81] Far from being an end in itself, it is a by-product of growth. In these terms, Lloyd turns doubt with respect to particular formulations of truth into belief, if not belief in any particular formulation, then in a "principle of truth" operating through all formulations and acting as a kind of humorous but persistent corrective agent for partiality, an instigating agent for growth. Thought, in short, is self-growing and self-corrective.[82]

A difficulty arises which is part of a many-sided tussle of this position with the canons of language and verifiability. When Lloyd insists that the metaphysician is a poet, the problem arises of determining what can be meant by true poetry and whether true poetry spoken by the metaphysician differs in kind from that spoken by the poet. But Lloyd would have the metaphysician paradoxical as well as poetical. Had he been content to leave the metaphysician a consistent poet, a stronger case might be made for the position. But poetry is expressed by paradox, and growth takes place by means of the action of polarities and by means of the violation of language. What, for example, can a paradox assert except everything or nothing? In either case its attempted assertions would be unstatable and meaningless. In Lloyd's own terms, the paradox must be meaningless, since neither side of a polarity exists, but only the interaction of both. Yet he holds, at the same time, that paradoxical expression is meaningful. He points out that the poetic and visionary character of philosophy is its virtue—and also its vice, in "quacks."[83] There are times when Lloyd is aware of the difficulties involved in his attempt to make philosophy violate language and yet speak meaningfully. Remarkably enough, in his very first article, he makes the following rather curious statement, with obvious satisfaction and a certain irony:

Philosophy from time to time has wanted the world to be something or other, this thing or that, very much indeed, and, in spite

of requests that were obviously very comprehensive, the world
has always complied. Hence philosophy's dignified position
today . . . . Philosophy as a profession knows no failures.[84]

At a much later date Lloyd is still apparently determined
to perch on Olympian heights and still determined to like his
precarious seat, proclaiming, "In a real universe everything
must be true of everything . . . ."[85] But, of course, if everything is true of everything, then it could be said with equal
justification that nothing is true of anything. Unfortunately,
if the all-inclusive view loses its criterion for meaningful
language, it loses its universe along with it! In the midst of
this debris, let us not forget the problem which brings Lloyd
to such devastation. As I see it, the problem takes two
forms. First, what, if anything, is meaningful poetry—how
can we distinguish it from meaningless poetry? And, secondly, what is the relation of the canons of scientific verifiability to the canons, if any are possible, of poetic verifiability? Lloyd's own implicit answer on this score seems to
be Jamesian. Inasmuch as he adopts the pragmatic definition for meaningful truth in James's sense, meaningful poetry
would be that in which we find worth and value for interpreting our relations to a world. But it is equally clear that
Lloyd is dissatisfied with this definition as oversubjectivistic.
Such a test would reveal something about man, only, and in
Lloyd's world man is not isolated from all other types of
being.

It might seem that philosophic truth at this point had
somewhat lost contact with the scientific enterprise. But,
on the contrary, Lloyd finds philosophic truth a dimensional
variation of science and, as such, built upon science yet not
reducible to it. One of Lloyd's articles[86] is an attempt to
demonstrate that philosophy has taken its starting point
from many sciences, each indicating a progressive stage in
the "naturalization process" by which man is made a citizen
of his world, by which man and his environment have come
into a closer and more vital relationship. Mechanicalism,
biology, and now psychology[87] have all been served by philos-

ophy in its task of broadening, extending, and "vitalizing" their perspectives. Speculative philosophy is "thinking after —in the sense also of through—scientific knowledge, poetry after positive experience, adventure that is able to employ, as it sets out, the best [scientific] equipment of its day . . . ."[88]

Philosophy, the instigator of the creation of new categories and of intellectual progress, the unifier and synthesizer of the sciences, the violator of traditional language, must not be "careless of science" or "deliberately superior"[89] to science, but must take scientific doctrines "only as mediating symbols or—a better word—analogies in the sense even of metaphors."[90] Philosophy must turn the institute of scientific knowledge for its own sake into the instrument of knowledge for the sake of more effective and wider use in appreciation and evaluation of the world:

True philosophy, responsible to its great calling, must be more than science . . . it must in fact be unscientific, but unscientific, not by any means in the sense of ignorance or contempt, but in the sense of free and appreciative use, through the very revelations of science seeing beyond what science itself with the very best instruments and methods sees or ever can see.[91]

Philosophy must generalize scientific knowledge and shape it into a poetic theory of the universe by exhibiting the interrelations of all forms of science in one life.[92] All of philosophy is, then (to use Kierkegaard's phrase), a "concluding unscientific postscript" to scientific knowledge.

Nor can philosophy as speculative reason abandon common sense. It must not only develop common sense more accurately, but must see beyond it. Speculative reason, Lloyd insists, is significant not because it is apart from common sense but because it infuses it: ". . . idealists need also to be more thorough or more radical by making reason really supreme, by recognizing a reason that is truly non-sensuous; being not aloof from sense . . . but even in and through the very life of sense itself."[93] Similarly, philosophy cannot abandon the scientific method. Lloyd treats the

relations of scientific method to what is, apparently, philosophic method in a fashion analogous to his treatment of
the relation of scientific truth to philosophic truth. The
scientific method must not be violated; it must be used as
a tool or instrument, and not as a master. "Especially,"
Lloyd cautions, "must philosophy never commit the error,
by no means uncommon among scientists, of actually or
virtually taking *useful* standpoints and methods as *literal*
indications of reality."[94]

Philosophy and science, then, are polarities, with philosophy as the negative and inclusive term. Hence, according
to his view, Lloyd can emphasize their relationship best by
exhibiting their distinction. With this in mind, he indulges
in a series of comments which are peculiarly effective in
leading the reader astray. For example, he says: ". . . that
lie about philosophy being unscientific was only a great truth
in masquerade."[95] He means by this only that philosophy is
a broader definition of a world than science because it utilizes
scientific doctrine for a larger point of view.

Perhaps one of Lloyd's most exasperating linguistic
devices is to identify philosophic truth with the "irrational"
because it violates a *specific, conventional* formulation of
what the rational is. We saw, for instance, that he identifies
pragmatism with the "irrational" because it denies the more
restrictive formulation of reason given by "abstract" idealists.
Lloyd insists that the pragmatic test for truth reasserts the
"spirit" of reasonableness without the idealist's limitations.
Pragmatism understands reason as a "wider principle" present
in all effective action. Hence, pragmatism is "irrational"!
Need I point out that Lloyd's ascription of the "irrational" to
philosophic truth must be understood in the same light?
Philosophic truth is not irrational in the sense of being transcendent, for it is present only in a related world. It is not
irrational in the sense of being a product of feeling, or Lloyd
would not call it "truth." If Lloyd means to indicate more
by the term "irrational" when it is ascribed to philosophic
truth, this can only mean *more* than the scientifically rational

in the sense of 'trans-rational' or 'inter-rational,' if you will.
If philosophic truth is "irrational," Lloyd can only mean
that it cuts across contextualistic boundaries.   In the interest
of psychological shock, Lloyd cannot resist distinguishing
philosophic truth in this "reasonably unintelligible" fashion.

How can Lloyd use language as a tool and yet demand
that it unlock a total world, tell a myth and yet tell a true
myth?   If philosophic truth is not commensurable with the
truth of the special sciences, in what sense can it be said to
be true?   How can philosophic truth have the characteristics
of both poetry and science at the same time?   If philosophy
is poetry, then the categories of truth and falsity are not
applicable to it in any *known* sense, much less is that mysterious category Lloyd employs, the "fictitiously true."   If philosophy is science, Lloyd need not have made the distinction.
Since Lloyd would tell a true myth, he has set the problem
of how a true myth can be distinguished from a false one.
Since he tries to recite poetry without abandoning the framework of the scientific method and pragmatic definition, he has
set the problem of how he can speak meaningful poetry.

Lloyd is aware of the dilemma.   He admits that philosophy can become overfree, that philosophic appreciation can
result in what might be called 'speculation' instead of being
'speculative,' and that philosophy's inexact enunciations can
become visionary and unintelligible when they should be
cryptic and terse: "There is a faulty, futile way of being
speculative, visionary, cryptic, the way of all quackery, and
there is the excellent way of genuine achievement."[96]   His
problem is to find a midpoint between science and poetry,
as well as between truth from a limited point of view and
truth from all points of view.   As the matter stands, if
scientific truth is too narrow for the task Lloyd sets for
philosophy, philosophic truth is too wide to have intelligibility.   How can he avoid narrowness on the one hand and
nonsense on the other?   It seems to me that until the relationship between truth which cuts across contexts and
pragmatically definable meaning is developed, Lloyd's diffi-

culties remain; and they remain for all those who would
broaden and deepen the meaning of pragmatic definition
and yet avoid license.

6. *"Philosophy . . . the Highest Comedy"*

Lloyd pours a philosophic libation to Puck. All humor,
he maintains, is based on incongruity, the unexpected, paradox. What then could be more comic than a philosophy that
makes paradoxical expression one phase of philosophic
activity? Philosophic growth demands that one point of its
journey be devoted to the attempt to express new views in
old language. The result is an incongruity which shocks into
laughter. Laughter functions to redress the intellectual and
nervous jolt concomitant with exposure of the incongruous.

Incongruity may be expressed on many intellectual levels.
Pun, slapstick comedy, and the philosopher's cosmic paradoxes are all generically identical, but each offers varying
grades and qualities of humor:

Puns at least, then, make extremes meet and, although their
comedy must always or almost always be very light or . . . very
puny . . . [acting] as a homeopathic cure—nevertheless they fill
the bill as to certain essentials . . . . [Like] vaudeville comedies
[they] are all too accidental or too superficial. They rest on no
comprehension, no insight, no real depth . . . . The pun is only
verbally deep. The vaudeville performance is silly, being only
accidentally deep. Yet in both we find the ingredients, however
poorly measured and mixed—excuse the intemperance of my
figure—of a potion that will make all who drink laugh.[97]

Choice between the types of incongruity depends on the
relative intelligence, appreciation, and abilities of the
observer. All men can appreciate puns on the level of
common experience, but the philosopher's cosmic puns
require intellectual skill and cosmic appreciation. Laughter
for the philosopher (who sees without eyes what others cannot see with them)[98] springs from the intellectual shock of
recognizing a yet unexpressed, new, and broader view in

the overtight clothing of traditional language: ". . . philosophy is constrained to be intemperate to the point of 'seeing
things.' "[99]   Insight, then, is accompanied by humor.   Seeing beyond accepted forms and standards, using language
in a shockingly unfamiliar way, the philosopher is a cosmic
comedian.

Since all thinkers are affected by these same conditions,
Lloyd takes cognizance of the Tower of Babel that must
result.   Speaking, one might suppose, from experience,[100] he
says, "Philosophy . . . is the gathering together in the name
of truth of two or more not one of whom ever knows what he
himself or any other is talking about."[101]   Lloyd's position,
however, would find such a situation most desirable, since,
at least (exempting "quacks"), it would be indicative of a
reconstruction in process.   If a test of truth is required on
such a view, Lloyd is ready with one.   The true is what
makes other people laugh and brings to its propounder a
laugh: "The pragmatist's test . . . can not hold a candle to this
test of provoked merriment."[102]

Lloyd's philosopher is not only a merry drunkard, but a
ribald one.   The philosopher's developing thought does such
violence to a society's fixed eternal truths, his unconven-
tionality so impiously demolishes the prevailing institutions,
that he hardly belongs in a well-ordered society.   The
philosopher lives "in a world in general," and this citizenship
makes him so universal as to be alien to the constrictions of
the culture in which he accidentally lives.   He promptly
removes its clothing, making "exposures" of "all that lies
beneath the outward appearances of men's lives, making
those appearances [and institutions] at most only the most
gauzy draperies . . . ."[103]   Nor does Lloyd forget the variety
of impudent exposures exhibited by finding meaning in the
commonplace, by asking the most basic and, in ordinary
terms, ridiculous questions.   Insight reveals that which is
so commonplace as not to have been noticed and hence as
to seem upon discovery almost miraculous.   According to
Lloyd, "The very essence of insight is discovery, not of any-

thing outside of life or nature, but of what dwells within life or nature, not of what something outside is, but of what this life or this nature really is."[104]   For Lloyd the visions of Aquinas, Spinoza, Kant, and Hegel are no more expressions of philosophic wisdom than the "tautologies and platitudes"[105] of Aristotle, who was "delightfully direct and flat"[106] and to whom he believes the following verses might be appropriately dedicated:

> Nothing to breathe but air—
>   Quick as a flash 'tis gone.
> Nowhere to fall but off,
>   Nowhere to stand but on.[107]

Last but not least, all philosophic activity is sublimely "impractical."[108]   In one place Lloyd says that the ideal (and philosophy, in the last analysis, seeks the ideal), which has always been accused of idleness and of not doing its share in the work of the world, has been put to work by the pragmatist.[109]   In another, he contrasts the philosopher and the practical man and comes to the conclusion that the philosopher is impractical because he really uses his experience, while the practical man spends, acts, and thinks only for return in kind.[110]   The philosopher, his occupation, and its goal are all impractical because "the philosopher's formula . . . means everything, the whole universe in fact, yet really is applicable to absolutely nothing."[111]

But finally, since ideals, for Lloyd, are rooted in physical soil, his ribald and drunken philosopher experiences the core of the religious life, for natural laughter is one ingredient of natural religion.   Lloyd's notion of cosmic humor is, in principle, much like Spinoza's view *sub specie aeternitatis;* while Spinoza seeks the longest view, Lloyd seeks the broadest.   Born of insight and understanding, cosmic or philosophic humor evidences intellectual and emotional appreciation, which for Lloyd is the essence of religious appreciation. In understanding natural processes, in participating in them, in belonging most intimately to a natural world, Lloyd's philosopher expresses joy in the activity of a universe even when personally a victim of it.   Cosmic humor is the basis of the religious experience of the free man, for "there can be no vision without laugter."[112]

7. *The Duty of the Comic Poet*

Apparently, the good philosopher functions on an intellectual level analogously to infinity in a world of things. He redefines and interrelates divergent intellectual enterprises in a larger and all-subsuming philosophic synthesis. He acts as a unifier by showing that all kinds of knowledge define one world and one life from divergent points of view. It is his duty to be meaningful, yet not literal; he must be poetic, yet build on scientific truth.   He must use the scientific method, yet "go beyond" it.   He must stand midway between science and silence by means of an identification of speculative thought with aesthetic appreciation.   He must take a position without taking a position.   In short, the philosopher must be a citizen of a universe so wide that he is forced to build a sort of linguistic no man's land which is at once analytical and poetic.

Ironically enough, such paradoxical and difficult duties were inspired in Lloyd by his allegiance to what might be called the "spirit" if not actually the "letter" of pragmatism and naturalism.   Insofar as he subscribes to the idea that truth is found in activity, Lloyd is brought to the notion that language cannot entirely encompass such truth.   Inasmuch as he subscribes to the idea that action is interaction and interrelation, he is brought to the problem of describing a totally interacting world.   Inasmuch as he subscribes to contextualism, he sets the problem of how language can be broadened to subsume many contexts and yet be meaningful.

Should there be a desire to classify Lloyd's views, to name the position which he hoped so desperately would be unnamable, let me simply say that such an enterprise would be not only difficult, but entirely fruitless.   Not only would the text contradict such an endeavor, but the enterprise would be seriously out of tune with his approach. Lloyd's is a philosophy which tries to swallow a world—whole. The indigestion is often evident. Certainly part of the comedy of the philosopher—that victim of overindulgence—is that in his effort to say everything, he risks saying nothing.

While Lloyd has caught the naturalistic temper and the pragmatic spirit at least as well as its foremost exponents, yet he makes these meaningful in the light of a poem. We might say with some justification that Lloyd is the idealist who writes a metaphysics for his naturalism, the idealist who pragmatically describes his absolute.

Surely the second act of Lloyd's comedy concerns itself with the way in which the reader is to take his point of view, the spirit in which we are to understand his metaphors. How can we, for example, determine where analysis ends and poetry begins? But perhaps these tragicomedies are obviated by the greatest paradox of all, the last act of Lloyd's drama. If Lloyd is to have a philosophic position, it already implies its antithesis. It is already swallowed up in a larger whole. It is already an institute which must become an instrument. It is already only a "formal letter" to be repudiated by a new, more comprehensive "spirit." This is the poetry, the humorous epic that the earnest philosopher must sing.

V

Social Community

1. *One Life; One World*

Ontology justifies Lloyd in a most thoroughgoing interna-
tionalism and cosmopolitanism. He scorns discussion of *a*
social community, committed as he is metaphysically to a
universal sociality. Geographic boundaries fail to isolate
groups from each other;[1] his relationalistic view makes such
physical limits meaningless.[2] Nationalism is just a habit of
mind, he asserts; it is an abstraction for community that dis-
torts and disguises its real nature.[3] It is significant to note
that on this basis Lloyd fervently supports the League of
Nations but protests its name, which seems to him to imply
that the member nations in some sense *created* community
rather than simply took cognizance of it. In behalf of a new
name he writes: "Adam, not Eve, must have chosen to call
the union a 'League.' Eve would once more have seen what
the new creature looked like and have had even the party-
ridden United States stampeding to join the United Nations!"[4]

Since any A, having a relationship with any B, is already
committed to infinite relationship, since every person in any
communal relationship is already related implicitly to a total
universe, or, as Lloyd puts it, since "society is a life, not a
fixed condition; a movement, not a creation of special time or
place,"[5] the principles of serial relationship insure that the

relations between A and B will be analogous to those with any other term.   To the extent that each term in a communal series is absolutely unique, Lloyd grants that the relationship of each man to any other inevitably differs in kind.   But, turning this fact into working capital, he now has the right to insist that the difference between an American and a Tibetan is no greater than that between siblings.   One culture differs from another no more diversely than brother differs from brother.   Furthermore, societies past, present, and future are interrelated: "Personally . . . all men whatever they may be as Babylonians, Egyptians, Jews, or Greeks, as Romans or Germans, as Englishmen or Americans, are of one time and place and of one life."[6]   Consequently, the cultural differences separating societies as well as those separating individuals are less wide and deep than they appear. While no society is completely dissociated and disparate from any other, undeniable diversity springs simply from the fact that a seemingly alien society expresses externally and overtly those aspects of human character existing only internally and covertly in us.[7]   Such societies, then, are explicitly what we are implicitly.   They exhibit what we hide, and vice versa.   Thus, examining the consequences of World War I, Lloyd sees the future as bringing a closer unity between ourselves and the Far East, for example, and prophesies what we might call "the meeting of east and west."[8]   He says that "all men are all things together."[9] What some are actually and conspicuously, others are only potentially and, in a sense, privately.   And again, "Every single person . . . however apart from his fellows . . . is but a revelation, a defined overt expression of something hidden, or at best only imperfectly known or expressed in their nature . . . ."[10]   Convinced that all share in one life, Lloyd centers his account of political and social matters around the primal fact of one world, one life, and one society.

In accordance with these theories, Lloyd refuses to localize sovereignty in any *particular* person or state, but finds it in the responsibility of each one with reference to the others.

Inasmuch as sovereignty springs from the fact of community that each person has with every other, it becomes an adverb modifying communal activity, and so, "The only real sovereignty is that of the social *whole*."[11]

Since sovereignty is an adverb modifying participation in world community, the idea of *national* sovereignty, so much strengthened by World War I, is the principal object of Lloyd's attack. "How several nations, for example, can be looked upon at one moment as each possessing an independent sovereignty and at another moment as parties under an international law . . . I cannot see,"[12] he says. In Lloyd's view a *union* of *sovereign* nations becomes theoretically a contradiction and practically a breeding ground for false hopes. Indeed, he uncovers a basic flaw in international organization as we today conceive of it. Significantly enough, in pursuit of this idea, Lloyd felt called upon, during the war of 1918, to protest against a victory by sovereign nations, preferring, instead, that the conflict be "drawn."[13] To this end he urged the institution of an arbitrating body which would function continuously throughout the war and which would have as its object a truce by agreement rather than victory by force of arms. His newspaper articles on this subject suggest that he felt a nationalist position, as it was then understood, to be contradictory and untenable for a military victor. One piece which was published in the *New York Times*[14] insists that economic and financial alliances rather than military victory are the keys to a peace dedicated to the securing of more significant types of international organization. Lloyd maintains that war is more than just a meeting of forces in kind; it is also a meeting of ideals and different kinds of living. He develops the matter further, elsewhere, by asserting that "there is no power like that which comes to life from the assimilation to each other of ways and forces that have met in conflict."[15] Thus, the conflict should be settled on a truly international basis and not merely on a nation against nation basis.[16]

Each *particular* society is only an artificial crystallization of a constantly restless process inherent in all. Each society, alike with all living things, is moving to its death. But social extinction duplicates personal death in that the dying life passes into a new form in the life of other societies.

Since all things must be understood in terms of their processes, nothing can be completely examined without an account of its history, or a description of its environing past and future, which form the links of the series within which it is but one member. Each society must be examined with reference to prior and subsequent cultures. While this principle is obviously justified, its application gives Lloyd much room for poetry and myth in historical interpretation. We have already raised the question of the verifiability of poetic and mythological explanations. It is not my purpose here to criticize Lloyd for lack of caution in historical analysis. Let it suffice to point out that for him the study of history has ontological justification, and this necessarily commits him to historical interpretation and a critical analysis of historical method.

2. *The Basis of Sociality*

For Lloyd, as for Aristotle, individuals are naturally social. In Aristotle, however, individuals are social by *their* nature, whereas in Lloyd, they are social in the nature of things. They are ontologically, rather than biologically or psychologically, social. Thus Lloyd is brought to the further conclusion that sociality itself is metaphysically original, a view which is consistent with both his dynamic relationalism and his theory of universals. This view forms the basis for a distinction between what he calls a "creationalistic" and a "naturalistic" conception of social theory and of historical interpretation.[17] Creationalistic sociologies concern themselves with the origin and the destiny of *a* society rather than with the nature and the function of sociality. They engage in legalistic controversy concerning the source and the justification of political rights, exemplified in America, for instance, by disputes about the rights of states and individuals and by idolatry of the Constitution.   Creationalistic histories of social development suffer from the same disease, being inordinately given to explanations of social change which presume abrupt beginnings and complete annihilations.   On the other hand, "naturalistic" social theory (which Lloyd takes his own social theory to be) is aware of the historical linkage between varying phases of social development.

In a particularly penetrating analysis[18] of the differing conceptions of the social-contract theory of government found in Hobbes, Locke, and Rousseau, Lloyd identifies all forms of the theory as creationalistic.   Social-contract theory characterizes a period of change between monarchy and democracy.   Such change Lloyd finds analogous to cultural development in mathematical theory, artistic production, and scientific conceptions.   Modern technological devices ultimately require a "naturalistic" theory to interpret them.

Lloyd's principal objection to a contract theory of society seems to be that it falsely implies that social life is formal, artificial, and external.   Distinguishing his own view from this, he insists that sociality is real in the sense of being present in all action, natural and internal in the sense of being part of the very characteristics that define a person. Akin to language in function in that it is a mediator between the members of one society, sociality provides the metaphysical basis for exchange of ideas and services between men.

The concept which Lloyd calls "mediation" facilitates his theoretical transition from sociality in general to *a* society in particular.   As mediator, sociality functions institutionally to form individual states and societies.   Sociality is physicalized and particularized.   The political state then expresses the principle of sociality openly and formally by institutionalizing it.   But, regrettably enough, institutionalized sociality is subject to the inevitable and fatal ailments of all institutions, their "original sins."

Lloyd maintains that the social-contract theory "outgrows" itself historically, and is only one phase of the development of society's self-conscious awareness of its foundations and enabling conditions. A society which understands its origin to be that of a lawfully instituted social contract is but recognizing the fundamental lawfulness of nature and evincing the respect of man for rationality. Thus the contract, whether so understood by the parties involved or not, is simply an innuendo for a broader lawfulness which underlies all social life and which, in due course, must take other, less formal, less legalistic and stagnant forms. The legal foundations of a society or the social contract is, then, "only a validating principle,"[19] or an abstraction for metaphysical sociality, which underlies social forms.

Although society is "organic" for Lloyd, he carefully distinguishes this conception from Spencer's social organism. Disgusted with what he considers a widespread misinterpretation of the notion of organism, he attempts to free this notion from the other views out of which it has sprung. He maintains that the characteristics he describes by the term "organic" do not include growth by increase in mass or in complexity of structure, nor yet interdependence of parts or survival of the whole despite the death of the parts. On the contrary, he understands an "organic society" to mean "a life, not a fixed condition; a movement, not a creation of special time or place."[20] The debt which Lloyd's ideas on community owe to evolutionary theory becomes evident, despite his rejection of Spencer's "mechanicalized" version.

Furthermore, Lloyd rejects the idea that a community is analogous to the 'class' of logic. Denying identity of characteristics, similarity, or common nature to the members of a social community, he asserts: "No common ritual . . . no common language, no common anything has ever either given men a common life or been developed by them to satisfy such a life."[21] Such "community" would be based solely upon aggregation and be the sum of identical parts. Lloyd marshals three reasons in behalf of this view. First, the identity derived by shared attributes is only superficial and suggests that social life is "in" the parties concerned rather than "of" them. Such unity would be structural rather than functional, and structural likeness fails to meet Lloyd's test for unity. Mere aggregation does not make a unity, he insists in many places. Secondly, even though the community were unified through similarities among its members, it would be equally disunited by the differences existing between them by virtue of their uniqueness. For Lloyd, difference serves as the foundation for, and not the destroyer of, both unity and community. A type of community based on the uniformity of the members, community as mere likeness, "were it ever realized, instead of being a basis of social life would be and could be only its undoing."[22] Finally, since each member of a community is uniquely distinct from the rest (which fact constitutes his very claim to a meaningful and responsible place in that community), the classification of people into the like and the unlike would not only be impossible, but would destroy the special unduplicable worth of each individual. Lloyd says, it will be recalled, that nothing is exactly like anything else and that nothing is "describable in literally the same way as anything else."[23] The idea of classification here, as elsewhere in his thought, meets with disapproval.

How then is social unity accomplished and on what basis does it rest? In what sense do the diverse and unique members of a society become organic? To answer these questions Lloyd defines community functionally. Community is gained whenever the group *participates in some action together*.[24] The state at large is organic inasmuch as its citizens share a life together. It is "a group of beings whose nature is one nature and one with all nature,"[25] he says rather cryptically, using substantive terms which tend to blur his meaning. By the phrase "whose nature is one nature" Lloyd means a unity gained through activity toward a common goal. "One with all nature" means that the social group exemplifies the traits of community along with all other types of groups, on any level of existence. Thus a community distinguishes itself as such through action. Its unity, says Lloyd, is dynamic, not static, "a spirit, not a material being; a principle, not a thing; a force not a status."[26] By calling social unity a "principle" and a "spirit," Lloyd emphasizes the superficiality of unity based on cultural origin, geographic location, race, color, or creed. It seems to me that in calling it a "force" he opens up new possibilities for the political, spiritual, and physical analysis of any society.

3. *Social Evolution*

Lloyd's society, like his metaphysical unity, is restlessly active, caught between the tensions which beset all organism, which internally split it into warring factions and which externally force it into partiality with respect to other societies. Eventually these tensions disrupt the society and cause its death. Eventually the "alienation" between society as a whole and a society as a set of factions becomes so complete that the "crisis in the series" develops and what Lloyd calls "precipitation" occurs. The particular society disintegrates and bequeaths its particular triumphs to the "larger life" of human society in general. Eventually the "principle of use" operates, making revered institutions weapons or instruments of attack in a warfare upon their sociological progenitors, the values which gave them not only birth but worth. Eventually, as "self-denial and sacrifice" become principles operative in social experience at large (as well as in individual experience), the society *must* decline, since the cosmic conflict of egoism and altruism always ends in "complete alienation." Eventually a revolution, either physical or spiritual, and *always* ideational, results in a changed attitude of a people toward itself. ·At this point the life of the society "bursts its bonds," as Lloyd expresses social demise, and its social forms gain a new context—it is "restored." Metaphorically, then, a society "gives its life" to a more inclusive and dimensionally variant society, as the Greeks gave theirs to the Romans, the Romans to medieval societies, and these, in turn, to us.[27]

Fatalities which *must* occur among societies follow from an ontologically necessary "dual allegiance" to both themselves and a world at large, and for this very reason are not to be mourned. The same dual allegiance between part and whole which on a social level causes the death of a society, forces its rebirth in a new variation; and thus societies are perpetuated in a continuous chain of culture. Lloyd's conception of the death and rebirth of a society is responsible for his numerous suggestive interpretations of historical events.[28] Although the terms "birth" and "death" are metaphorical, because historical concepts are hypotheses, not fixed realities, for "my history, in some sense necessarily is a work of fiction,"[29] the processes involved are, in Lloyd's opinion, verifiable.

Lloyd cannot resist an identification of his conception of the dual movement, dual responsibility, and dual functions of a society with his notions of intension and extension (see Chapter I, section 8). Thus "social intension" represents those forces which separate an individual society from the "otherness" outside of it; it is sociologically manifested by what Lloyd calls the "inner life" or relative state of the values of a society; and it is an expression of the desire for self-maintenance inherent in any society, as in any organism.

It will also be remembered that Lloyd's principle of intension was analogous with what he called "control" as over against "spontaneity" or "impulse,"[30] or, to translate this in still another way, analogous with 'thought' as over against 'emotion.' In this new context the principle of intension examined sociologically suggests the "rehearsal" (on the part of a society) for the life to come,[31] or, to put it another way, the imaginative (although perhaps unconscious) review by a society of the consequences of its past life and activities. This "ideal experimentation" (if I may use Charles Peirce's expression) represents to Lloyd "life preparing for a leap"[32] and is really another variation of his basic theme of the necessary connection of the past and the future with the present, the connection which makes possible a theoretical account of a framework within which social change takes place.

Extension as a social principle, on the other hand, represents the society's responsibility to nature as a whole. Analogous with "impulse" or the demand for action, it signifies the presence of a new dimension of social life which is already asserting itself. It signifies that something is newly active in a society, which will eventually cause the breakdown of the old. Since the battle is as much internal as external, as much physical as ideational, this dual activity of any society leads Lloyd to say that the presence of an external foe is evidence of internal strife.[33] In the physical and ideational struggle that develops, the selection of a *particular* foe gives tacit but nonetheless clear-cut witness to the nature and character of the internal confusions. The enemy becomes that other society which most overtly expresses a society's own internal and covert dissension. Furthermore, in the course of the struggle the opponents must necessarily meet on "common ground," and since in battle they function as polarities and thereby "share the same law," "common ground" seems to imply that foes come to share weapons, methods, and techniques.[34] Before the battle is done, the two sides will have exchanged places, and a qualitatively different fusion of the two will result from the exchange. Thus, Lloyd never expects a peaceful society; he is never convinced that any war can end wars. But nonetheless, though social struggle can hardly be eliminated, he hopes that the ever-necessary battles will take place on levels somewhat higher than that of physical combat, and envisages new and less crude techniques of conflict. Since the wages of war seem to be the loss of personal identity and a mimicking of the enemy, Lloyd vigorously attacks the notion of carrying on war to *preserve* anything.

4. Analysis of History

Lloyd's conception of "dynamic history" is a protest against what he terms "materialism" in historiography. The vitalistic historian must be an evolutionist, and his history must be primarily concerned with human values. It must, therefore, understand change as dimensional in the sense of something more than alteration in time and space; it must respect the law of continuity; and it must insist on the relativity of ideas to contexts. To distinguish it more adequately from a "mere record of natural causes and effects"[35] without personality or life, Lloyd carefully outlines a number of major characteristics of materialistic historiography which the *Philosophy of History* aims to correct and which the "History of the Humani" exhibits corrected. His article on the subject, "History and Materialism,"[36] is so satirically drawn and so cleverly expressed that it is worthy of some attention. It has four main targets.

(1) Lloyd first attacks the historian who holds that historical events are cyclical. Though he grants the idea some meaning, he repudiates historical repetition understood as mere duplication of earlier occurrence. Such history is blind to qualitative variation and contextual difference. Lloyd maintains that repetitive history is "a scaffolding, not a real history,"[37] in that it assumes events to have only space, time, and quantity, and he examines two versions of this position: first, that two *types* of events occur, each following the other, in rhythm, and, secondly, that great changes are "reactions."

In regard to the first of these, Lloyd points out that the "pendulum" concept of history is actually a case of mistaken identity. It attempts to describe polarity relationship, but fails to recognize that *both* movements of the pendulum are incident to *one action,* and therefore that both are ever contemporaries. Lloyd blames the fault on a mechanistic interpretation of the vibratory theory of motion which has found its way into the theory of history, and he observes that even the pendulum never swings back to its old position.

In regard to the second variety, Lloyd objects that "reactions" imply spontaneous alteration which completely supplants a prior situation. Change as re-action, he maintains, is as sudden and mysterious as "revivalistic conversion" (and exhibits fully as much supernaturalism). To illustrate, he selects the most extreme example of change, that of social revolution, and reasons that its apparent abruptness is deceptive. Lloyd entirely denies revolutionary change in this sense and insists that even revolutions are actually examples of evolution. Long in preparation, so-called revolutions are always outgrowths of earlier conditions and are inevitably less violent breaks with the past than they appear to be on the surface.

Thus all types of historiography based on a sense of repetitive change suffer from being "formula-bound" to some standard arbitrarily selected by the particular historian, in terms of which he reinterprets history as "only a gathering of illustrations of the working of his special straitjacket."[38] Furthermore, Lloyd insists that the chosen standard is usually derived from and is a product of the contemporary scene. It is, therefore, at best inadequate, and at worst completely inapplicable to the past to which it is being applied. But most often the arbitrary measuring rule is only an exhibition of the personal background and temperament of the historian and reflects his biased judgment.

(2) With the historian of "dead" and "wooden" history disposed of, Lloyd next attacks his counterpart and extreme opposite, the equally materialistic historian who is given to statistics and sees in history only a multiplicity of facts that have no other unity save their association in time and space. Such a historian is indifferent to ethical values,[39] makes of history a "mere record," and is solely concerned with material conditions such as climate, natural resources, and geographical location, as if a static account of the scenery environing "living, breathing, failing, and triumphing men"[40] would be adequate to describe living events.

(3) Next Lloyd singles out for criticism the historian who treats his material in terms of eras and epochs, who produces the "date-ridden history," which, Lloyd protests, is the epitome of a materialistic attitude; such history makes "man

for dates" rather than dates for man. Apparently recalling his own early educational experiences, Lloyd grants that although this historiographical sin is now more or less out of fashion, it nonetheless appears, in two fresher and more subtle forms: first, as an attempt to extend the period to the whole of history (approaching the process of history as though it were one vast period); and, secondly, as an attempt to "relate a man or an event, a great thought or a great deed . . . to the times,"[41] which means, I believe, to reduce events to the sum of their causes, and to suppose tacitly that events have to *be* related by the historian when such a relation is actually always intrinsic and necessary.

Lloyd's objections apparently mean that the date-ridden historian ultimately conceives of environment as simply 'there' to be discovered. With environment static in the same sense as the 'era' is understood to be, this historian has recreated materialism by depriving the environment of its own life. He must necessarily hold that space is a container and that matter is the stuff contained, which inevitably devitalizes his account.[42]

(4) Finally, Lloyd challenges historians who overtly or covertly express an idea of progress as a march to some distant goal of perfection. The idea that we grow *out of* or *toward* something, leaving a trail of discarded values behind, comes in for its own share of punishment. Lloyd complains that this sort of history hypostatizes perfection into a state of being, thereby making a complete and absolute separation between the real and the ideal (and incidentally destroying a naturalistic basis for ethics). The 'out-of-and-toward' interpretation disregards the law of continuity and sees history's past achievements as a record of mere eliminations and accretions. Failing to recognize the contextual character of historical judgment, it makes invidious distinctions between different historical periods on the basis of some present standard of progress; it takes the *known* past for the *real* past,[43] as if current judgments of that past were not inevitably conditioned by continuously altering present interests.

When this happens the past cannot escape "the ignominy or the flattery of the pharisaical epithets of less and more, worse and better, that a superstitious, unappreciative, self-deceived present would cast on [it]."[44]

In all four types of materialistic historiography Lloyd finds the general fault of treating the part as the whole, of taking the means for the end. The historian who treats a part as the whole considers both men and events to be isolated phenomena unrelated to the rest of mankind's history, sprung from nothing, illustrative of nothing, and independent of past and future; he sees his history as an end in itself, instead of as a means for deriving from the past a set of working hypotheses which could provide a meaningful interpretation of current life and a significant education for humanity's future.

Indeed, Lloyd's vitalistic historian might well have the motto 'History for life, not life for history.' He must treat such historical concepts as reactions, revolutions, periods, and social forms as hypotheses and not as exact duplicates of any situation. He must not regard historical theories as phenomena having no duty to known experience, but must understand past, present, and future as a continuous, unified process, for "history is an affair of the whole."[45] The new historian must have a proper conception of ontology and must understand matter, as we have seen,[46] not as a special thing or a distinct group of phenomena, but as a general function capable of as many applications or expressions as there are relations in experience. If it follows these strictures, the vitalistic approach may then offer a *pattern* of living activity by which history gains life, movement, and dramatic character, and is vital rather than "fatal" and mechanical. With this perspective "history may gain anew the humanity and dramatic interest that to many it has appeared in serious danger of losing."[47]

5. *History as Evidence of Value; the Social "Occupations"*

Lloyd's history differs entirely in both intent and content from what is ordinarily understood as cultural history, and it regains "humanity" by describing a varying pattern of "bodily and spiritual" *value relations* which underlie historical events; it does not simply recount those events. Holding that events cannot be understood except in terms of a *pattern* of cultural values which are implicit in them and responsible for them, Lloyd seeks principles upon which activity is dependent. In opposition to a history which is meaningless except as a "description of the scenery" and an "analysis of character" inferred therefrom, Lloyd hopes to explain culture in terms of the human values found in it, and sets about the development of a kind of sociology of ethics designed to illuminate history by illustrating the interrelations of specific types of value complexes. He describes and interconnects varying cultural attitudes, intellectual disciplines, and personal occupations. History, in short, reflects changing cultural values.

History, however, must not only be understood in terms of a set of valuational relationships; it must provide a *pattern* or order of these relationships. Lloyd describes a series of "stages" or "occupations" which he feels underlie history. His completed but unpublished "History of the Humani" is devoted to this analysis, which, he remarks, "had long been a preoccupation" of his. One chapter, "The Reign of Science in the History of a Race," Lloyd published in article form[48] to determine public response. Despite the fact that interest in the article was apparently slight, his preoccupation with this endeavor never diminished.[49]

Lloyd's five "stages" (or, more properly, "phases") are more than types of valuational interest and choice found in the development of any person, society, or civilization. They are differing degrees of spirituality and awareness, and, as such, Lloyd sees them representing changing ways by which organisms face and temporarily solve their major conflict, that between a particular group and nature as a whole, between a society and a universe of societies, between a people's life and the larger, fuller life of the natural environment.[50] Since those "battles of the soul" are activities, Lloyd finds their movement analogous to the general movement of all things, described in the analysis of process as "centripetal" and "centrifugal" movement.[51]   Drawing again on the action of these correlative phases of process which combine to provide the movement in *any* organism, Lloyd uses them to produce the five phases of value underlying the movement of human history.

Lloyd employs various terms in speaking of the five basic stages, calling them sometimes "phases of the human psyche," sometimes "situations" or "occupations," and sometimes, and perhaps most significantly, "attitudes."   Aware of the arbitrariness of distinguishing them at all, he will vary their number from five to four[52] and insist that they form a process which it is actually impossible to subdivide.

The account of the five stages that appears most frequently runs as follows: first, "law," which Lloyd characterizes as a "simple assertion of the human *against* the natural"; secondly, "art," which he suggests is "the intrigue of the human *with* the natural"; thirdly, "science," which is described as "candor toward the natural and alliance with utility"; fourthly, "philosophy," which he typifies as "the gift of the human to the natural with the [consequent] liberation of the spirit"; and fifthly, "religion" (denoting here something akin to Dewey's later interpretation of the meaning of religion), which Lloyd characterizes as "the gift of the natural to the spirit."[53]   When from a larger view he reduces these attitudes to "situations" (the "moral," "aesthetic," "practical," and "natural"), their character as descriptions of value relations emerges more clearly.

What does Lloyd mean by his five valuational attitudes underlying human choice, which, in turn, determines human events?   It is important for proper understanding of this endeavor to be clear from the outset that Lloyd is *not* writing history.   In his "History of the Humani" he begins *in vacuo*, as it were, painting the values of a mythical society.   He unfolds a general picture of the stages of culture which his fictional society undergoes, isolates the values attendant

upon its sociological development, and weaves their alterations into a pattern.   He considers such things as the location of the sovereignty, the occupation of laborers, the
manners and customs of that society.   In this way, he hopes
to develop general standards by which to judge a society
and to establish sets of value relations which may illuminate
our own present and suggest our own future.

In Lloyd's fictional society, the "legalistic" value relation
is the first to emerge.   Apparently in an attempt to account
for the origin of civilization, Lloyd says that "when men meet
on common ground and in common ways . . . an advance is
certain to be made sooner or later in spirituality [inner life]
and civilization [external environment]."[54]   Thus, as soon as
men united into nomadic tribes, the legalistic stage was born,
since tribal life brings conflict with other tribes.   Conflict, in
turn, fosters "self-control" or skill in use of the environment,
which "always brings new depths to the inner life, new
qualities to the outer, vicarious environment, and new form
and meaning to the mediating language."[55]   Lloyd is making
the point that Peirce makes on a methodological level,
namely, that progress begins with doubt and dispute.   But
not only is it necessary for man to conceive of his environment as other than himself and therefore to use it as what
Lloyd would call a "freed medium of expression," he must
begin to experiment with and manipulate that environment
in order to advance his civilization.   To illustrate the point
Lloyd describes a child who, upon coming into painful contact with a bureau, enters "the life at once of spiritual activity
within and vicarious activity without"[56] when he uses part of
his environment, a block, for example, to hit back at the
bureau.   He not only becomes self-consciously distinguished
from his environment, but he begins to utilize it experimentally for his needs.   Lloyd can then draw an analogy
between his meaning of civilized life and "reading to self,"[57]
in which one reads "his life at large to self, vicariously maintained."[58]   Man becomes civilized when he perceives his
environment as something apart from himself, for his use.

With men united in groups and aware of their distinction from the environment, Lloyd is ready to describe the most elemental battle in the history of the human psyche. He gives an impressionistic picture of environing conditions at this point, and examines the set of values he calls "legalistic" or the "simple assertion of the human against the natural."[59] Finding a duality of man against nature in this first, valuationally primitive, stage of civilization, Lloyd describes the situation as one in which the environment is something "outside" of man to which he has difficulty in adjusting. With little adaptation to his natural circumstance, man's life is physicalistic, lacking in imagination or control, characterized by might, which Lloyd calls "the clash of arms and armor."[60] In this situation the dangers to the individual are primarily physical damage; wars and invasions typify it. The stage is considered "legalistic" because it attempts to make formal but positive statements about the customs, rituals, and taboos which have developed. A legalistic milieu tends to a division of labor and classes and provides the first elements of distribution and exchange in a society. But, by and large, the first cultural stage shares with the first stage in the child's learning process the recognition of a separate and hostile environment which requires the formulation of strict codes of conduct to permit life in and with it.

The second stage in Lloyd's "life to self"—in which man is not aloof from the physical world but utilizes and adjusts to it—is the "artistic" or "aesthetic" (Lloyd uses both terms), which he describes as "the intrigue of the human with the natural."[61] Here the duality of man and nature breaks out in a dynamic exchange between them. The characteristic affairs are military and romantic, and there is a change from open warfare to the delays and so-called peaceful settlements of artful diplomacy. Now man's response to nature is one of capitulating strategy. The new battle provides its own weapons of "striking dress" and "pointed manners," by which Lloyd means that the adornments of life, such as surroundings, architecture, personal decoration, and attitude toward one's society, are artful and designing (in both of the associations of these terms).   Under the disguise of the artful rituals of institutions, people are condescending and sentimental rather than candid.   Since this phase of culture is characterized by the creation of objects of sensuous beauty, the environment is able to maintain vicariously man's life in a more extended form.   The social hazards for man in this phase are to sensibility and self-consciousness.

The third stage in the process, which Lloyd characterizes as "scientific," involves much more "candor" toward the natural.[62]   With the greater interchange between man and his environment achieved in the previous stage, the duality between man and his world becomes more open and intense. Here the society makes "alliance with utility" and achieves that utility by the use of "standard measurements," such as the rules of logic, the formulae of the scientist, and the currency of international banking.   This "rational game of standard methods and instruments"[63] makes possible the game of science on the abstractly intellectual side and the game of commerce and industry on the practical side.   Thus the new battle is one of *kinds* as well as *magnitudes* or sheer physical weights, a subtlety foreshadowed in the preceding stage.   Since diplomacy has led into the "calm game of reason," the dangers of this new sociological period are to property, material opportunity, and occupation.

The fourth stage of the developing society Lloyd calls "philosophic."   The relations of man with his environment have now reached the place where a "gift of the human to the natural"[64] is possible.   This stage is already foreshadowing the next in that a new dimension in the relations of man with his environment is observable.   Here the standard measurement of the age of science has become "unlimited" in the sense that the mechanical routine of the scientific method has been superseded by what Lloyd calls individual talent.   This means that the deadlock of method is broken by something superior to the measurable conditions, namely, the use of those conditions, in place of formal compliance with them, by talented individuals. Now the "invasions" which take place are no longer those of conquering armies, as in the first stage, but those of new customs and ideas. Here the formal measures of the age of science are set free from their "mere letter" as man begins to use them. Man learns that the discipline of the standard measurements is for *his* use, not that he exists for their uniformity. The philosophic spirit is set free from confining standards, and the battle of "will" or spirit, rather than that of intellect, begins to take place. The great hazards of the period are subjective attitudes and individual license with respect to standard measurements. The period will be characterized by reform, invention, and revolution in practical matters, and the cultural victims will be found on what seems to be a battlefield of character.[65] Since here the individual is more reconciled to his natural environment and learns to trust it more, nature becomes the philosopher's tool.

The fifth, and for practical purposes the last, stage which Lloyd envisages, the stage in which this particular set of battles with the environment comes to a close and new unannounced ones come into being, the stage of the actuality of the new dimension in human values is that of "religion," which, in the manner of Lloyd, can be characterized as the gift of the natural to the human—"the final winning of body and soul."[66] In this stage the environment is no longer considered "outside" man, but becomes part of his inner life because of his complete adaptation to it. In this stage the physical foundation of value is not attacked, not made suspect, and not made mechanical, but is understood as the aspect of man's life which permits his experience to be crystallized and his values to be preserved. Here what Lloyd calls complete "self-control" (perfected will) is gained, and the individual enjoys a free mind in a natural body. Man is now ready for new battles qualitatively different from those of the winning of the environment and the winning of the proper perspective on his physical life with which previously he was totally yet unconsciously engaged. Now, having

digested and absorbed the environment, having released all
the technological and spiritual powers incident thereto, man
stands with the gift of a new dimension in his relations to a
world, ready to make new conquests in some further direction and to fight new battles which are quite incommensurable with those just won.   The last stage of history is merely
a last stage with respect to this particular battle of adjustment to the environment.   Unwilling to suggest the areas of
experience in which the future battles of the psyche will take
place after nature is won by means of the five struggles he
outlines, Lloyd concludes his analysis in a tentative vein.

Lloyd is careful to point out that these five stages in
human development are phases of *one* process,[67] important
primarily as phases of relating activity binding the process
of cultural development into a unity.   As process, the five
are at once both functionally contemporaneous and temporally sequential.[68]   They comprise a "general situation" of
which the particular stages are just "moments."[69]   Since
"relational activity" is genus to "temporal movement" as
species, the stages are not only temporal unities in succession, but, understood as a group, they compose a total relational activity as well.   Lloyd's social "occupations" are
contemporaneous in the sense that each of the five types of
evaluation, characterized broadly in terms of "soldiers,"
"artists," "scientists," "thinkers," and "religionists" are present
at all times in the history of a society: ". . . each [of the five
activities is] at every time a special part in the always divided
labor of civilization and at some particular time the promi-
nent and commanding part."[70]   At any particular time one of
the values held dear (by one group) permeates each of the
other types of occupations with its character.   These groups
are not meant to be social classes, for each person engages in
all of these types of evaluation at once, and this progress of
values not only represents the development of human society, but is found in miniature in the development of each
child into an adult.

Lloyd asserts that his "stages are fictional"[71] and gives

three reasons. First, since each unit is a division of a continuum, the boundaries of each must necessarily be arbitrary and inadequate. As an abstraction from total interrelatedness, no stage, as described, can provide a satisfactory and true account of experience. Secondly, since discussion of each stage entails classification of its properties, we can define only the "typical," for, as will be recalled, the philosopher's theories are about everything *in general,* but applicable to nothing in particular. Therefore, we cannot hope to present more than an impressionistic account. Finally, since the real lies in the relations of things, Lloyd's entire purpose in developing the stages is to illustrate certain relationships through which he sees a principle at work, rather than to describe actual events. Thus his "History of the Humani" is dedicated to a development of the *principles* to which the relations between these stages attest; it is those principles which indicate the directional pattern in the history of human events.

It is significant that although Lloyd's metaphysics is opposed to this type of enterprise, his Hegelian strain forces it upon him. While the stages, like schemata in general, merely define activity abstractly,[72] Lloyd loses no time in defining it. Although they are about a general situation[73] of which the particular instances are just 'moments,'[74] Lloyd cannot refrain from a complete description of them which grows in richness of detail with each account. To modify these conflicting pulls upon him, Lloyd continually suggests that his elaborate picturizations must be taken "with a grain of salt."[75] He paints them, however, with such gusto and in such lively colors, that not only can his reader easily be deceived into thinking the account empirically real, but Lloyd actually succumbs to his own spell. Completely losing sight of his stages as mere servants, Lloyd permits them to gain mastery in his thought. Though he asserts that they are fictional, he makes them actual. That Lloyd does think of his stages as historically sequential is quite clear. He not only applies them to ancient Greece, but risks a prophecy

that "Christendom is now nearing its age of philosophy."[76]
If only because he succeeded in giving such a strikingly
accurate picture of modern values, Lloyd must be forgiven
his weakness.   But a further possible difficulty arises.   Does
Lloyd's general analysis of process and continuities force him
to the position that the stages are *necessarily* sequent?
Lloyd can hardly be taken to task for maintaining his social
occupations to be empirically real, or for holding that at any
one time one of these activities is dominant.   He says, also,
however, that the *order* of the dominance of the stages
presents a natural "line of succession."[77]   Does the theory
of polarity, process, and interrelatedness make the "natural
line" a necessary order?   One might even ask a further
question, namely, whether there is not also present here the
implication of an inherent teleology of moral progress.[78]

Lloyd distinguishes between the theoretical sequence of
his stages qua stages and their empirical sequence as *dominant* phases of a society's activity.   The stages are in empirical sequence only relative to a particular situation, "mindful
of a context."[79]   But even the substitution of the term "dominance" for "stages" and even the added qualification of their
contextual relativity have not eliminated altogether a suggestion of a *necessary order* in the dominance of these relative
stages and the consequences of this necessity.   Inasmuch
as Lloyd insists that each stage is a "dimensional variation"
of the earlier one, each is already dependent on the *particular* previous stage.   Indeed, he takes great pains to show
how the *particular* deadlock in a preceding stage produces
the *particular* characteristics of the next one.   But despite
these difficulties Lloyd has, with vitalistic fervor, made historical change something more than an accidental concres-
cence of causes and has humanistically grounded events in
the soil of human evaluation, where they rightfully belong.

6. *Social Goals*

Looking at the five phases of social process as a development, Lloyd sees them as a progress toward a more facile,

functional relationship between man and his environment.[80] He is really ascribing social change to the relating activities of the knower, who acts as the principal unifier of the environment. Offering a kind of 'historical psychology,' Lloyd is interpreting history, or the changing environment, as an exhibition of man's biological, spiritual needs. He sees "will" or "life" bubbling over into polarities of "inner" and "outer," now to be understood in terms of his five levels of value found as data of the environment.

Lloyd states the goal of social activity in another provocative way. The changing occupations of man move, he says, toward a "release from any uniformity—from class life, from 'bodily mass-play,' "[81] and from duplicative group activity—and he envisages the ultimate goal of the individual to be activity which fully expresses his metaphysical uniqueness. The final battles of philosophy and religion are battles in which mankind no longer fights en masse or in chorus: ". . . men are no longer in any visible way grouped together . . . ."[82] The social goal of each individual is to bring his own special genius and relating ability to bear on his experience, to illuminate his activity thoroughly with his own unique perspective. Like Leibniz's monads, each of which faces the world with a differing perspective and each of which has a necessary place in the completion of that world, Lloyd's individuals need to express fully their personal genius and capacities in action. Thus conceived, the activity of each would be vital, induplicable, thoroughly responsible, and a truly creative part of the self-active world, rather than a mechanical duplication or mere echo of another's genius. Lloyd's plea for originality and creative responsibility in personal action is fundamental in his ethics. It is obvious that a casuistic ethics of rule and rote evokes his greatest anathema. And it is obvious that his ethics permits judgment only relative to a context. But it is remarkable that this ethical expression of a relativistic, naturalistic, and pragmatic outlook finds its roots in a metaphysics of historical stages.

Lloyd's account of the development of individual uniqueness in a society without geographic boundaries is not to be
misunderstood as a plea for the goal of a 'classless society.'
Both faction and person must always operate in the social life
as polarities.   They are equally original, equally necessary
furniture for social life, and equally contributory to it.
Society must have classes because social development
depends on diversity and conflict.   A society is always composed of conservatives and radicals,[83] or, as Lloyd sometimes
puts it, of loyalists and anarchists.[84]   Every society requires
classes within the framework of which each individual will
operate as creatively as possible.   It may be noted that the
idea of a perfectly unique member of a class functions again
as a "limiting notion."   The completely individuated class
functions as the overdifferentiated A, while the classless
person functions as the undifferentiated A.   The two notions
are contradictory, and simply serve to describe erroneously,
but to explain accurately, social excellence.

Lloyd sees the direction and the goal of society and those
of the individual as two sides of the same process.   He takes
each stage to be aiming at a limit rather than at a final end.
The limit he envisages is a "free soul and the natural body,"[85]
or, put another way, the "real adaptation"[86] of man to his
environment.   The whole process of history is a cumulative
preparation for freedom in nature, for the gradual breaking
down of man's reserve and aloofness toward nature[87] through
greater ease and effectiveness in its use as a tool.   In one
sense the process of history is the acquisition of greater facility in the use of language,[88] in both of Lloyd's meanings of
that term.   Expressed another way, it is the development of
a naturalistic attitude, implying the "naturalization" of man
in his natural world.[89]   This view reflects Lloyd's own
pragmatic and naturalistic temper.   But it should be noted
that Lloyd's conception of "naturalization" is not to be confused with naturalism as a set of intellectual presuppositions
about the nature of a world.   It stands rather for an attitude,
a habit of mind, an approach to experience.   While Lloyd as

idealist seeks metaphysical guarantees, as naturalist he understands the naturalistic temper to be one free of irrelevancies and doctrine. He supports a naturalistic attitude, but does so by means of a metaphysics tinged with idealism.

7. *Person and Faction*

Lloyd's analysis of the person vs. the faction is one of the more significant aspects of his thought on social community. Both person and faction are created and distinguished from each other by the same activity which separates a particular society from a world at large. They are polar opposites. Their relationship duplicates the larger relationship of a society with a society of nations. Born of activity and process, the person and the faction are themselves forever contemporaneous functions, forever irreducible, and forever, at war in the maintenance of their different goals and responsibilities. According to Lloyd, their conflict insures unity.

Lloyd's allegiance to the significance of individuality taken together with his insistence that the whole is a "ratio" and not a mere aggregation of parts produces striking results. The person becomes "the whole" and the class "the part"! Functioning analogously to a whole, the person cannot be understood merely physically,[90] and the self is therefore "denied local habitation."[91] The individual, as a result, "saves human nature from the disruption and stagnation to which specialism and its formal establishment always tend."[92] The class or faction, functioning analogously to a part, is special, particularistic, repetitious, imitative, and habitual. To apply this analogy epistemologically, the person, representing the knower, acts to incorporate a multiplicity of relationships in a unity. To apply it biologically, the person, representing the organism, is a whole utilizing the particularities of the environment. To apply it socially, the person is implicitly and potentially what the society is explicitly and actually. In short, the person functions like a small cosmos, while the faction represents the function of the matter and physicality of that cosmos. The person represents the organic; the faction, the mechanical. The person is a herald of the future, the faction a reminder of the past; the person represents intellectual spontaneity and drive, the faction, crystallized intellectual fermentation. But as polar terms the person and the class share in the maintenance and productiveness of experience.

Inasmuch as "factional life, like that of corporations, lacks soul," Lloyd says, "it tends to become formal and mechanical . . . it is static";[93] it is a mechanism (tool) for the organism (vital activity of the individual). In holding that all institutions must submit, along with the physical environment, to being only tools for present human activities, to being only the means for the ends required by developing life and spirituality, Lloyd exhibits his revolutionary and iconoclastic tendencies. No institution can be granted sanctity; neither Church nor State, social group nor professional dignity is sacred.

With terminological abandon and psychologistic overtones, Lloyd sees the individual as analogous to "right-handedness," while the environment, more sluggish and resisting and only half awake, as it were, is analogous to "left-handedness." These terms imply indirectly an earlier contention of Lloyd's that the environment gains more meaningful life only when known by the knower and only to the extent that it translates or crystallizes, in a physical sense, the knower's spiritual initiatory action, of which it, as mere physicality, is incapable. In consequence, divergence and breach between persons will never be so difficult to repair as those between factions.[94] Persons represent the more meaningful links of the great chain of living action; hence personal enmity is cosmically more amenable to correction than factional war. States, pressure groups, ruling classes are not only more prone to war than persons, but tend to continue the battle to the point of annihilation. The person, Lloyd says, "is himself the living, urgent unity of experience . . . ."[95] And again, "Personality as a living, integral expression of the whole of experience . . . bridges all the chasms of history; the chasms of race, of caste, of epoch; of nationality, of party, of any form of division of human nature."[96]

8. *Conservative and Liberal: Miser and Spendthrift*

Lloyd finds the virtues and vices of the person best expressed by the appellations "miser" and "spendthrift."[97] The miser is one species of transgressor in the sense that he hoards his activity and inventiveness; he imitates and conserves the past and holds it sacred; he hesitates to initiate bold action. By acting thus he illicitly adopts the role of the institution, rather than playing that of the person; he duplicates the halfhearted life of the clod. Failing to utilize his unifying capacities on the new problems born of a changing context, he openly exhibits the limitations of his society and is taken captive by them. Although the miser's function is damnable enough, it is nevertheless necessary. The miser represents the positive polar term required for dimensional change, and with such a metaphysical burden, his sins must be redeemable. But the mediocre, the average, the one who neither spends nor hoards, is the real non-entity, the placeless, functionless culprit of Lloyd's social community. Lacking the courage to reform and the humor necessary to accept regress, the mediocre is unable to appreciate the great, the inimitable whom he would try to imitate, and is capable only of condemning the sins of the transgressor, which he himself hides. The most outstanding example of the mediocre is, for Lloyd, the merely professionally developed, the individual who is midway between the miser and the spendthrift. Skillful, he plies his techniques without genius; he is above the commonplace, but below the great. The professionally mediocre person is more damned than the unprofessional mediocre one, just because he could be great, while the latter has less opportunity to be great.

The spendthrift, or genius (Lloyd takes Socrates and Christ as examples), freely uses his body, his environment, and the institutional forms of his society as means to "life" as the end. Functioning as a "whole," in the most significant degree possible for an already limited part, he contains all the possibilities for action that a material world presents. Utilizing the limitations of his surroundings, acting in terms of an empirically given context and confining conditions, the spendthrift takes "captivity captive."[98] Imaginative realist, he uniquely makes use of 'the given' to purchase a more meaningful spiritual life. "Greatness [genius]," Lloyd says, "has ever translated seeming fate into human purpose,"[99] necessity into opportunity.

It will be recalled that Lloyd's theory of environment found the physical surroundings to be a "standard measurement," a sort of currency which permitted ideational exchange between man and environment and which was the basis for the linguistic exchange between man and man. "Miser" and "spendthrift" are terms for those who either conserve or spend their standard currency.

Transgressor and reformer[100] are equally iconoclasts and lawbreakers. Both share piety and deviltry. As polar opposites, they "share the same law," for the same principle is at work in each. The distinguishing feature between their antiauthoritarian activities rests on whether or not they are purposefully aware of their disrespect. The transgressor breaks the law *unaware* of his shameless exhibition of the social sin responsible for the values his errors attest. For example, the thief is made captive by his society's permeating lust for the accumulation of physical goods and is unaware that he is exhibiting what may be that society's carelessness of individual necessity. The race-hater unconsciously reveals his society's aggressive competitiveness and its resultant failure to value any and all human beings. The spendthrift or reformer, exemplified, for example, by Socrates, consciously uproots dogmatic conviction with experimental, tentative conviction and deliberately combats sophistry with directed sophistry.

Regardless of their distinguishing characteristics, however, the transgressor and the reformer function in a polarity relationship, the first acting as the positive pole and the second as the negative pole productive of the new dimension. The miser is a successful failure, while the reformer is a failing success. Personal vices thus become cosmic benefits, if we may rephrase Lloyd in Mandevilleian language.

9. The Institution and Its Original Sins; the Person as Savior

Since, according to Lloyd, the term "institution" means "any manifestly established mode of activity"[101] in a society, the institution is the breeding ground of factionalism and the faction is the core of institutionalism. Lloyd makes a fertile analysis of the virtues and, particularly, the vices of institutional life. The institution, functioning as a part, embodies both virtue and vice in its partiality. Factionalism, that "hot-bed of specialism,"[102] provides for the growth of skill and for the insurance of technical development, regardless of the tendency of such development to be formal, mechanical, static, and in chorus. It permits insight even though such vision is limited by its habitual and mechanical character and is therefore routine and diminished in importance. Thus factional life sustains and preserves the developed past for our use.

An institution's original sins are too original to be unredeemable, Lloyd maintains.[103] Since its transgression consists in partiality, the institution errs (as much as Lloyd could ever grant 'error' in a necessary world) by reason of the four mortal failings of dogmatism, opportunism, materialism, and schism. Dogmatism causes it to assert its isolation and self-worth at the expense of other parts or phases of life and to bedevil itself with notions of its own infallibility and superiority. Opportunism, always institutionally bred, causes the institution to utilize *anything* as means to justify its own ends, which it sees as superior to all others. But not only does the sin of opportunism destroy other phases of human activity in its own behalf, it often utilizes *persons* as its fodder. The institution which thus sacrifices the individual hastens its own demise, because the person is, as it were, the savior, the great ethico-religious unifier. Lloyd finds it no accident that Machiavelli and the Roman Church flourished contemporaneously,[104] because both used persons as servants of institutions. The third sin of any institution, materialism, causes it to treat itself as a whole rather than a part and thereby to interpret all life in terms of its own prosperity and loss.

While dogmatism, opportunism, and materialism are the underlying causes of an institution's demise and eat at its vitals, schism is the immediate cause. When an institution commits the error of treating itself as a whole rather than a part, it attempts to encompass too much. An institution that succeeds in functioning as an all-embracing end must unfortunately measure its success by its imitation of the actual function of the whole, which, it will be remembered, was to divide into parts! Significantly enough, Lloyd finds that the factions that *do* develop in any institution suffering the penalties of institutionalism actually represent what it has overlooked, forgotten, professed blindness to, or ruled out of existence. Thus he finds that the many phases of life prove larger than the institution, despite its pretensions. Falling into factions, the institution, if I may put it this way, pays its debt to doubt, which it failed to conquer by its insistence on its all-inclusiveness and supreme importance. Diseased by schism, the institution bloats and dies, a victim of overindulgence.

The function of the person, then, is to correct for such institutional partiality by acting "whole-ly," in a sense in which he alone is properly capable and of which the institution is only a poor imitator. But because the person exemplifies, but does not duplicate, this ideal of absolute unity in his activities, and because "action is more spiritual than any institution,"[105] the person becomes the principal source of religious meaning, which can now be found in whatever the person does "efficiently," for "God is immanent in what his creatures do, their acts having a positive share in his creation . . . ."[106] The person is efficient in his metaphysical and religious function when he successfully manifests his unique

prerogatives of "expressing" the principle of unity in experience, when he exhibits "skill in social life."[107]   He becomes
"responsible" insofar as he "translates" his factional, group,
and professional experience into all other parts of his life.
In utilizing his factional experience as a means to an end and
repudiating the tendency of the institution to become an
end in itself, he binds his experience into a unity by means
of genius rather than by means of the compulsion used by
the institution.

Lloyd speaks of the person's function as "translation."
By translation the person interrelates a chaotic environment
in qualitatively new ways.   Alone capable of expressing the
relations between things, he translates these into his own
tongue and is thereby instrumental in developing new
(although not necessarily 'higher'[108]) levels of value experience by *creatively* adapting his *technical* skill to the various
relations of life.   While professional skill provides the rules
of grammar for the person's interpretation of his world and
his spiritual life, personal genius provides its unique vocabulary.   Thus by bringing *skillful* originality and professional
genius to the task of significant action, the individual serves
as an agent of exchange between, and an exhibitor of the
unity and interdependence of, the mechanical and physical
sides of his life on the one hand and the organic and spiritual
sides of it on the other.   By skillful and original action, then,
Lloyd makes the person prove the interdependence of
philosophical insight and scientific knowledge, the interrelation between theory and practice, and the ultimate connection between spirit and its "material wings."[109]

While the person exhibits the unity of experience potentially, the institution exhibits it actually.   The person expresses the unity of experience potentially in that (1) he may,
but need not, fulfill his cosmic task and (2) he can only relatively and partially fulfill it.   The institution, on the other
hand, "actually" exhibits the unity of experience, in the sense
that it crystallizes or solidifies man's past activities in the physical objects, customs, and traditions which compose his en-

vironment. Standing as a physical monument to these, the institution offers the past to the present as tangible, explicit, and, therefore, clarified; it serves as an instrument for future decision.

10. *The Fiction of the Great Man*

With the concept of individuality so central, it is hardly surprising that the idea of "the great man" plays a role in Lloyd's thinking. The leader performs the proper tasks of the person, but he performs them with greater gusto and finesse. Fearlessly extravagant with his environment, he often sacrificially donates his own body to the new social era in preparation.[110] He is a leader in that he not only "expresses" and "liberates" himself, but sets the conditions for the liberation of an entire group as well. Unfortunately, only subsequent history can attest social genius. Only from a later vantage point, and even then only in terms of a special teleological bias, can events reveal human greatness. Thus Lloyd informs us that the great man is "a good deal of an abstraction, being more thinkable than findable; in other words, having a wider reach and deeper root than merely findable things of time and space."[111] He is, in fact, "a noble fiction," a sort of afterthought, best seen in retrospect.[112] He is the product of interpretation in the light of special values.

Lloyd finds Socrates and Christ the most significant of the great men, and erects *Citizenship and Salvation* as a poetic shrine to them. Characterized by Lloyd as "a biological study of self-denial,"[113] this first book sees Socrates as an example of a person using his physical life for the fulfillment of the organic life of the society as a whole. Socrates translates his insight into the implications and consequences of Sophism, and exposes the ultimate defect of Sophism by his personal death. Socrates, Lloyd says, "turning the utilitarianism of his day completely back on itself, used all Athens for the development of his thought."[114] Taking advantage of Greek inability to act in unison, Socrates insisted on individuality at his trial, thus transforming necessity into opportunity and expressing the potentiality open to the Greeks. By his death Socrates demonstrated for the Greeks the fuller possibilities of their life, turning "the miserly, sensuous life that they had been leading rather unreflectively than consciously, into an avowed ideal."[115] Making them "resolve to be what they [unconsciously] had been,"[116] Socrates prepared the way for the Roman conquest, by which the entire society duplicated Socrates' personal death.

Christ equally, but in a new context, illustrates the same principles of inspired and sacrificial use of any and all material for a "new life." A section from *Citizenship and Salvation* on the function of Christ and his greatness is worth quoting, for I am sure that it stands as the only account of its kind:

Now at the Crucifixion the Jew's formalism, with its empty faith and hollow spiritual life, came into use; it came into use completely, explicitly . . . it became a . . . useful tool . . . an instrumental formalism . . . or a basis of positive action. In fact, the Crucifixion did nothing more nor less than give the Jew a trade or profession, of whose activity it was itself typical. . . .

I have described the Jew's formalism as at once acting in the future and looking at the past or as a sort of walking backwards, and I have shown how the birth of Christ was involved in it. But at his death Christ made fully manifest the nature of formalism; he revealed the future as its ideal or motive; and he made his people, even in their opposition to him, adopt his Christian standpoint. He made them face about. He gave them a future. He defined their formalism by giving it an end, sacrificing himself to it that they might be set free . . . . In treating [Christ] as an impostor they [the Jews] had no choice but to become loyal at least to the principle [anticipation of the future] for which he stood. If he was not their Messiah, then the Messiah was still to come; and upon their return to this forgotten and all but lifeless faith the formalism that had been developed among them became instrumental, and they came into a trade or profession. They were transformed . . . from idolators and traditionalists into lenders. The Crucifixion was itself an act of lending . . . .   The Jewish formalism . . . [being] an altogether abstract basis of social intercourse, an wholly external medium of exchange, it created a mental attitude that was preparatory to . . . a very worldly activity . . . .

Money . . . is the past treasured solely for itself, and so embodied in a medium wholly external to its possessor . . . it·is a material counterpart of the unity of the self or of a common or universal self in society . . . .   And so, at last, in the Jews becoming by nature money lenders we have the special way, the worldly way, in which they adopted Christianity . . . money is a worldly counterpart of Heaven . . . .   Thus it relies, does it not? on an unseen future, on faith . . . on worldly credit . . . .[117]

Surely the great man is a noble fiction!

11. *Social Will*

In search of a significant conception of "social will" Lloyd eliminates several possibilities.   First, he repudiates the idea that the social will can be located in a leader: leadership, being individualistic, gives contrary testimony.   Secondly, he repudiates the idea that social will is found in any individual state or nation, since a localized sovereignty is only an incorrect habit of mind, a contradictory concept.   Thirdly, he rejects the idea that the social will should be understood as a *common* will, for Lloyd's organicism and his consequent theory of the individual and the class combine to make him insist that no common attribute ever gave man a common life.   And, fourthly, he scorns the idea that the concept of the social will means the numerical sum of an aggregate of wills, since an aggregate shares nothing.

To explain the meaning of social will, Lloyd looks to the constantly divided unity he defined as "society."   Since society is characterized by factionalism or the interrelated tensions of adaptation and resistance on the part of its members acting in groups, the social will amounts to a conscious and deliberate effort to maintain unity through diversity—a purposefully adaptive agreement to differ.   Each person being bound to the implications of all of his social contem-

poraries and expressing unity while challenged by the wealth
of difference his neighbors present, the social will must be a
deliberately sought poise obtained by creative adaptation of
each to all the rest.   Nor is social will, as Lloyd defines it,
mere toleration of difference, but rather a utilization of difference for a creative unification of individuals through their
participation in common activities.   The social will is found
in shared practice and coöperative activity toward common
goals.

It will be noticed that Lloyd puts his question concerning
the nature of social will somewhat differently than had
earlier accounts.   He does not ask in whose hands sovereignty lies, for such imposed will could hardly be called
'social' in any sense.   He rejects Rousseau's "will of the
majority," because a sheer numerical aggregation of ayes
and noes is both mechanical and unshared.   He also rejects
Rousseau's formulation of the "general will," because it inad-
equately defines what society *ought* to desire.   Thus Lloyd
is really asking, 'What kind of activity is both desirable and
truly social?'   He emerges with an account of social will
similar both in phraseology and intent to Dewey's description of "the social."

12. Social "Forms"

Finally, Lloyd offers a significantly unusual account of
the meaning of such social forms as individualism and socialism, aristocracy and democracy.   Rejecting the presupposi-
tion that these concepts in any sense represent "forms" each
with a special and fixed set of distinguishing characteristics,
Lloyd defines them as *principles of activity*.   Since *each*
set represents a polarity, each is found to be always contemporaneous with the others.   Thus a society can never be
characterized as 'individualistic' or 'socialistic,' nor does individualism give way to socialism, but, rather, individualism
and socialism are ever-present *principles of relationship*, the
character of which continually alters and by its alteration
develops new social dimensions.

Lloyd makes a particularly fruitful study of the meaning of the democracy-aristocracy polarity in varying historical contexts.[118]   He emphasizes the contextuality of the meaning of democracy and maintains that we too often understand it as entailing a fixed, rather than a relative, set of defining characteristics. "Equality," as one of these fixed conceptions, has been made an absolute dogma, and this is "to betray its origin in vital human experience . . . to render it impracticable and so to cause the democratic movement inspired by it . . . to be seriously misunderstood and retarded."[119]   Undertaking to show these origins and the threads of relationship which run through the contextual variations of the history of democratic ideals, Lloyd points out that democracy is a principle operative in medieval and Roman periods as well as now. For the medievals the notion of democracy involved a conception of equality in which men were equal in *another* world. Thus medieval society harbored a supernaturalistic, future-if-not-now democracy which served to correct for and finally to undo a worldly inequality of military and religious aristocracy. The military might of the Roman Empire illustrated the principle of aristocracy, and acted in a physical sense as did its counterpart the Church in a spiritual sense. Thus, whereas the democratic ideal found its fulfillment in another world, the aristocratic ideal, its polar term, found expression in worldly and military power.

Tracing the development of the democratic ideal of equality, Lloyd turns to the seventeenth and eighteenth centuries, where he finds it undergoing a dimensional variation in that it was there placed in experience rather than in extra-empirical realms. But the concept of equality was then most worldly, in fact crude, in that it pertained to the equal right of each individual to basic and quite brute physical things, namely, life, liberty, and the safe possession of property. This expression of the ideal of equality was relative to and contextual with an aristocracy which must ever accompany it, an aristocracy of money and property incident to the rise of capitalism and contextual with the definition of equality as life, liberty (in the physical sense), and property.

In the nineteenth century Lloyd finds the contenders again altered in character. There an aristocracy of reason and of machinery accompanied an equally legalistic and mechanistic democracy. But this warring polarity once more produced a new dimensional variation. Lloyd sees today's aristocracy as one of labor and skill. The counterbalancing democratic ideals require for their adequate and appropriate expression much more than mere physical life and property, since now democracy understands its institutions as "means, not treasures or idols; public utilities, not just sanctuaries."[120] Contemporary democracy must, in turn, alter the concept of equality to mean that men are equally entitled to "worthwhile work" (a useful and rewarding occupation), "education" (or freedom to learn skills), and "commerce."[121] Sometimes Lloyd expresses this last right as the right to leisure,[122] by which he means the "unhampered opportunity of using and enjoying the present highly developed machinery of social life,"[123] and sometimes as freedom to use the means of communication for personal development. Lloyd's social organicism and religious humanism change the concept of equal human rights from rights to things or physical objects to rights with respect to participatory activities, from the elementals upon which life depends to the fruits of an industrial society. Lloyd's new bill of rights "might be set down as Work, Welfare and Worth,"[124] but hardly in an unqualified sense. Note the following account of the new social and political goals which Lloyd finds *unsatisfactory* because they are only the *forms* of social reform without real substance, only the letter and not the spirit of what he sees as our most immediate needs:

Cooperation, profit sharing, labor-representation among directors, protective labor legislation, public health measures, state-medicine, welfare associations and social service have all been efforts, direct and indirect, at the solution of the problem and may be said, all of them, to be influences for industrial democracy; but for the most part they have been palliative measures rather than candid and adequate solutions. Hardly have they really changed the status of labor or in any important degree increased the responsibility of capital industrially.[125]

Lloyd, in short, regards as only half a loaf those social goals upon which today's hopes rest!

In Lloyd's analysis, democratic ideals represent a negative polarity or a denying of the previous expression of democracy, while they *include* it in a new qualitative variation; a qualitatively different *kind* of democratic activity develops, bound but not enchained by its relations with the past. Democracy is an expression of "liberalism" relative to a particular context. This analysis may suggest that our conceptions of liberalism today are dogmatic and unhistorical. Lloyd develops a kind of evolution of dimensionally varied social concepts which provides him with both an interpretation of history and a specific example of metaphysical change.

Lloyd castigates his countrymen and begs for the perspective necessary for a more meaningful expression of the nature of our equalities. The "natural rights" so uncritically claimed by today's democrat are only one expression, he insists, of a continually developing concept: ". . . natural rights, in a very real sense . . . must evidently be earned or realized, however 'natural' . . . . Natural rights not just are; they become, as society comes to be capable of them."[126] Once the type of equality is understood, the nature of the demanded rights is seen to be relative to an ever-changing context. But, even further, the process of social leveling which we understand so absolutistically and the democratic rights which we defend so staunchly are actually not ends in themselves. Even socialism "is constantly acquiring new objects or fields for its application."[127] Applying the point to democracy, Lloyd maintains that democracy conceals its true design, for it really serves a more significant type of aristocracy; it "mediates between a passing and a rising aristocracy";[128] it is the "indispensable condition of progress from one level of life to a higher level."[129]   For Lloyd democracy is not significant because it is a leveler of social classes, but because it represents a *process or principle* of leveling which operates to redefine political rights and to act as a means to mass elevation.   In the history of the world, then, "democracy [along with its ever-changing expressions] is no golden age; but the gold of all ages, which some new aristocracy is ever ready to spend and, spending, to enjoy."[130]

Adventurous Ethics

I. ETHICS AS INQUIRY

1. *The Experimental Basis of Ethics*

Appeal to any but a natural basis for ethics, whether this basis be an exalted supernatural deity who imposes ends on man or a sanctioning absolute that directs man's progress to a final goal, is not only conspicuously absent from Lloyd's thinking, but utterly contrary to it. Insisting that "morality as based on enlightened action can never entertain an absolutely blind religion of external fate, or destiny, of sheer chance or arbitrary miracle,"[1] Lloyd gives the ethical question a natural origin and a natural resolution.[2] He objects to the separation of ethics from other types of human activity: ethics is the study of environment as comprising the conditions of action.[3]

If the ethical question is part of the rough and tumble interplay that is experience and has its origin in a natural, changing world, the question of what one *ought* to do "is a most natural incident of a changing life."[4] With 'ought' as a product of universal change, Lloyd's answer has been so framed that it refuses to limit ethics to a special set of questions and a special area; and accordingly all phases of man's experience are subject to ethical connotations. There can be no experience which is intrinsically devoid of moral quality, any more than there can be phases of experience which are intrinsically exempt from scientific verification. The objective scope of ethical inquiry being no less broad than that of scientific inquiry, Lloyd is in a position to extend the *method* of scientific inquiry to ethical inquiry. Thus ethics as a *science* of human relations cannot plead special license; it must submit to the qualifications and restrictions imposed by the scientific method.

2. *Ethical Relationalism*

So far as the problem of moral choice is concerned, Lloyd struggles to express the foundations of an objective relativism in ethics as he has done in metaphysics and epistemology. "The distinction . . . between good and evil," he says, ". . . should be judged relatively to the specific situation"[5] unless ethics is to be "legalistic"[6] and casuistic. I take this to mean that since the nature of the thing valued depends in part on the nature and disposition of the valuer, since the thing valued is always good *for* something, *for* someone in particular and never good in itself, the good is relative, not absolute. At the same time, Lloyd defines ideals most objectively: "Nature-born ideals are ideals whose realization one can plan, as one plans any common action . . .";[7] and elsewhere he says that ethics is "the science which studies and interprets the conditions of action with a view to action."[8] In short, the valuable *for* something is found objectively and experimentally to be good for the particular valuer. It is objectively good relative to and limited by the particular value situation at hand. Ethical judgment is relative because part of its ultimate basis is the individual's desire for fulfillment, understood with reference to his particular and specific social context. Ethical judgment is objective because the soundness of that desire for contributing to personal and social fulfillment can be tested either by direct experience or by imaginative preview[9] of its consequences. The consequences of any act not only determine the desirability of the act, but express that desir-

ability by an 'ought.' Lloyd's analysis of both rigorism and
hedonism as abstract and meaningless ideals, his insistence
on determining the good by the consequences of action, and
his assertion that the good is relative imply, if they do not
argue, an objective relativist position.

Since the good in one situation is evil in another, the
answer to any particular ethical question depends on the
conditions of action. Lloyd is impressed with this approach
and announces rather triumphantly that he is defining ethics
"almost pragmatically."[10] Ethical answers are, then, constructs designed to facilitate use and to further successful
activity in the very same way that scientific answers are.
Lloyd's assertions on this score point to the often forgotten
fact that our choices are not made in terms of either good *or*
evil, but in terms of a less clearly recognizable complex of
both elements. Nothing is either absolutely good or absolutely bad, he maintains, for good and evil "literally involve
each other" and are "mutually inclusive."[11] I take this to
imply that when ethics abandons absolute standards of good
and evil and substitutes for them 'better' and 'worse,' we
are in a favorable position to appreciate what is most frequently the case, namely, that ethical choice must often be
made between 'bad' and 'worse.' Lloyd exorcises absolutism's black and white world and substitutes a gray one.

Defending an ethical contextualism with vigor, Lloyd
calls Dewey to account for identifying Kant and Frederick
the Great as brother proponents of absolutism. He contends that Dewey fails to interpret Kant in his historical
context, and he reinterprets the categorical imperative as
proposing ethical relativism rather than absolutism and as
"a call to rigorous conduct under whatever law experience
at the time may warrant."[12] The imperative is formulated
generally enough to be adapted to any context, Lloyd suggests, granting that his own reading of Kant "might even be
called pragmatic."[13] He regards the very formulator of the
categorical imperative as one of the progenitors of ethical
naturalism![14]

If ethical questions are relative to the situation, so are their answers. Lloyd denies that ethics is peculiarly "normative"[15]—a position which I take to be not only an assertion of the equality of ethical questions with scientific ones but also a denial of any type of overall ethical standard. Ethical questions have many answers, Lloyd points out, each relative to a point of view. Every real question, he maintains, "is a leading question. Thus it can never have more than a tentative reply. A reply that claimed more than tentative value, than the value of a working hypothesis, would betray its origin most shamefully."[16] Since ethical answers are characterized by tentativeness and fallibility, their value for conduct springs from their being useful, not final.[17] Ethical analysis is sound to the extent that it serves to clarify the question asked, to define the area of choice, and to promote human fulfillment.[18] Ethics, then, is "the study of the conditions of action manifested in the course of action—which is exactly what science is . . . ."[19]

In terms of this ethics of "principle" not "programme,"[20] Lloyd draws what amounts to Dewey's distinction between a critical and a conventional morality, between an ethics of principle and one of rule, between an ethics of a fixed conception of the good and one without such a restriction. For both Lloyd and Dewey ethical principles are developed only in and through analysis. For both, analysis and interpretation are in part socially conditioned. As a result, Lloyd is in as good a position as Dewey to put traditional morality to rout. Though he takes little advantage of his opportunity to develop corollaries for the new ethics of changing rather than fixed goals, I would like to suggest that Lloyd's formulation, as well as Dewey's, provides for the fact that analytical principles *themselves* must be interpreted. Each *particular* ethical question, arising as it does in a different social milieu, requires a skillful selection and interpretation of the principles applicable to it.

3. *Embarrassing Consequences of the Good-Evil Polarity*

While Lloyd's metaphysical position permits him to state
the foundations of an objective relativism with respect to the
problem of ethical choice, it involves him, at the same time,
in a difficulty peculiar to itself when the problem of the
nature of good and evil is raised.   As long as Lloyd confines himself to particular cases, he is able to assert that
ethical judgment is relative to the context.   As soon as he
considers good and evil generally, a difficulty develops which
threatens to obliterate any distinction between them.

Let us recall one or two prior analyses to throw light on
the matter.   Attacking atomism in all its guises, Lloyd
relates all things to "one life."   For example, he maintains
that isolated events can never be shown to have any causal
connection with their effects; a particular motion atomized
into a mass of isolated parts is subject to Zeno's paradoxes.
But when each effect is understood as related to a universe
of causes, it is reinterpreted as being necessary.   When
motion is understood as the expression of the existing relations of one process, then analysis may safely proceed.   So
here, Lloyd understands good and evil as related to one life,
one society, one world: "They [good and evil] are the differentiated conditions of a life or an activity that, being indivisible, gives to all of its conditions mutual dependence and
determination."[21]   Good and evil are related to one life;
what is good in that life is evil at the same time, and vice
versa.

Let us consider the matter another way.   Metaphysically
speaking, good and evil constitute a polarity relationship,
hence, all good is adulterated with evil, and all evil with
good.   Ideals, apparently, are mixed with their opposites,
"a man's vices being also his virtues."[22]   As long as this
means that the good from one point of view is evil from
another, Lloyd is simply asserting that each choice is
attended by a complex of good and evil consequences.   But
he means something more.   Good and evil are *"neither*
absolute nor relative, because [they are] themselves a rela-

tion."[23] Any particular ethical problem when isolated and abstracted from the total situation—from the total life of which it is a part—would receive only a relative answer. Good and evil would be properties of different contexts. But when we consider the nature of good and evil from the larger frame of reference, within the one life, they are properties of one context. Good and evil share the *same* context, as do all polarities.[24] Lloyd emerges with the conclusion that "in a society that is an organism, all are good together and all are bad together."[25]

The difficulty can now be expressed. Although one alternative of ethical action may present a complex of both good and evil results, it is either good or evil relative to another alternative. Lloyd's analysis of polarity relationship, however, requires that each alternative is both good and evil relative to the same context, namely, the larger life which they both share. As a result, the basis of choice is obliterated. Even an evil alternative does good office, for it is implicitly good, if not explicitly so. Equally, a good choice is implicitly evil.[26] What it means under such circumstances to adopt a good rather than an evil alternative is far from clear. Lloyd's "total life," it seems, turns out to be excessively hospitable.

4. Adverbial Ideals

Since all ethical answers, like scientific ones, are imaginative constructs from some point of view, they are, as we found, useful rather than final.[27] This seems to have two meanings: first, ethical answers are useful to the inquirer; and, secondly, they make use of earlier answers. If answers are useful to the inquirer, if knowledge is something to be used, not hoarded,[28] ethical ends must always be sacrificed as a means to something else. If true morality depends on conflict and change, not on rigidity,[29] the notion of ends-in-themselves—that last bulwark of ethical absolutism—must go. Since we "idealize our object according to what its nature suggests to us through the possibilities it has in

itself,"[30] our goals must alter.   And, as a result, Lloyd urges
his readers to find new values to replace the present "bankrupt" ones for which "a receivership, doubtless, should have
been declared long ago."[31]   Goals must be created and discarded on the basis of their usefulness for the pursuit of
effective, satisfactory, and fulfilling natural activity staged in
ever-varying contexts.

According to Lloyd's principle of use, new answers make
use of old.   He generalizes from the relativity of the means-
end distinction in the personal value situation to account
for the relativity of group or cultural values.   Ends and
goals once held sacred become "secularized" into instruments
or means for the development of newer, more applicable,
and more meaningful ones.   Lloyd makes Dewey's point
that critical morality takes its departure from conventional
rule, and holds, further, that all new social ideals use old
ones instrumentally.   Lloyd's emphasis, however, is somewhat different.   While Dewey finds at least some worth and
value in traditional rule, inasmuch as it represents the
funded experience of the race, Lloyd insists that traditional
rule has no meaning for new generations until it is reformulated and redefined.   Perhaps the outcome is the same for
both.   Perhaps Lloyd's variation is only verbally divergent,
but when Lloyd formulates the point, it has a peculiarly
iconoclastic ring.   Quite candidly he says that culture involves the traditional patriotism, piety, and morality becoming things to use, not save,[32] and thus makes public sacrifice
of what he sometimes calls the "outworn values of traditional
faith"—political, economic, and religious.

Lloyd, as well as Dewey, is convinced that ideals are
certified rather than destroyed by their relativity.   Having
translated ideals into principles—ways of acting, adverbs
rather than nouns—Lloyd weaves his new idealism into the
warp and woof of experience by calling attention to the
newly opened expanse of human possibility in the selection
and formulation of goals.   Ideals understood adverbially or
as principles of ethical activity, need no longer force a variety

of personal experience into narrow regimented channels, but permit the free play of human genius, of experimental ability in their interpretation. Lloyd rejoices that values are fluid and adaptable.[33] With an indefinite number of possible goals, or, as Lloyd puts it, as many ideals as there are conditions of life,[34] the adverbial ideal calls for experimental genius in ethical matters as well as in scientific ones. When Lloyd banishes the older, ideal *summum bonum* to assert an ethical naturalism he retains the concept of the ideal. But the objectively relative ideal gains significance *because of* its relativity and not *in spite of* it.

The view of ideals as relational, Lloyd feels, is strong enough to withstand even the objections of mechanistic determinism. The onward flow of necessity can only repudiate the "letter" or the *particular formulation* of the good; it can never destroy the *principle* of good as perfection of function and fulfillment of action, the principle which lies at the heart of all formulation. Final programs of perfection become meaningless with each new generation. Disillusionment and confusion are inevitable when values thus conceived are altered and reformulated.

With ideals as "working hypotheses,"[35] Lloyd maintains that we can no longer speak of ethical activity as some kind of progress away from one thing and toward another; this jeopardizes the principle of continuity in human history. No longer can ethics be thought of as an enterprise devoted to discarding animal nature. The penalty thereof is loss of the physical cloth from which ideal values are cut. A consistent ethical naturalism demands the fulfillment of animal nature, not the abandonment of it. Lloyd develops what is essentially Santayana's notion of "spirituality." *Because* ideals are formed by the recognition of things as conditions for one's activity, because the ideal is the "transfiguration of the commonplace,"[36] a physical world should be cherished for the part it plays in spiritual fulfillment. "The spirit needs the flesh,"[37] and the flesh gains value from its contribution to such fulfillment.

If nature provides the rich soil in which values grow, Lloyd is equally insistent that the same nature is capable of bringing them to fruition. A material world advances in step with its creatures and expresses the things which their skills and genius provide. Nature, never really brute because inclusive of man, who adds something more than animal existence, never really hostile to our poetry or intolerant of our schemes for betterment, because so intimately related to us, never out of step in the evolutionary process, because companioning man, is, as we have seen, "fully capable of expressing or mediating [translating or jelling values into solid form] the spiritual life."[38] In these terms, the ideal becomes the adequate expression of human possibility, not the attainment of some fixed goal.

Lloyd is dissatisfied with the language provided by earlier supernaturalistic thought to express the ways of men with ideals. It has been customary to speak of ideals as if they were things in space. Objecting to such terms as "above," "beyond," "hereafter," "striving toward," and "progress from," he calls for a language more in keeping with a naturalistic view. Nor can he resist linking the earlier type of term employed by ethical theory with mathematical conceptions of space as three-dimensional. The conception of a fourth dimension he sees as a development in mathematics analogous with his own conception of this new naturalistic "qualitative variation" in ethics: ". . . today's beyond and hereafter must get their meaning in the fourth dimension."[39] The context demands that we discuss moral ideals qualitatively or "intensively" rather than spatially and quantitatively. Despite this plea, Lloyd, perhaps fortunately, did not actually undertake to reorder ethical language in so drastic a fashion.

Lloyd, like Dewey, attacks both ethical rigorism and hedonism, which, he says, "belong to the class of doctrines, or intellectual formulations, commonly known as apologetics."[40] But while Dewey finds that these older ideals must be retained, retranslated, and synthesized, Lloyd believes that they present the crux of the antinaturalistic attitude. The ideals of both rigorism and hedonism are *extra*natural[41]—one above nature and one below nature. While rigorism brings "super-natural" sanctions from another world, "always darkly suggestive of something new, of something to come,"[42] hedonism brings "infra-natural"[43] ideals which fail to credit nature with being all it is. The "natural," for Lloyd, includes not only the physical basis for values, but their ideal fulfillment as well. Both rigorism and hedonism are extranatural in that they artificially dichotomize experience into unconnected physical and ideal parts. Dewey makes the point by asserting that both rigorism and hedonism require interpretation in terms of particular situations, since, as they stand, we might well ask, 'Duty to *what?*' 'Pleasure in *what?*' but Lloyd puts it more cryptically. He maintains that rigorism and hedonism, giving no answer, emphasize the need for one.[44] As soon as either is made the ideal, it becomes generalized, abstract, and without any determinable character. These ideals, "besides being otherworld visitors, are also bound to be formal and empty."[45] Neither "singly [n]or collectively [do they give any] intelligible indication of *what* man ought to do."[46]

Applying his distinction between personal and factional experience to the problem at hand, Lloyd is able to characterize both hedonism and rigorism as expressions of the factional, rather than the personal, aspects of human life. Both represent ethics as an institutionalized ideal or "social profession"[47] over against "ethics as personal experience."[48] Either duty or pleasure, alone, is partial, empty, formal, and mechanical. Only when redefined and fused in conduct can they operate as meaningful ideals. Toward this end Lloyd appeals to the metaphysical role of the person. Only the *acting* ethical agent, motivated by the 'ought' of duty, can exercise choice, and only he can find fulfillment in the exercise of that choice.

5. *Cosmic Gambling*

Since our judgments are tentative, since the good is relational, and since man is as uncertain of his goals as he is of their attainment, "inquiry . . . is a condition of morality."[49] If action is to be responsible in a nonresponsible world, the experimental attitude regarding choice must be the core of morality. Making a distinction between the critical morality of the thinker and the habit of the practical man, Lloyd defends the halting and uncertain path of the former. The scientific attitude is not merely applicable to ethical questions, but its adoption is itself a part of any morality.[50] In fact, according to Lloyd, confidence in the experimental attitude is the *sine qua non* of any conduct worthy of the term 'moral.' Precisely because morality necessitates the treatment of any experience as means to larger areas of fulfillment, and because the moral man "spends" rather than "hoards" experience,[51] the adoption of the experimental attitude is an unconditional requirement for the ethical life. Experience becomes the fallible but eminently useful tool for shaping newer and more rewarding values. Thus Lloyd entirely excludes both the practical man and the holder of traditional faith from the domain of ethical action.

Ethics, Lloyd maintains, is a game of chance in which the individual challenges the universe, as it challenges him.[52] Problematic alternatives offer the duty of choice to the inquirer, who would be ethically irresponsible were he not required to choose and to abide willingly by the consequences of that choice. Denying a pessimistic note in the assertion that inquiry implies that all one can ask is a confession of past error, Lloyd reminds us that experimental verification gives us "the companionship of all the centuries,"[53] the abiding help of corrective experience, which brings to each generation of gamblers the largess of the race.

Ethical experimentalism, relying on the correction of experience, constitutes the "gallant life"[54] of facing risk of person and probability of failure with equanimity and hope, rather than with fear or dread. In fact, ethical endeavor gains religious significance insofar as it is a hopeful assumption of the risk involved in choice which, in turn, is made on the basis of limited knowledge and which promises only uncertain results. The individual becomes ethically religious only insofar as he takes this "sacred chance" or makes the experiment which forms character[55] and only insofar as he acts without guarantee or assurance of future reward or punishment.

Lloyd delineates the difference between sacred and profane gambling in a small article, "Games of Chance," which describes itself as "A Timely Essay on Certain Possibilities of Gallant Living," a "blood test"[56] of the body social. The essay seeks to set forth the basic social attitudes illustrative of profanity and productive of the "professional gambler," who exemplifies only a local and insignificant species of general social gambling.[57] General social gambling is defined as "inordinate greed" for easy return without effort,[58] and a number of illustrations of this are developed. Among the species of profane winners—the cosmic villains who play with loaded dice and seek "stale possession" without the courage to face risk—are those who would be excused from the consequences of their actions on the ground of good motive or intent as well as those who would sanction such sentimentality, those who lead "disorderly" lives without ends or goals, those who depend upon circumstances of birth and privilege for quick and unearned return, and those who are consciously and irresponsibly incompetent. All of these, according to Lloyd, cheat chance by stacking the cards to their own profit. Each profanes experience and, through habit, becomes unable to play fairly. To play fairly, to engage in sacred chance, is to "let chance work" by risking action in terms of limited knowledge, by standing corrected if necessary, and by gaining the reward of fulfilled values if experience concurs with judgment.

In this fashion Lloyd arrives at the formulation of what Dewey calls "critical" morality, in contrast to its conventional imitation.   But, in his paradoxical manner, Lloyd goes considerably further than Dewey by asserting bluntly that the moral man is a "lawbreaker."[59]   Whereas Dewey is willing to dignify traditional codes as being invested with the funded experience of the race, Lloyd is a more thorough iconoclast.   Ruthlessly attacking the traditional code even as a framework within which critical morality operates, he contends that "all reformation is bound to do violence to the law."[60]   This sets the problem of the difference between the criminal and the reformer, and Lloyd undertakes to clarify it.   While the criminal is impulsive and unaware of the meaning of his action, the reformer is reflectively aware of his role and conscious of his function of redefining the good.   While the criminal serves no law, the reformer serves a higher law on the altar of which he offers the conventional code as sacrifice.   While the malefactor is in bondage to the situation, the reformer grasps it.

The reformer, however, not only alters the external situation, but acts as savior for the malefactor.   Serving a more comprehensive law, namely, the internal law of his own being, the reformer preserves his own unity and integrity, because the person is more sacred than any institution, more sacred than the laws which he breaks.   Serving a more comprehensive law, the reformer understands the evils of the situation which have enslaved the malefactor.   While the criminal responds in kind to the evils of his environment, thereby displaying the emptiness of mere imitation, the reformer conquers them by turning necessity into advantage, and thus evidences his originality and ethical genius.   The reformer shows the malefactor the way; the malefactor, in his turn, "saved his fellows by taking their sins upon himself."[61]   Lloyd characteristically says that he wants to translate the old adage 'It takes a rogue to catch a rogue' into "It takes a reformer, at once lawless himself and so broadly and vitally sympathetic, to save a malefactor."[62]   But it must be clear through this Lloydian whimsy that the reformer— artist, scientist, and daredevil—exploits experience, which is the medium of his art, by tentative excursions into unknown ethical territory. Now Lloyd is in a position to redefine the element of mystery in experience, of which supernatural religions have made so much capital and with which they have made so many converts. He traces it historically. No longer is the mysterious *outside* of knowledge, forever dark and impenetrable, as in the Middle Ages, and demanding a sharp break between faith and knowledge; no longer is it the yet-to-be-known of science, compelling the dichotomy between science and religion so typical of the nineteenth century; it is now the element of exploration and risk in every experience of ethical action, an element which unites man's faith, his knowledge, and his experience into a freer-working unity.

But although inquiry is the chief condition of morality, Lloyd is dissatisfied with this unqualified conclusion. It is too reminiscent of idea-ism. Men must not only inquire, but must *persistently desire* to inquire; they must not merely *know* the good, but must act on it. In short, the moral life must *do* as well as think and feel. Action requires the response of all man's capacities. The surprise, satisfaction, and excitement of inquiry and verification is an experience that unites thought, feeling, and biological drive in a complex demanded by experimental, as against habitual, activity. Thus conceived, ethical action, or cosmic gambling, provides stimulation of all human capacities, and thereby expiates that trio of ethical sins, overintellectualized morality, stylized action, and exclusive emphasis on pleasure.

Responsible adventure, candidly challenging nature, has its worth for the individual, whether it is successful in the usual sense or not. Success and failure are polarities: no action is completely successful, none is a complete failure. If completely honest, the ethical trail blazer can never entirely lose the game, regardless of superficial appearances. From an overall view, there are as much knowledge and experience to be gained from relative failure as there is satisfaction from relative success.[63] From this long-time vantage point, under this particular view of eternity, a universe finds no goats among its honest but venturesome sheep, despite their frequent mishaps. Lloyd's vision provides him with a kind of cosmic humor, which "gives relief in responsibility, not from it; cherishes frailty; feels the success of failure, and enjoys not less honestly than keenly, the impartiality of nature."[64]

Cosmic humor is not the only cushion against the bumps and bruises in the battle for the good life. The ethical adventurer is permitted one faith as salve for his wounds, namely, the hope that experience is a completely impartial arbiter. In the light of this faith, the ethics of experimental inquiry is now synonymous with religious experience. Now the adventurer can laugh, not in relief but in joy, for his ethical enterprise has gained new worth. The *religion* of enlightened morality is not blind, but sees with a mixture of fact and imagination, reality and fancy, which Lloyd compares to that experienced during the night run of a train. It is a "mingling of efficiency and chance, of certainty and mystery, of a present view clear and liberative and a vision straining to catch the weird shadows or half-shaped images of the future."[65] The ethical adventurer, combining skill with art, knowledge with faith, makes his bet with nature in the spirit of religious dedication.

6. *The Brave New Humanism*

Since the maintenance of society is a communal effort, Lloyd's ethical traveler is not alone in his wanderings, nor are his companions deprived of the social benefits of his experiments. As in scientific endeavor, the research of each aids all, while the artistry of one produces a work of art for his neighbors' enjoyment. Each abets the others in attaining his own fulfillment. Individual members set the moral pace and confer benefits on their fellows by their "adventures in personality,"[66] and the life of the entire society gains a new quality thereby. All things, "the things about us, the powers within us, are all material for what is ideal,"[67] and the realization of ideals depends on "direct, well-controlled and enlightened"[68] social action. Hence the efforts of each bring others to their full worth. Lloyd's "new humanism"[69] emerges not merely as sanction for the nurture of human values, not merely as provider of the experimental attitude to formulate these values, but as a social creed with religious significance. This humanism is not to be construed as a merely individualistic humanism. Although the individual never loses his importance as an ethico-religious unifier, yet in one sense he is a means to an end. He contributes to the life which society is leading.

With the experimental attitude at the heart of morality, Lloyd's new world can move forward to the enunciation of new and more meaningful ideals adequate for our particular present cultural situation. As a qualitatively variant set of ideals to replace older ones born of a supernaturalistic religion, Lloyd offers the tentative, humanistic goals of political and economic democracy, among which are: assurance of physical well-being, which he understands to be the basis of all else; education to the limit of the capacities of each individual; "worthwhile work" providing opportunity to use learned skills; social recognition of the dignity and worth of each individual; and leisure for each to enjoy the fruits of technological development. While these *particular* ideals spring from the conditions of our present life, they too will eventually become outdated and bankrupt if and when society moves to a new ethical dimension. Thus Lloyd offers humanism, but looks beyond its present expression to even greater fulfillment of the many facets of human personality.

II. RELIGIOUS HUMANISM

1. *The Religious Motivation in Lloyd*

A naturalistic interpretation of religion is not only the result of Lloyd's philosophic position, but one of the motivating forces of that position. This judgment is perhaps supported more by insight into Lloyd than by evidence. Yet considerable evidence can be presented.

Lloyd's first philosophic endeavors are concerned with a redefinition of religious experience. His student "Notebooks" are liberally sprinkled with startlingly mature religious assertion. Two of his early articles[70] are passionate defenses of a naturalistic position against the charges of atheism. His first book, *Citizenship and Salvation* (1897), sets about an identification, in principle, of the roles of Socrates and Christ as reformers, and winds up with a thoroughly secularized and humanized conception of the "Christ-motive"[71] in experience. His second book, *Dynamic Idealism* (1898), has the curious appendix "A Study of Immortality in Outline,"[72] which is designed to supersede the older Christian views on this subject with a naturalistic one. His third book, *Philosophy of History* (1899), includes among its "Historical Studies" a chapter called "Reason and Religion"[73] which is quite irrelevant to the main theme of the volume but which presents one of the problems in terms of which the intellectual tools developed in the book are displayed. *The Will to Doubt* (1907) is a forthright defense of the piety of the sceptic. Many of Lloyd's articles, also, ring with overtones of religious interest. Here and there, as if in afterthought, he introduces an interpretation of some religious concept in a context far removed from it.[74]

Lloyd's religious naturalism was well developed early in his life. Even as a boy, the directions of his thought were evident. He refused to enter the ministry despite obvious inducement. His resistance suggests a mind already stocked with religious conviction, already sure that religion is thought[75] rather than credal adherence and ritualistic observance. A few years later, while yet a student, he wrote that "belief and creed are only stumbling blocks to real faith and Christian feeling."[76] And still later he asserted that "a religion turned non-sectarian shows man truly living and moving and having his being, not aloof from God, but in God."[77]

Considerable internal evidence points to the fact that the outlines of Lloyd's thought imply a naturalistic interpretation of religion. Inquiry and experiment are "sacred gambling."[78] In many places Lloyd defends the philosopher's right to express himself poetically; and then, in one context, he says, ". . . morality and religion are related to each other, and to human conduct, as understanding and imagination . . . as prose and poetry."[79] His metaphorical approach itself testifies to a conception of his own enterprise as the height of religious expression. Furthermore, Lloyd's naturalism is humanistic rather than positivistic, and, historically speaking, the humanistic type has most often concerned itself with exploring the implications of naturalism for religious experience. Thus, from both internal and external evidence, I feel that Lloyd's religious perspective was not only the outgrowth of his thought, but was, as much, its nurturing soil.

2. Pious Atheism: the Traditional Church

Among Lloyd's articles written before the turn of the century there is one which launches a fierce attack on the Church.[80] It apparently represents a defense against the charge of atheism leveled at Lloyd by his confrères. Declaring that the charge of atheism is brought against thinkers by those who have *"no familiarity with thought itself,"*[81] he sets the core of the religious experience in the use of intellectual method. Only ignorance of the nature of the method of inquiry can prompt the "strange question"[82] of whether the thinker can have a "genuine idea"[83] of God. Lloyd maintains that if religious experience is characteristically marked by some kind of faith, those who condemn the thinker should examine the experimental method, with its risk and its tentative results. The experimental method provides ample evidence of a faith, if not in creed, then in nature and experience. Maintaining that "atheism" is always a profane word used only by "hardened natures,"[84] Lloyd satirically explains that "resentment [by traditionalists] against offenders [alleged atheists] is natural, just because their deeds are such an unwelcome exposure of the acts and impulses of their judges."[85]

To meet the attack, Lloyd caustically turns the tables and accuses his accusers. The traditionalist is idolatrous and atheistical. Orthodoxy, he says, makes progress an "exhuming and reviving process."[86] It would "advance backward," measuring its strides by the amount of literal revival of the old it is able to achieve. As a result, the creeds and dogmas of the Church have no relevance to the day's problems or to the day's needs. Traditional creeds "hoard" the past[87] and are "misers" of experience. They refuse to spend or utilize things past for new growth. They, like practical men,[88] spend only for return in kind. They demand personal salvation or a hoarding of their persons in return for a hoarding of creed.

The traditionalist, Lloyd maintains, is defeated before he begins. He can never completely duplicate the past because he must *select* that which is to remain. *What* he selects is determined by present problems. Hence, even the *way* in which he views the past must be altered by present conditions.[89] His goal ever recedes. Eventually, the cosmic miser will suffer the due consequences. As things move, develop, and change, natural necessity must "take our very Gods and our very religions from us,"[90] as well as all attendant beliefs. The gods, products of mortal fashioning, are subject to mortality, like those who would be their slaves.

Lloyd turns from the symptoms to the causes of the disease. Traditional religion, he asserts, is cursed by a *crude* materialism. It often conceives of God in spatial terms. It treats "the whole" as a part.[91] It understands immortality as elongated duration and hence it tries to preserve its creeds indefinitely. Apparently, a society of the "bottled, tinned and canned,"[92] being quantity-minded and imbued with automatism, would preserve its verities like a jar of fruit. A scorching attack on eternal truths follows, which is elsewhere supplemented by an anthropological exploration into the nature of gods and ideals.[93] Anthropological history indicates that indefinite numbers of experiential things have been made into gods or ideals.   For that matter, Lloyd maintains, any and all things in experience can be idealized, since the ideal is the fulfillment of the functions of things. Men deify the thing which best represents the state of their intellectual and moral development at the time.   The truly religious man of today, he concludes, must forfeit all creed and dogma.   He must countenance his god's mortality, his creed's demise, aware of the tentativeness of his passing view.

As early as the "Notebooks" Lloyd says, "Never have I realized so fully the imperfection of all our creeds and beliefs and wished so sincerely for a more perfect conception of God."   But it was not long before he publicly sacrificed all "letters" to the completely "nude" spirit,[94] which can no longer profess a fixed creed.   He soon abandoned the search for a "more perfect conception of God" and held that all conceptions of God are relative.   But Lloyd is not crying in the wilderness.   His tone does not echo the same type of disillusionment with which, for example, Bertrand Russell, in particular, and Santayana, to a lesser degree, ask, 'Now what can an enlightened spirit believe?'   More consistent in his iconoclasm, Lloyd refuses to raise this question, because it asks only for a new creed.   His refusal to be disturbed by the state of doubt rewards him with the gift of perspective, if not of belief.

Continuing his attack on a credal conception of religion, Lloyd insists that creeds are verbal icons, symbols of an "idolatrous religion"[95] which is "so much more a matter of phrases than of responsibilities."[96]   They are literal, uninspired, and lacking in poetry, and they therefore fail to stimulate the imagination, which is the real genius of man. Creeds can make no contact with living issues, and hence dichotomize life and values.   The dichotomy in turn fosters an almost inescapable duplicity and hypocrisy in the adherents of creed, who assert value in the Church and find it actually in life—extramurally, as it were, in the secular, in daily experience. "Institutions, you know," Lloyd says pointedly, "can be beside themselves as well as individuals."[97] On these grounds he opposes faith in dead credal issues to reason as found in living experience, faith understood as a garment, a cloak to put off and on at will, to faith as an achievement in action—acting in good faith, as it were, on tentative conclusions.

Creeds, then, become ends in themselves and thereby usurp the place of religious experience. Ritual, expressing belief in creed, suffers from the same "materialistic" contagion.[98] Ritual is mechanical and meaningless. Its lofty purpose is tangibly to reassure the churched impious that they have conformed.[99] Both creed and ritual are versions of the "stat" principle,[100] or undue reliance on standardized evaluation. Ritual reduces each participating member to the "equal measure" of conformity. It obfuscates the originality of each, and is more appropriately part of the "militarism" of the Middle Ages. In short, creed, for Lloyd as for Dewey, spells the death of religious experience. Since the heart of that experience is, for Lloyd at least, in doubt and not in belief, credal adherence rules it out in the first place.[101]

Lloyd's humanism and relationalism combine to offer still another objection. Creeds isolate and separate men, when religious experience would give them what Dewey calls "a common faith." They are a fruitful basis for social distinctions. They classify men,[102] whereas Lloyd insists that significant distinction is not found between groups as such but between persons.[103] To hinder coöperative life is to be irreligious, and hence worse than to be nonreligious.[104] If religious form is *ever* necessary, its purpose should be primarily to unite man with his natural world, which in turn relates man to man. Only when men are united by means of a shared environment, shared language, and shared goals can they gain common courage, hope, and incentive to action. Failing this, religious creed is only so much vested interest designed to maintain a bankrupt *status quo*.[105]

But perhaps worst of all, creed is faith separated from inquiry. It is faith without duty to knowledge,[106] demanding the special privilege of isolating itself from life as experienced. Lloyd makes short work of the matter: ". . . to deny inquiry the right of entering certain fields is only, as history has made clear again and again, to make questionable just what would be kept sacred . . . . To exclude anything from inquiry is to mistrust it."[107] And again: "Inquiry and its reasoning must always lose much of their zeal and purpose if . . . [one is] told that the sphere of human life is a divided sphere, in part questionable and rational, in part beyond question and irrational. Either part cannot but compromise the integrity of the other."[108] This type of faith appeals to the "ouija-board mentality" and the supernaturalistic frame of mind. It relies on revelation and miracle to establish answers distinguished by their childlike finality.

The Church is addicted to perfectionism and otherworldliness. The practice of speaking of ideals in spatial terms, as "out," "above," "beyond,"[109] has sent men on a fruitless religious quest which minimizes present imperfections in the hope of future miraculous rectifications. Present remedial action then becomes unimportant. Present action demanded by present need is reduced to pallid duty; an energetic pursuit of timely goals is rendered unnecessary.

Many of these unhappy results spring from the fact that the Church is an institution. Like other institutions, it faces an inevitable battle with the "vital" in experience. Like other institutions, but in a greater degree, the Church understands itself as an end rather than as an instrument for the fulfillment of human life as end. The Church is dogmatic, opportunistic, and riddled by schism.[110] Foes outside (positivistic scientists) mimic the failings of their religious contemporaries. To underscore the indictment which the fact of schism so brazenly and openly announces, Lloyd advises the institutional-minded that much of the most "truly religious work . . . is now [secular and] carried on outside the visible religious institutions."[111]

3. *Clerical Culture*

The Church is not alone in its creed, dogma, ritual, isolation, and duplicity, for positivistic science appears as its contemporaneous polar term. Lloyd tries to demonstrate their kinship. Positivistic science substitutes formulae for dogma.[112] It asserts knowledge for its own sake, if not creed for its own sake. It "exposes" the religion of its day; it is openly what supernaturalism is covertly. Religion takes its dogma and ritual as fixed and literal truth, and positivistic science takes its dogma or formulae and its ritual or method in the same absolutistic fashion.

Lloyd draws sociological implications. The traditional Church and positivistic science combine to provide a general cultural pattern consistent with their assumptions. This pattern is "medievalistic," "militaristic," and "materialistic," measuring both secular and religious values by physical size and temporal duration. Absolutism in political and intellectual spheres duplicates the spiritual tyranny of the Church. Speaking from a larger point of view, Lloyd maintains that absolutism in all its forms results from what might be called a general "isolation-ism."[113] Because man is isolated from nature, he is isolated from his fellow man in a fashion so pervasive that competition rules every area of experience. Economic, political, and even ethnic groups echo the religious competition for personal salvation and wield the type of tool appropriate to a struggle on this level, namely, tools of force and physical might. All groups mirror the religious struggle for the preservation of creed by battling to maintain the *status quo*.

Since values and experience are dichotomized, all groups struggle to preserve even the most unsatisfactory and inadequate social forms. Traditional ideals of conformity prevail. Men stifle their independence of thought and action on every level of their experience for the sake of singing "in chorus."[114] Under these conditions, they turn as facilely to political demagogues for this world's goods as they turn to their gods for the goods and services of the next. It follows that success or failure is understood to be due to chance, luck, and other such outside forces. When religious salvation is believed to be achieved by grace, when social salvation depends on the accident of birth, then political and economic salvation are likely to depend on the whim of tyrannical governments. Education in such a society is conceived of as "the maintenance of some cult, of some given set of institutions and beliefs . . . [an education] in casuistry and cant, [making] life as double as it is pretentious . . . ."[115] The society as a whole is beset by "occupational protectionism" or "one-hundred per-centism" in its desire for "standardized quantity output and accumulation of some appropriate product, be this product dollars, automobiles, scientific results, graduates, teachers, 'whites,' Americans, Christians . . . . [This narrow occupationalism] may seriously threaten civilization and lead to something at least no better than 'Kultur.' "[116] Men in such bondage Lloyd calls "soldiers" (Christian or cultural), since, puppet-like, they do someone else's will and sacrifice their lives for they know not what.

Supernaturalistic religion links this sorry chain of personal and cultural circumstances. While no link is the primary cause, all bespeak a philosophic orientation best expressed by what Lloyd calls "official" supernaturalism.[117] Since a religious perspective dares to be the largest and risks embodying the fundamental attitudes of man toward his world, it must accept the responsibilities of its width and be declared the unifying agent by means of which the parts of a culture cohere. Obviously, significant reform must come on the religious level. With that in process, the varied attitudes and goals in other aspects of life will alter accordingly. Religious experience must then be redefined, and Lloyd sets about doing this in the light of biology and evolution.[118] Though Lloyd never devotes another article to combating the charge of atheism, he never entirely forgets the matter. He frequently approaches it indirectly and becomes ever more insistent in developing the two opposed culture patterns and in exhibiting the "sacred" character of the experimental method, working both themes out on many alternately satirical and intensely assertive pages.

4. *Naturalistic Piety: Religious Experience Redefined*

Lloyd's redefinition of religious experience takes place in an evolutionary world without origin or fixed destiny.[119] It lacks *a* God because *a* God doesn't exist. Creation is no longer a "fixed programme," but a principle of development worked out by the creatures in a creative world. Whatever a world becomes depends on them. Since man is at home in the universe, since he springs from natural soil and is capable of natural fulfillment, his faith should be placed in that soil, his hope in that fulfillment.

The first premise of the new perspective makes religion a way of life, not a way of dogma, a way of action, not a way of mere belief, a way of deed, not creed.[120] "Action is more spiritual than any institution,"[121] Lloyd says, and again:

. . . religion as mere ecclesiasticism, religious bigotry that has its own exposure in heresy, religious cant that is so much more a matter of phrases than of responsibilities . . . sectarianism in the sense of religious caste, religious ignorance that justifies itself by avowing—in the very face of history—that faith has no duty to knowledge, these are all marks of atheism in religion . . . .[122]

With this fundamental alteration in perspective, Lloyd turns to the most significant of all man's actions, namely, his way of thinking—his way of establishing a tentative basis for action, his method of inquiry—where the heart of the religious experience is located. Ethics and the natural sciences are unified by their common participation in adventure and "holy chance." The fusion of both in action defines the religious experience. Emphasizing the union of knowledge and desire, the fusion of facts and values, and the identity of what ought to be found good and what is found good, Lloyd says, ". . . the thinker is one who identifies the knowledge of science with the impulse of religion."[123] Since truth is not absolute, since knowledge is not certain, the new religion must be exploratory, not explanatory. The religious spirit is best exemplified by submission to the groping search of inquiry: "All honest inquiry . . . may be associated with prayer. Often, bringing enlightenment as it does, it is a very efficacious prayer."[124] Thus the religious experience is found in the use of the experimental method in solving problems, in meeting questions and in seeking valuable action.

What, then, in such a view, is the meaning of "God"? Lloyd has better reason than most other naturalists for retaining the term. To use his own expression, he must be "profane"; he must shock and challenge his century out of its complacency by using old words to express new meanings.[125] An account of Lloyd's meaning of the term "God" must begin by identifying the natural with the divine: "What is that we call Nature? What, but the real basis of the possibility of all facts and their unification in law! And what may God be? What, but the equally real basis of the possibility of all values and their unification in ideal and purpose!"[126] God is to be found in the relations of which the world is composed. Hence Lloyd, stating his conclusion, says, "With Darwin . . . there came to expression a still broader and deeper pantheism; God was so expanded as to be identified with or declared immanent in the great unity of all life."[127] It will be remembered that relationship, by which all things are defined, is dynamic, moving, or growing. Hence a more complete definition of deity makes God that which is "inspiring or animating the natural with unlimited freedom and possibility."[128] God, therefore, is identified with the possibility of growth and development in the relations between things. God, if I may adapt a phrase of Lloyd's, is the challenging possible[129] of all experience, to which man above all other creatures can most significantly respond.

Men's gods are "sublimations of their own nature."[130]

Lloyd carefully points out that "sublimation" means the idealization of the fulfilling, successful, or rewarding action —action which fulfills intellectual, emotional, and animal needs. He even exclaims on one occasion: "God's creative life is whatever any of the creatures of any age or garden do *efficiently*."[131] Needless to say, Lloyd means much more by "efficiently" than 'expediently.' Effective action is the infusion of knowledge and value into action from a wider and broader point of view, for religion is thought or life facing all its responsibilities or seeking the consistent expression of all its relationships.[132]

To discern God in any efficient action involves obvious difficulties. It bestows religious significance on the mouse which efficiently salvages the cheese from the trap and on the murderer who efficiently wields a meat cleaver on his neighbor. Lloyd is aware of these difficulties and heavily qualifies his notion of the religious as the efficient. By this particular definition of deity he is seeking, if unsuccessfully, a way to broaden the religious experience and make it a possible dimension or quality of all human action when that action is viewed from the largest frame of reference. He is emphasizing the fact that ideas as plans of action warrant the predicate 'holy.' For Lloyd religious experience is neither thought unrelated to action nor emotion unrelated to thought. These considerations pave the way for a later and more significant perception, namely, of "man as a responsible partner in the creative life of God . . . ."[133]

Let us recall the function of the person from this vantage point. Man, as we saw, is the most significant and effective example of "acting whole-ly."[134] Since God is the principle of organic wholeness, man himself is the ethico-religious unifier of the world via his action. Action is religious inasmuch as it represents values informed with facts.[135] Hence Lloyd finds the divine primarily in man, as he cognitively-evaluatingly acts, and secondarily in other creatures, who are part of a total interrelational pattern of existence. God is never found anywhere but in nature, for "God and nature have ever been very near."[136]   God is a way of acting which the world manifests.   Lloyd's God, like Spinoza's, is everywhere in varying degrees and can be expressed by many and diverse predicates.

Lloyd, like Spinoza, hardly needs to prove the first principles of his point of view.   To ask for a proof of God is the height of materialism.   It treats the possibility of development in the world as if it were a thing.   The question "lacks candor"[137] because it offers the possibility of denying experience, for Lloyd maintains that to ask about a thing is already to have given it being of some sort.[138]   God as organic relationship cannot be denied, for we define the possibilities of that relationship as we move, know, or value our world. Asking proof of God is really asking, 'Is this experience true?' instead of what we should ask, namely, 'What does this experience mean?'

With God defined as the possibility of valuable action or growth, prayer becomes, for Lloyd, inquiry,[139] and responsible thought becomes spiritual opportunity.[140]   Lloyd uses the term "inquiry" with good reason.   First, prayer is not simply thought or meditation, but thought about action in a world.   It is not Spinoza's "contemplation," but the planning of action, the intellectual concomitant of interaction with the world.   Secondly, prayer is not directed toward "ideals" in Santayana's sense; for Lloyd, *all* action has ideal fulfillment. Even quite mundane activity would be entitled to the term 'prayerful' under certain circumstances.   As Lloyd puts it: "Worship is skill in the social life, not ritual; and the church is society itself, not a mass of bricks and stained glass."[141] This, of course, is another of Lloyd's attempts to widen the area which supernaturalism reserves for religious experience. Prayer is enlightened action, activity fused with knowledge, which is curious, groping, tentative, and exploratory.   It is action at once aware of its responsibilities to consequences and ready to assume them in order to express more fully and effectively its relationship with a universe.   Prayer is action which is both daring in exploration and submissive to consequences, which is both adventurous and humble.   Prayer is action which willingly adventures in a sea of uncertainty for the sake of value, not "cultured routine" or "domesticated ease."[142]   As will be recalled, the experimental attitude is not just a *means* to morality, not merely the proper method for answering ethical questions, but is itself a *part* of morality. For Lloyd, the experimental attitude and the moral attitude are identical.

Lloyd emphasizes the point that prayer is a method, a temper of mind, an attitude toward any activity, rather than the self-conscious performance of a ritual, and that it is in behalf of man's good, not God's.   Even as a student Lloyd said, in terms which resemble the traditional ones, though the sentiments can hardly be called such: "The love of one's fellow man, the conservation of one's life to all that is good, noble, and pure is more than prayer and worship because it is prayer and worship in action.   Unconscious worship in action is the best worship."[143]

The meaning of 'faith' must be revised in the light of this interpretation of the meaning of God and prayer if Lloyd is not to violate his view that the candid questioner never rules out experience, but asks its meaning.   All relationship, it will be remembered, is eternal.[144]   Faith, according to Lloyd, is neither faith in the absence of evidence nor faith in spite of evidence.   It is certainly not a feat of anti-intellectual endurance.   Nor yet is it faith on the basis of evidence.   It is not faith *that* something is true, not even faith that a method of inquiry is sound.   Lloyd is too crucially aware that all truth is tentative and ever subject to revision to accept any such meaning.   Hence, as a foundation for his view of faith he says: "Faith ceases to be faith of course when it gets a doctrinal content."[145]   What then is faith without a doctrinal content?   Lloyd's answer is that it is the faith of the sceptical inquirer, who thinks, acts, and finds value in the very face of the fact that his thought, action, and values will be altered and revised.   It is faith that experience will grow, develop, and correct for partiality, faith that action and interaction are the source of that growth. The new faith no longer strives for a fixed answer, but persistently struggles for tentative ones. But this is no easy scepticism, this scepticism without disillusionment, for "naturalism is a more difficult idealism [philosophy] than supernaturalism of any sort has ever been."[146]

In Lloyd's case its difficulties are linguistic as well. In behalf of the principle of continuity Lloyd refuses to commit even the term 'supernaturalism' to the ashes. By means of a distinction between the supernatural *"in parte"* and the supernatural *"in toto,"*[147] he redefines the supernatural in naturalistic terms! The supernatural *"in toto"*—the "fulfilled" version of supernaturalism—is the organic which requires the physical, which is the functioning of the physical, and which cannot be reduced to the physical. It is the growth, thought, and evaluation which the natural creatures of a natural soil exhibit.

Christianity, to the spirit of which Lloyd is always loyal, is reinterpreted. In one of his many attempts to make it meaningful he says:

. . . science has . . . helped Christianity to a clearer consciousness of itself. . . . The Resurrection, the Immaculate Conception, the Divinity, the Immediacy of the Kingdom of Heaven, the Sacrifice, and the Brotherhood of Man are doctrines which one and all testify that our real being, our real individuality, lies not in a separate existence . . . but in the abiding relations of our present life . . . .[148]

To interpret Christ as a mere "physical appearance and reappearance nearly two thousand years ago" is to "parody."[149] Translating these views into traditional terms, which can so easily be misunderstood by the casual reader, he says that Christ is a "principle" and as such

. . . was really not born as men are born . . . [but] lives in our lives today . . . more than the creature of a single moment or a single place and more than the creature of another world . . . today he is in us, being one with the relations of family, the relations of society, the relations of nature, in which we have our being now and hereafter.[150]

Needless to say, the ribald spirit with which Lloyd is possessed smiles at the "new philosophy," his "heroic idealism," the definitions of which are couched in language so thoroughly acceptable, in superficial appearance, to the medieval mind. "Here," he says, "has been no justification of any orthodox husks."[151] The "natural laughter"[152] which must be part of natural religion has already gotten "beyond the eyes."[153] Lloyd's smiling piety springs from understanding and a great faith which the traditional religionist could scarcely appreciate. It actually achieves the iconoclastic "violence of the spirit"[154] while appearing to be orthodox; it demolishes the idols of the past by usurping them. Lloyd finds cosmic justice in such verbal hospitality to older views. His iconoclasm asserts a wider point of view and expresses his principle of cosmic inclusiveness, the arch foe of institutionalized sectarianism.

Perhaps, however, speaking humanistically, the ultimate in cosmic humor is reached as the line between comedy and tragedy disappears. While man is earth-bound and soil-rooted, his activities witness fulfillments never completely equatable with his biological background. While man masters nature's processes, he is nonetheless part of them. Since his goal is to interact successfully with a world, he must welcome *all* natural processes, of which successful interaction is one. Hence, even on his death, man must coöperate in dignity and grace with the same natural necessities which give all investigatory activity worth.

5. *Humanistic Naturalism*

The new religious perspective, like the old, must be set in its attendant culture. Lloyd sketches out a possible future on the basis of the implications of the new view. The new world will be committed to the philosophic view that the goal of man is to understand himself and all his activities

as a part of nature, without reservation. The future requires, I take it, a realism which is "not simple or naive,"[155]
a pragmatism with an explicit metaphysics,[156] a naturalism
which is not merely a denial of supernaturalism, but a positive redefinition of the natural as the organic,[157] and a
humanism which understands man in a new, wide sense as
related to, not isolated from, the natural world.[158]

The new naturalism is not just a theoretical position but
a way of life—an attitude toward oneself and one's environment. This naturalism as an acquaintance with nature has
a history and is an outgrowth of the past. Consider this
significant passage:

Naturalism, however, is or at least may be a very different thing
towards the end of a civilization from what it was at the beginning . . . . It is one thing to be able to use positive laws and
humanly fashioned weapons . . . still another to use rationally
and objectively accurate measures, methods, and machines, all
bringing men, if not yet to a vitally intimate, at least to a formal
and mechanical acquaintance with nature . . . [but] it is the
supreme thing . . . to live by right of understanding and developed character and will the unrestrained life of nature . . . . Man
is great, of course, as a maker and user of laws and as a maker
and user of machinery, but greatest when he has fought his way
to the freedom and power, the inestimable power, of adopting
nature as the medium of expression for his life.[159]

The new culture would seek natural human values in a
present world, under present conditions. "Sacred chances"
must be taken for the betterment of the conditions of man's
life. Christianity must be "secularized";[160] it must return to
the "real and practical"[161] and concrete, and be "socialized"[162]
(in Dewey's sense of the term 'social'), for it has no good other
than the furtherance of human physical, intellectual, and
moral welfare. In the new culture the function of the Church
would be to aid the struggle for new political, economic, and
social goals to serve as the physical conditions of society. In
this connection Lloyd says:

With such sanctification and elevation of the natural and secular there set in a process that has brought to us . . . a radical change in the basic instrumentation of technique of the whole life of Christendom [society] . . . . Once Christendom "belonged," body and soul . . . to the aloof and supernatural institution; but its "belonging" or real membership to-day would seem to have been transferred . . . [to] the great communal complex of adjusted and coöperating machines . . . membership in the earlier mechanical and mediating institution, God directed and man-powered . . . must have been training for the greater freedom of our present social life with benefit of the objective, humanly free, natural mechanism, the "Iron Man" or Giant Automaton, by which the institution has been followed.[163]

But the new culture, organic rather than mechanical, must recognize that

. . . we must candidly appraise our modern knowledge and then with faith and courage launch whatever adventures in politics, economics, morality or religion may be indicated. Just this, nothing less, would seem to be the present duty, our day's biological or anthropological need; and to satisfy it all the various modernisms [realism, pragmatism, and naturalism] must boldly and strongly, not weakly, meet their respective fundamentalisms, political, economic, moral or religious, in kind; that is, not just intellectually, not by arguments as to fact or natural law, but with such values, with such quickening motives, as will actually sustain life to-day. By two things men may not live wholly and honestly to-day: mere bread and blind orthodoxy . . . .[164]

The new adventures, then, concern a different *quality* of life, a new humanism. Lloyd concludes "The Time of Day" by defining the "great adventure of our time."[165] We can no longer isolate ourselves from the rest of the world, he maintains, nor have narrow orthodoxy in religion. Questions of whether or not one believes in God are "irrelevant" and "futile."[166] We cannot be misers of the past, cannot turn back the clock, cannot abandon science, but must accept its challenge. Our age of machinery, then, "ought to challenge the humanities, not discourage them, and develop person-

ality, not kill it."[167]   Maintaining that "adventures in personality," or adventures in quality not quantity, are among those
of the present age, that its opportunities are in anthropology
and technology, Lloyd exhorts his readers on to "more bold
and pious adventures in naturalism and in humanism, in
power and in character."[168]

The political form of the new culture, as is consistent with
its philosophical presuppositions, must be internationalistic.
Sovereign states must give way to a world state of sovereign
individuals.   Since the human personality is no longer understood as physically bounded, neither can its state be so.
Since truth is relative, the new political method must be
democratic in a sense not previously conceived of.   In this
fashion, it can recognize the political, social, and economic
worth of each individual, to *whom* the truth is relative and
whose experimental activity in behalf of all types of good
is all that can now be meant by 'the religious': ". . . the ideal
life today exists—does it not?—in an adequate expression of
worldly relationships, spirituality being no cloistered existence but active adaptation to affairs of the day."[169]   And in
an encompassing statement about his brave new world to
which naturalism and pragmatism are irrevocably committed,
Lloyd says:

. . . human conscience must equate itself candidly and confidently
with the knowledge of nature's laws . . . .   [We must have] in
general direct responsibility to the known facts of life . . . the will
of today should apply itself to the removal of such things in life
as retain the attitude and manners of life still having a frontier.
Thus, if political divisions there still must be, they should be . . .
only with the consent of the parties concerned.   In general,
militarism must be cast out . . . as belying, what the life of the
peoples is already become, an international life.   And sectional
differences and privileges must be reduced . . . the will of today
should apply itself to a change in the recognized equal rights
of men.   Those old rights, life, liberty, and safe enjoyment of
property, were only anti-militaristic . . . today men must be
granted more inclusive rights, rights that are even in some sense
anti-industrialistic; such rights, I suggest, as useful occupation . . .

an education that will develop skill . . . and enjoyment of the means of communication and transportation . . . . Only with these more inclusive rights, I am sure, recognized and extended among men, can the industrial organization, under which the world has been settled, be finally put to productive or creative use . . . .

A world of untold opportunity . . . [of] realizing the spiritual in the actual, stands before the will of the present day.[170]

Lloyd envisages a future in which men engage not in physical combat but in battles of character, which are no longer

. . . bodily mass-plays; men are no longer in any visible way grouped together; and so may not battle in any formally organized social movement; . . . [their] new freedom has involved their release from any uniformity . . . [for] they have entered into the still richer and worthier fellowship of a free open unity, always so much bigger and deeper than uniformity, and creative life, so much more vital than routine [a creative life which] . . . belongs to free persons living in the universe.[171]

For Lloyd's religious humanism, "the truth that faithfully and responsibly defines the conditions of life to those that live is the only real, because the only effective or answerable prayer."[172]

NOTES

INTRODUCTION

[1] For better or worse pedagogically, Lloyd spoke to students as he spoke to mature philosophers. His work with students was as much responsible for his offerings to learned journals as the other way around. In the margins of his lectures for Ancient Philosophy (1907) and for Introduction to Philosophy (1913) are to be found notes incorporating the conclusions of previous publications and pointing the way to later ones.

[2] See "Alfred Henry Lloyd, 1864–1927," by Arthur Lyon Cross, DeWitt H. Parker, and R. M. Wenley, *Journ. Philos.*, XXV(1928), 124–30.

[3] See "Some Important Situations and Their Attitudes," *Psych. Rev.*, XIV(1907), 37–53.

[4] "Tocianism," a satire on a lecture on art appreciation. Lloyd invents the term "Tocianism," the first five letters of which stand for "The Open Circle in Art," and uproariously parodies a lecture on its meaning and significance via a set of personally drawn and Thurberesque charts with running commentary. The paper was delivered privately to a group at the University of Michigan.

[5] "Evolution Evolved—A Philosophical Criticism," *Monist*, IX(1899), 197.

[6] *Philosophy of History* (Ann Arbor: George Wahr, 1899), p. 114.

[7] E.g., "The Possible Idealism of a Pluralist," *Am. Journ. Theol.*, XIV(1910), 406–21.

[8] See letter from James to Dewey, March 23, 1903, in Ralph Barton Perry, *The Thought and Character of William James* (Boston: Little, Brown, and Co., 1935), II, 521.

[9] Herbert W. Schneider, *A History of American Philosophy* (New York: Columbia University Press, 1946), p. 478.

[10] *Op. cit.*, XI(1933), 328–29.

[11] *The Will to Doubt* (London: Swan Sonnenschein and Co., 1907), p. 153.

[12] Lloyd said that Pascal was not a philosopher: "He was probably never really interested in working out a system of philosophy" ("The Mathematician Pascal, as Philosopher and Saint, 1623–1662," *Scient. Monthly*, XX[1925], 140).

[13] Quoted on the title page of *The Will to Doubt*.

[14] See "Evolution Evolved—A Philosophical Criticism," *Monist,* IX(1899), 198.

[15] The subtitle of *Dynamic Idealism* (Chicago: A. C. McClurg and Co., 1898).

[16] See "Monuments," *Inlander,* III(1892), 133–36; "The Reaction," *Inlander,* V(1895), 311–15; "A Psychological Interpretation of Certain Doctrines in Formal Logic," *Psych. Rev.,* III(1896), 422–26.

[17] "Also the Emergence of Matter," *Journ. Philos.,* XXIV(1927), 309–32.

[18] "Some Unscientific Reflections upon Science," *Science,* N.S., XIV (1901), 22.

[19] A style, however, which Lloyd's reviewers alternately mourn and criticize.

[20] See Palmer's "Introduction," in *Contemporary American Philosophy,* ed. G. P. Adams and W. P. Montague (New York: The Macmillan Co., 1930), I, 30.

[21] Boston and New York: Houghton, Mifflin and Co., 1888.

[22] See "The Glory of Democracy—Poetry, Comedy and Duty," *Internat. Journ. Ethics,* XXVIII(1918), 179–96.

[23] See Chapter II, section 12, and Chapter IV.

[24] E. S. Bates in the *Dictionary of American Biography* (XI[1933], 328) says that Lloyd held the Walker Fellowship, but *The University of Michigan: An Encyclopedic Survey,* Part IV (Ann Arbor: University of Michigan Press, 1944), p. 675, says that he held the Chapman Travelling Fellowship.

[25] "The Philosophy of Herbert Spencer," *Scient. Monthly,* XI(1920), 98.

[26] "Luther and Machiavelli; Kant and Frederick," *Journ. Philos.,* XVI (1919), 233.

[27] "The Glory of Democracy—Poetry, Comedy and Duty," *Internat. Journ. Ethics,* XXVIII(1918), 184.

[28] "Germany and the Germans," *Springfield Daily Republican (ca.* 1899).

[29] See Marc Edmund Jones, *George Sylvester Morris* (Philadelphia: D. McKay Co., 1948).

[30] See Marjorie H. Nicolson, "James Marsh and the Vermont Transcendentalists," *Philosoph. Rev.,* XXXIV(1925), 28–50. From 1866 to 1871 Angell had been president of the University of Vermont, which was "the originator and center of the new movement" *(ibid.,* p. 45).

[31] John Dewey, "From Absolutism to Experimentalism," in *Contemporary American Philosophy,* II, 18.

[32] R. B. Perry, *op. cit.,* II, 520. Italics mine.

[33] See Morris' article on Trendelenburg reprinted in Marc Edmund Jones, *op. cit.* Morris here maintains that in Trendelenburg "efficient causality becomes Means, Substance becomes Organism, Inheritance—the relation of parts to a whole—becomes the relation of members to the organism, Quality becomes Organic Activity, and so on" (p. 375).

[34] "Ethics and Its History," *Am. Journ. Sociol.,* XI(1905), 239.

[35] "The Institution and Some of Its Original Sins," *Am. Journ. Sociol.,* XIII(1908), 539.

[36] John Dewey, "From Absolutism to Experimentalism," in *Contemporary American Philosophy,* II, 19.

[37] "The Possible Idealism of a Pluralist," *Am. Journ. Theol.,* XIV(1910), 406–21.

[38] I learned of this tradition from conversations with several of Lloyd's friends and associates at the University of Michigan.

[39] "Alfred H. Lloyd," *Philosophia*, III(1938), 12–22.

[40] See "Realism, Naturalism and Humanism," in *Contemporary American Philosophy*, II, 262.

[41] R. B. Perry, *op. cit.*, II, 375.

[42] *Ibid.*, pp. 521–22.

[43] "The Time of Day," *Scient. Monthly*, XVII(1923), 563 n.

Chapter I

[1] See Chapter II, section 13.

[2] "Also the Emergence of Matter," *Journ. Philos.*, XXIV(1927), 309–32.

[3] See "The High Comedy of Philosophy," *Monist*, XXIII(1913), 532; "Philosophy in the Service of Science," *Scient. Monthly*, X(1920), 467; and "The Doctrinaire in Time of Crisis," *Internat. Journ. Ethics*, XXVI(1916), 484 ff.

[4] See "A Psychological Interpretation of Certain Doctrines in Formal Logic," *Psych. Rev.*, III(1896), 422–26.

[5] See "The Stages of Knowledge," *Psych. Rev.*, IV(1897), 164–79. This matter will be considered further in Chapter III.

[6] See "Radical Empiricism and Agnosticism," *Mind*, N.S., XVII(1908), 175–92.

[7] See Chapter IV, section 2.

[8] See *Dynamic Idealism* (Chicago: A. C. McClurg and Co., 1898), pp. 36–40.

[9] *Ibid.*, p. 36.

[10] Chapter III will be devoted to relationalism in epistemology.

[11] "Evolution Evolved—A Philosophical Criticism," *Monist*, IX(1899), 197.

[12] "Relativity and Reality," *Journ. Philos.*, I(1904), 663.

[13] *Dynamic Idealism*, p. 43. Italics mine.

[14] "Evolution Evolved—A Philosophical Criticism," *Monist*, IX(1899), 211; see also *Dynamic Idealism*, pp. 56–57.

[15] "Evolution Evolved—A Philosophical Criticism," *Monist*, IX(1899), 204–5.

[16] See "Negation and Direction," *Philosoph. Rev.*, XXV(1916), 383–406.

[17] See "A Study in the Logic of the Early Greek Philosophy: Pluralism —Empedocles and Democritus," *Philosoph. Rev.*, X(1901), 264; "Evolution Evolved—A Philosophical Criticism," *Monist*, IX(1899), 208; and "The Philosophy of Herbert Spencer," *Scient. Monthly*, XI(1920), 101.

[18] *Leadership and Progress and Other Essays of Progress* (Boston: The Stratford Co., 1922), p. 109.

[19] See below, section 11.

[20] See Lloyd's phrase "the including whole" in "The Possible Idealism of a Pluralist," *Am. Journ. Theol.*, XIV(1910), 419.

[21] "Evolution Evolved—A Philosophical Criticism," *Monist*, IX(1899), 211.

[22] "The Social Will," *Am. Journ. Sociol.*, VIII(1902), 356.

[23] "Evolution Evolved—A Philosophical Criticism," *Monist*, IX(1899), 207.

[24] *Dynamic Idealism*, p. 43.

[25] "Problems of Human Conduct."

[26] See "Negation and Direction," *Philosoph. Rev.*, XXV(1916), 383–406; see also, "A Study in the Logic of the Early Greek Philosophy: Being, Not Being, and Becoming," *Monist*, XII(1902), 404–15.

[27] See Chapter III, 'The Process of Knowledge.'

[28] See "Dualism, Parallelism and Infinitism," *Mind*, N.S., XX(1911), 213 ff.; "The Poetry of Anaxagoras's Metaphysics," *Journ. Philos.*, IV(1907), 88 ff.; and "A Study in the Logic of the Early Greek Philosophy: Being, Not Being, and Becoming," *Monist*, XII(1902), 405 n.

[29] "Dualism, Parallelism and Infinitism," *Mind*, N.S., XX(1911), 221; see also "Negation and Direction," *Philosoph. Rev.*, XXV(1916), 383–406.

[30] "Negation and Direction," *Philosoph. Rev.*, XXV(1916), 392.

[31] "A Study in the Logic of the Early Greek Philosophy: Being, Not Being, and Becoming," *Monist*, XII(1902), 413 n.

[32] For elaboration see below, section 9, and Chapter II, section 1.

[33] "Physical Psychology," *Psych. Rev.*, VII(1900), 174.

[34] "Negation and Direction," *Philosoph. Rev.*, XXV(1916), 392.

[35] *Ibid.*

[36] The use of grammatical categories here, as elsewhere in this book, I owe to the influence of Professor John H. Randall, Jr.

[37] "Relativity and Reality," *Journ. Philos.*, I(1904), 665 n.

[38] "A Study in the Logic of the Early Greek Philosophy: Being, Not Being, and Becoming," *Monist*, XII(1902), 413 n.; see also "Professor Fullerton on 'The Doctrine of Space and Time,'" *Psych. Rev.*, IX(1902), 174–80.

[39] "Dualism, Parallelism and Infinitism," *Mind*, N.S., XX(1911), 214 ff.

[40] See "The Poetry of Anaxagoras's Metaphysics," *Journ. Philos.*, IV (1907), 85–94.

[41] "Dualism, Parallelism and Infinitism," *Mind*, N.S., XX(1911), 213.

[42] The parallelism in the order of the terms has been deliberately reversed—a matter which will be explained in Chapter II under a general account of the activities of polarities.

[43] See, for example, *Philosophy of History* (Ann Arbor: George Wahr, 1899), p. 100.

[44] The use of the term "series" is elaborated in the next chapter.

[45] "Negation and Direction," *Philosoph. Rev.*, XXV(1916), 394.

[46] Unity and community constitute a polarity which in Chapter II will be seen to be subject to the laws of polarity relationship.

[47] See "Evolution and Immortality," *Monist*, X(1900), 399–402; see also "Dualism, Parallelism and Infinitism," *Mind*, N.S., XX(1911), 212–34. This analysis of monism, pluralism, and dualism as abstractions for certain kinds of function must be recalled and reapplied to Lloyd's own "infinitism."

[48] "Pragmatism and Metaphysics," *Journ. Philos.*, XIV(1917), 478.

[49] For a general account see *ibid.*; see also "Dualism, Parallelism and Infinitism," *Mind*, N.S., XX(1911), 212–34, and "Evolution and Immortality," *Monist*, X(1900), 397–421.

[50] "Pragmatism and Metaphysics," *Journ. Philos.*, XIV(1917), 480.

[51] *Ibid.*, p. 482.

[52] C. M. Perry insists that Lloyd is a monist of the Hegelian variety and asks, "Did dimensional analysis break the *spell of unity* for Lloyd and lead him to a dimensional pluralism *in addition to* organic unity?" ("Alfred H. Lloyd (1864–1927)," *Philosophia*, III[1938], 21; italics mine).

[53] A distinction between an 'organic world' and a world 'as an organism' indicates that relationships exhibited by so-called nonbiological things are exhibited as well by biological creatures—although the reverse is not true. See "The Organic Theory of Society," *Am. Journ. Sociol.*, VI(1901), 577–601.

[54] *Dynamic Idealism*, p. 53.

[55] See "Evolution and Immortality," *Monist*, X(1900), 398.

[56] *Dynamic Idealism*, p. 55. Italics mine.

[57] *Ibid.*, p. 117.

[58] As Lloyd puts it, ". . . even plants are conscious and the very animals think . . . ." (*ibid.*, p. 21).

[59] See "The Passing of the Supernatural," *Journ. Philos.*, VII(1910), 533–53.

[60] See Chapter III for a development of this point.

[61] See *Dynamic Idealism*, p. 52.

[62] *Ibid.*, p. 47.

[63] *Ibid.*, p. 16.

[64] Lloyd's panpsychism, however, is not to be understood as an "arbitrary personification of nature. It is and it always has been a personal relationship to nature" (*ibid.*, p. 221).

[65] *Ibid.*, p. 232.

[66] See Chapter II, section 8.

[67] This is the basis of Lloyd's psychologism.

[68] Lloyd justifies anthropomorphism on the grounds that it is not the concept which is at fault, but, rather, a narrow interpretation of the concept.

[69] "The Passing of the Supernatural," *Journ. Philos.*, VII(1910), 542. Italics mine.

[70] *Ibid.*

[71] *Ibid.* Italics mine.

[72] See "Relativity and Reality," *Journ. Philos.*, I(1904), 660–65.

[73] "Evolution Evolved—A Philosophical Criticism," *Monist*, IX(1899), 197.

[74] See *Dynamic Idealism*, p. 48.

[75] See Chapter IV, section 3.

[76] "Philosophy in the Service of Science," *Scient. Monthly*, X(1920), 467.

[77] *Ibid.*, p. 474.

[78] Lloyd says: "The doctrine of will is intimately connected with that of the feeling of effort . . ." (*Dynamic Idealism*, p. 210).

[79] "The Time of Day," *Scient. Monthly*, XVII(1923), 576.

[80] See, in general, *Dynamic Idealism*, pp. 166–77 and 209–18.

[81] "Incarnation: An Essay in Three Parts," *Am. Journ. Theol.*, XX(1916), 78.

[82] See *Dynamic Idealism*, p. 209.

[83] Quoted from Lloyd's personal lecture notes for his course on Political Philosophy (1912–13).

[84] *Ibid.*

[85] "The Stages of Knowledge," *Psych. Rev.*, IV(1897), 169.

[86] "The Social Will," *Am. Journ. Sociol.*, VIII(1902), 341.

[87] Lloyd, however, often uses such terms as "impulse" or "instinct" to refer to will, possibly because he lacks adequate terminology, possibly because he is overfond of old bottles for new wine, but more probably because he simply wants to emphasize the dynamic, spontaneous character of will.

[88] Lloyd's concept of will is not 'romantic' if we mean by this any emphasis on the tragic or on *Weltschmerz*, but it is 'romantic' if we mean 'adventurous.'

[89] George Sylvester Morris, "Friedrich Adolf Trendelenburg," in Marc Edmund Jones, *George Sylvester Morris* (Philadelphia: D. McKay Co., 1948), p. 375 (originally published in the *New Englander*, April, 1874).

[90] *Ibid.*

[91] John Dewey, *Psychology*, 3rd rev. ed. (New York: Harper and Bros., 1893), p. 423.

[92] *Ibid.*

[93] The meaning of the term "will" in Lloyd's *The Will to Doubt* (London: Swan Sonnenschein and Co., 1907) is irrelevant to this discussion, for the book is about the fact of doubting and its implications. Lloyd's choice of a title is apparently designed to relate the book to James's *The Will to Believe, and Other Essays in Popular Philosophy* (New York and London: Longmans, Green and Co., 1897) and to suggest that belief is no more fundamental than doubt in human experience.

Chapter II

[1] "Reality" is an *inclusive*, not an exclusive term for Lloyd. It simply means 'nature' including man.

[2] *Dynamic Idealism* (Chicago: A. C. McClurg and Co., 1898), p. 46.

[3] Since knowledge is a relationship, all things are potentially knowable if not actually known—and the number of possible scientific laws which formalize relationship is indefinite.

[4] *Dynamic Idealism*, p. 59.

[5] *Ibid.*, p. 41.

[6] *Ibid.*, p. 53.

[7] See, for example, Lloyd's phrase: ". . . consciousness, being due only to the interaction of organic parts, being vital or essential in organic life itself . . ." (*ibid.*, p. 70).

[8] In Lloyd, 'the ideal' *is*.

[9] "A Psychological Interpretation of Certain Doctrines in Formal Logic," *Psych. Rev.*, III(1896), 426.

[10] *Ibid.*, p. 423.

[11] *Ibid.*

[12] The article cited above, in note 9.

[13] See *Dynamic Idealism*, p. 58; see also the phrase, "a single and an indefinitely differentiated life" (*ibid.*, p. 92).

[14] In one sense, however, Lloyd's logic is entirely concerned with language, since the entire environment is linguistic (see Chapter III, section 9).

[15] *Dynamic Idealism,* p. 43.

[16] "The Poetry of Anaxagoras's Metaphysics," *Journ. Philos.,* IV(1907), 86; see also "Kant and after Kant," *Journ. Philos.,* XII(1915), 374.

[17] "The Poetry of Anaxagoras's Metaphysics," *Journ. Philos.,* IV(1907), 86.

[18] *Philosophy of History* (Ann Arbor: George Wahr, 1899), p. 131.

[19] "The Poetry of Anaxagoras's Metaphysics," *Journ. Philos.,* IV(1907), 89; see also "Dualism, Parallelism and Infinitism," *Mind,* N.S., XX(1911), 218, 219, and 226.

[20] See "Negation and Direction," *Philosoph. Rev.,* XXV(1916), 383–406; see also "The Logic of Antithesis," *Journ. Philos.,* VIII(1911), 281–89.

[21] "The Case of Purpose against Fate in History," *Am. Journ. Sociol.,* XVII(1912), 492.

[22] *Ibid.*

[23] See "Negation and Direction," *Philosoph. Rev.,* XXV(1916), 383–406.

[24] See *Dynamic Idealism.*

[25] See "The Function of Philosophy in Reconstruction," *Journ. Philos.,* XVI(1919), 505–18.

[26] "Also the Emergence of Matter," *Journ. Philos.,* XXIV(1927), 325. Italics mine.

[27] See "Relativity and Reality," *Journ. Philos.,* I(1904), 660–65.

[28] See "The Duplicity of Democracy," *Am. Journ. Sociol.,* XXI(1915), 1–14.

[29] See "Scholars of the Cloister: A Defense," *Internat. Journ. Ethics,* XII(1902), 477–86.

[30] "Negation and Direction," *Philosoph. Rev.,* XXV(1916), 383.

[31] See "The Logic of Antithesis," *Journ. Philos.,* VIII(1911), 281–89.

[32] *Ibid.,* p. 281.

[33] See *ibid.,* p. 282.

[34] "Negation and Direction," *Philosoph. Rev.,* XXV(1916), 384 ff.

[35] *Ibid.,* p. 384.

[36] See, for example, "The Logic of Antithesis," *Journ. Philos.,* VIII(1911), 282; *Dynamic Idealism,* p. 18; *Philosophy of History,* p. 100; and *The Will to Doubt* (London: Swan Sonnenschein and Co., 1907), p. 231.

[37] "Dualism, Parallelism and Infinitism," *Mind,* N.S., XX(1911), 229.

[38] See "Evolution and Immortality," *Monist,* X(1900), 397–421.

[39] *Ibid.,* p. 402.

[40] "Dualism, Parallelism and Infinitism," *Mind,* N.S., XX(1911), 229.

[41] See *ibid.,* pp. 212 ff.

[42] *Ibid.,* p. 213.

[43] *Ibid.,* p. 218.   Italics mine.

[44] See "The Logic of Antithesis," *Journ. Philos.,* VIII(1911), 286 n.

[45] "The Poetry of Anaxagoras's Metaphysics," *Journ. Philos.,* IV(1907), 90.

[46] "A Study in the Logic of the Early Greek Philosophy: Being, Not Being, and Becoming," *Monist,* XII(1902), 410.

[47] "The Meaning of $\sqrt{-1}$," *Journ. Philos.,* V(1908), 143.

[48] See "A Study in the Logic of the Early Greek Philosophy: Being, Not Being, and Becoming," *Monist,* XII(1902), 404–15.

[49] See "Epistemology and Physical Science," *Philosoph. Rev.*, VII(1898), 374–81; see also "The Meaning of $\sqrt{-1}$," *Journ. Philos.*, V(1908), 149.

[50] See "History and Materialism," *Am. Hist. Rev.*, X(1905), 728.

[51] *Dynamic Idealism*, p. 49. Italics mine.

[52] *Ibid.*

[53] *Ibid.*, p. 50.

[54] *Ibid.*, p. 51.

[55] "Evolution and Immortality," *Monist*, X(1900), 407.

[56] *Dynamic Idealism*, p. 49. Italics mine.

[57] See "The Possible Idealism of a Pluralist," *Am. Journ. Theol.*, XIV (1910), 406–21.

[58] "Evolution and Immortality," *Monist*, X(1900), 407. Italics here and in the four quotations that follow all mine.

[59] *Dynamic Idealism*, p. 49.

[60] *Ibid.*, p. 51.

[61] *Ibid.*, p. 49.

[62] *Philosophy of History*, p. 50.

[63] *Dynamic Idealism*, p. 78.

[64] *Ibid.*, pp. 76–77.

[65] *Philosophy of History*, p. 25.

[66] *Ibid.*, pp. 25–26.

[67] *Ibid.*, p. 26.

[68] *Ibid.*

[69] *Ibid.*, p. 34.

[70] See *Dynamic Idealism*, p. 42.

[71] *Philosophy of History*, p. 35.

[72] *Ibid.*, pp. 22–36.

[73] See "Also the Emergence of Matter," *Journ. Philos.*, XXIV(1927), 329.

[74] "Evolution and Immortality," *Monist*, X(1900), 403.

[75] *Dynamic Idealism*, p. 84. Italics mine.

[76] *Ibid.*, p. 79.

[77] *Ibid.*, p. 80.

[78] "Evolution and Immortality," *Monist*, X(1900), 405 n.

[79] *Dynamic Idealism*, p. 82. That is, a world is think-able, see-able, move-able (see *ibid.*, p. 71).

[80] See *Philosophy of History*, pp. 21–36.

[81] *Dynamic Idealism*, p. 79.

[82] *Ibid.*, pp. 78–79.

[83] See *ibid.*, p. 35; see also "Five Great Battles of Civilization," *Am. Journ. Sociol.*, XIX(1913), 166–87.

[84] "Evolution and Immortality," *Monist* X(1900), 408.

[85] See *ibid.*, pp. 402 ff.

[86] *Ibid.*, pp. 404–5; see also "Physical Psychology," *Psych. Rev.*, VII (1900), 172–77.

[87] *Philosophy of History*, p. 36.

[88] "Evolution and Immortality," *Monist*, X(1900), 406.

[89] Compare Samuel Alexander, *Space, Time and Deity* (London: Macmillan and Co., 1920), Vol. I, Bk. 1.

[90] See "Evolution and Immortality," *Monist*, X(1900), 406.

[91] *Ibid.*, p. 405.

[92] *Ibid.*, pp. 407–8.

[93] See "Kant and after Kant," *Journ. Philos.*, XII(1915), 373–81; see also *Philosophy of History*, pp. 37–53 and 80–93.

[94] "Kant and after Kant," *Journ. Philos.*, XII(1915), 375.

[95] Lloyd uses this term, in many places, for organic interaction. It is synonymous with "mediation." For some examples see "The Organic Theory of Society," *Am. Journ. Sociol.*, VI(1901), 577–601; "Five Great Battles of Civilization," *Am. Journ. Sociol.*, XIX(1913), 166–87; and "The Personal and the Factional in the Life of Society," *Journ. Philos.*, II(1905), 337–45.

[96] *Philosophy of History*, p. 40.

[97] "Conformity, Consistency, and Truth: A Sociological Study," *Journ. Philos.*, X(1913), 285–86.

[98] *Philosophy of History*, p. 34.

[99] See "Some Unscientific Reflections upon Science," *Science*, N.S., XIV (1901), 13–22.

[100] See "Negation and Direction," *Philosoph. Rev.*, XXV(1916), 395 ff.

[101] See *ibid.*

[102] "Relativity and Reality," *Journ. Philos.*, I(1904), 663–64.

[103] See "Evolution and Immortality," *Monist*, X(1900), 397–421.

[104] See Chapter I, section 5 .

[105] "Evolution Evolved—A Philosophical Criticism," *Monist*, IX(1899), 206.

[106] See "When Gods Are Born," *Internat. Journ. Ethics*, XXIX(1919), 277.

[107] "Dualism, Parallelism and Infinitism," *Mind*, N.S., XX(1911), 216.

[108] See *The Will to Doubt*, pp. 224–247, and *Philosophy of History*, pp. 131–41; see also "Negation and Direction," *Philosoph. Rev.*, XXV(1916), 383–406, and "The Duplicity of Democracy," *Am. Journ. Sociol.*, XXI(1915), 1–14.

[109] See "Psychophysical Parallelism: A Psychological Episode in History," *Journ. Philos.*, XIV(1917), 561–70.

[110] See Chapter V, section 5.

[111] See "The Passing of the Supernatural," *Journ. Philos.*, VII(1910), 533–53.

[112] The question may be raised: If the very meaning of "organism" was conceived in terms of its being a whole for its parts and a part in a larger whole, what is being added by the present account of change? Difficulties of this sort will be considered in section 13 of this chapter.

[113] See "The Glory of Democracy—Poetry, Comedy and Duty," *Internat. Journ. Ethics*, XXVIII(1918), 179–96.

[114] See "The Passing of the Supernatural," *Journ. Philos.*, VII(1910), 541 ff.

[115] *Ibid.*, p. 540.

[116] See *ibid.*, pp. 536–43.

[117] *Ibid.*, p. 536.

[118] Lloyd seems familiar with Jamesian and Deweyan pragmatism, but is apparently unaware of Peirce.

[119] See "The Passing of the Supernatural," *Journ. Philos.*, VII(1910), 533–53; "Negation and Direction," *Philosoph. Rev.*, XXV(1916), 384; and "The Reign of Science in the History of a Race," *Mind*, N.S., XXI(1912), 506.

[120] See "Ethics and Its History," *Am. Journ. Sociol.*, XI(1905), 248; and "Conformity, Consistency, and Truth: A Sociological Study," *Journ. Philos.*, X(1913), 288.

[121] See "The High Comedy of Philosophy," *Monist*, XXIII(1913), 534 ff.

[122] See *Philosophy of History*, p. 81.

[123] On these grounds he alters, for instance, the phrase 'adaptation of man to his environment' to "progressive variation in their manner of inter- action or in the mediation of their essential and persistent relationship" ("Philosophy in the Service of Science," *Scient. Monthly*, X[1920], 469).

[124] See "Some Important Situations and Their Attitudes," *Psych. Rev.*, XIV(1907), 48; see also "Some Unscientific Reflections upon Science," *Science*, N.S., XIV(1901), 13–22.

[125] *Philosophy of History*, p. 57; see also p. 73.

[126] See *The Will to Doubt*, p. 221.

[127] See "The Social Will," *Am. Journ. Sociol.*, VIII(1902), 343.

[128] "Conformity, Consistency, and Truth: A Sociological Study," *Journ. Philos.*, X(1913), 286.

[129] "Incarnation: An Essay in Three Parts," *Am. Journ. Theol.*, XX(1916), 73.

[130] "The Passing of the Supernatural," *Journ. Philos.*, VII(1910), 548.

[131] "Evolution Evolved—A Philosophical Criticism," *Monist*, IX(1899), 218.

[132] Lloyd says that "for an organism to be is to progress" (*Philosophy of History*, p. 201 n.).

[133] *Ibid.*, p. 93.

[134] *Ibid.*

[135] "History and Materialism," *Am. Hist. Rev.*, X(1905), 734.

[136] See "Evolution Evolved—A Philosophical Criticism," *Monist*, IX (1899), 205.

[137] See "Negation and Direction," *Philosoph. Rev.*, XXV(1916), 383–406; see also "The Meaning of $\sqrt{-1}$," *Journ. Philos.*, V(1908), 141–50.

[138] "When Gods Are Born," *Internat. Journ. Ethics*, XXIX(1919), 277.

[139] *Ibid.*

[140] See *Philosophy of History*, p. 92; see also "The Reign of Science in the History of a Race," *Mind*, N.S., XXI(1912), 486–507, and "The Duplicity of Democracy," *Am. Journ. Sociol.*, XXI(1915), 7, 8.

[141] See "The Time of Day," *Scient. Monthly*, XVII(1923), 456–57; see also "Five Great Battles of Civilization," *Am. Journ. Sociol.*, XIX(1913), 166–87.

[142] See "When Gods Are Born," *Internat. Journ. Ethics*, XXIX(1919), 277.

[143] See *Philosophy of History*, p. 88.

[144] "The Power behind the Throne," *Journ. Philos.*, XI(1914), 676.

[145] *Ibid.*, p. 678.

[146] "Five Great Battles of Civilization," *Am. Journ. Sociol.*, XIX(1913), 175.

[147] See "The Passing of the Supernatural," *Journ. Philos.*, VII(1910), 533–53.

[148] See "A Study in the Logic of the Early Greek Philosophy: Being, Not Being, and Becoming," *Monist*, XII(1902), 407.

[149] See "The Possible Idealism of a Pluralist," *Am. Journ. Theol.*, XIV (1910), 420. Lloyd translates "Whatever is, is right" into the proposition that the ideal can "actually take to itself whatever the earth, however earthly, may happen to contain" (*ibid.*). Since anything can have ideal fulfillment, Lloyd takes the Leibnizian joker to be supremely moral and heroic.

[150] Lloyd's optimism is not the result of a personal temper, but is a consequence of his doctrine of polarities, which pushes him, despite his preference, into these unfortunate consequences. He makes many attempts to avoid an optimistic outcome, but without success.

[151] See *Philosophy of History*, pp. 68–69 and 76.

[152] *Dynamic Idealism*, p. 49.

[153] This is not meant in either a Berkeleian or a Kantian sense; see Chapter III, and "Evolution and Immortality," *Monist*, X(1900), 405 n.

[154] "Evolution Evolved—A Philosophical Criticism," *Monist*, IX(1899), 201.

[155] *Citizenship and Salvation, or Greek and Jew* (Boston: Little, Brown and Co., 1897), p. 3.

[156] See "The Philosophy of Herbert Spencer," *Scient. Monthly*, XI(1920), 97.

[157] *Philosophy of History*, pp. 106–7.

[158] See *ibid.*, pp. 103–12.

[159] See *ibid.*, p. 112.

[160] *Ibid.*

[161] See *Dynamic Idealism*, pp. 200 and 212.

[162] See Chapter III, section 4.

[163] *Philosophy of History*, p. 104.

[164] "The Philosophy of Herbert Spencer," *Scient. Monthly*, XI(1920), 104–5.

[165] See "Evolution and Immortality," *Monist*, X(1900), 397–421.

[166] See *Dynamic Idealism*, p. 132.

[167] See "The Philosophy of Herbert Spencer," *Scient. Monthly*, XI(1920), 108.

[168] *Ibid.*, p. 111.

[169] *Dynamic Idealism*, p. 235.

[170] "The Organic Theory of Society," *Am. Journ. Sociol.*, VI(1901), 577.

[171] *Ibid.*

[172] *Ibid.*

[173] *Citizenship and Salvation*, p. 3.

[174] "Philosophy in the Service of Science," *Scient. Monthly*, X(1920), 471.

[175] *Ibid.*, p. 468.

[176] "Psychophysical Parallelism: A Psychological Episode in History," *Journ. Philos.*, XIV(1917), 570.

[177] "The High Comedy of Philosophy," *Monist*, XXIII(1913), 525.

[178] "Psychophysical Parallelism: A Psychological Episode in History," *Journ. Philos.*, XIV(1917), 567.
   [179] See "Philosophy in the Service of Science," *Scient. Monthly*, X(1920), 466–74.
   [180] See Chapter III, section 13.
   [181] "The Possible Idealism of a Pluralist," *Am. Journ. Theol.*, XIV(1910), 421.
   [182] "The Function of Philosophy in Reconstruction," *Journ. Philos.*, XVI (1919), 509.
   [183] See "The Time of Day," *Scient. Monthly*, XVII(1923), 449–61.
   [184] *Ibid.*, p. 453.
   [185] "When Gods Are Born," *Internat. Journ. Ethics*, XXIX(1919), 283.

CHAPTER III

[1] *Dynamic Idealism* (Chicago: A. C. McClurg and Co., 1898), p. 106.
   [2] Lloyd indicates that he was accused of "materialism" by his colleagues: ". . . the implied idealism of the assailant is undoubtedly of a piece with gross materialism itself" (*ibid.*, p. 73).
   [3] "Evolution Evolved—A Philosophical Criticism," *Monist*, IX(1899), 206.
   [4] See Chapter II, sections 2 and 3.
   [5] *Dynamic Idealism*, p. 59.
   [6] "Mind" is one expression of consciousness. It is the adaptation and adjustment of organism on the level of human ideas, whereas "consciousness" is a broader term connoting the relational adjustment and differentiation of even 'inanimate' things.
   [7] See *Dynamic Idealism*, p. 60.
   [8] It will be seen, in section 5, that what in the present context is being called 'sensation' should be, more accurately, called 'perception.'
   [9] Ample empirical evidence has since been brought to bear on this contention that any instance of sensation is characterized by a fusion of sensuous response: food is unappetizing when served under purple light, for example, and the blind accurately describe facial characteristics by touch.
   [10] *Dynamic Idealism*, pp. 64–65.
   [11] *Ibid.*, pp. 69–70.
   [12] See *ibid.*, p. 81.
   [13] "Some Unscientific Reflections upon Science," *Science*, N.S., XIV (1901), 19.
   [14] *Ibid.*
   [15] See Chapter IV, section 5.
   [16] See "Epistemology and Physical Science," *Philosoph. Rev.*, VII(1898), 374–81; "Physical Psychology," *Psych. Rev.*, VII(1900), 172–77; and "Some Unscientific Reflections upon Science," *Science*, N.S., XIV(1901), 13–22.
   [17] *Dynamic Idealism*, p. 122.
   [18] "A Study in the Logic of the Early Greek Philosophy: Pluralism—Empedocles and Democritus," *Philosoph. Rev.*, X(1901), 269.
   [19] This point will be elaborated in Chapter IV.

[20] "The Stages of Knowledge," *Psych. Rev.*, IV(1897), 171.

[21] Lloyd says that everything "has the companionship . . . of a larger, a deeper, and a broader and more lasting expression of itself" ("The Social Will," *Am. Journ. Sociol.*, VIII[1902], 339).

[22] That the universe maintains itself as a kind of thing provides it, even for Aristotle, with *nous*. Lloyd departs from the Aristotelian spirit, however, in that each thing is unique and hence functions as a universal.

[23] See the discussion of "a universe lives" in Chapter I, section 11. The present assertions are parallel to the earlier ones, because thought and life are coextensive in Lloyd.

[24] "Psychophysical Parallelism: A Psychological Episode in History," *Journ. Philos.*, XIV(1917), 562.

[25] See *ibid.*, p. 563.

[26] Lloyd would say, to act "with" a world not 'in' one. See "Evolution Evolved—A Philosophical Criticism," *Monist*, IX(1899), 206.

[27] *Dynamic Idealism*, pp. 102–3.

[28] "The Glory of Democracy—Poetry, Comedy and Duty," *Internat. Journ. Ethics*, XXVIII(1918), 195–96.

[29] See Chapter I, section 5.

[30] See "Also the Emergence of Matter," *Journ. Philos.*, XXIV(1927), 309–32.

[31] Lloyd says that he "hesitates at anything like a rigid schematism" (*ibid.*, p. 314); see also, "Stages in themselves are not history any more than positions are a curve or than places are a journey" (*Philosophy of History* [Ann Arbor: George Wahr, 1899], p. 130).

[32] See "A Study in the Logic of the Early Greek Philosophy: Being, Not Being, and Becoming," *Monist*, XII(1902), 404–15.

[33] See "The Stages of Knowledge," *Psych. Rev.*, IV(1897), 164–79.

[34] *Ibid.*, p. 166.

[35] *Ibid.*, p. 167; see also *Dynamic Idealism*, p. 234, and "A Study in the Logic of the Early Greek Philosophy: Pluralism—Empedocles and Democritus," *Philosoph. Rev.*, X(1901), 269.

[36] "The Stages of Knowledge," *Psych. Rev.*, IV(1897), 167.

[37] *Ibid.*, p. 178.

[38] *Ibid.*

[39] *Ibid.*, p. 179.

[40] *Ibid.*

[41] *Ibid.*, p. 178.

[42] See "Radical Empiricism and Agnosticism," *Mind*, N.S., XVII(1908), 175–92.

[43] See Chapter IV.

[44] The two forms of the idea of "sensation" in the history of philosophy constitute a smaller polarity duplicating the larger one between the respective emphases on knower and on known considered in isolation (see the first principle of the logic of antithesis, in section 3 of Chapter II).

[45] Lloyd's analysis suggests that perception and conception are also analogous to body and mind. It will be recalled that all things are "relating activities." All things then are combinations of body and mind, of matter and self-direction. Body is analogous to relationship—to A relating itself to the rest of the world—while mind is analogous to activity—to A defining

itself or to A's *entelechy*. Now, perception is analogous to a principle of relationship, or matter, while conception is analogous to a principle of organization, or mind. Perception is of matter; conception, of mind. The knower perceives a related world; he conceives an organized and systematized one. .

[46] See *Dynamic Idealism*, pp. 111–22; see also "The Stages of Knowledge," *Psych. Rev.*, IV(1897), 169 ff.

[47] *Dynamic Idealism*, p. 162.

[48] See *ibid.*, p. 112.

[49] See "Physical Psychology," *Psych. Rev.*, VII(1900), 172–77.

[50] "Active" in the narrower sense of the term. Metaphysically, the unconscious person, like the clod, is relationally active. See "Time as a Datum of History," *Philosoph. Rev.*, VIII(1899), 45–46.

[51] See *Dynamic Idealism*, pp. 166–77.

[52] *Ibid.*, p. 114.   Italics mine.

[53] *Ibid.*, p. 113.

[54] See "The Stages of Knowledge," *Psych. Rev.*, IV(1897), 169 ff.

[55] *Citizenship and Salvation, or Greek and Jew* (Boston: Little, Brown and Co., 1897), p. 9.

[56] "Five Great Battles of Civilization," *Am. Journ. Sociol.*, XIX(1913), 170.

[57] See "History and Materialism," *Am. Hist. Rev.*, X(1905), 749.

[58] *Ibid.*

[59] See "Five Great Battles of Civilization," *Am. Journ. Sociol.*, XIX (1913), 173.

[60] See "The Organic Theory of Society," *Am. Journ. Sociol.*, VI(1901), 589 ff.

[61] "Five Great Battles of Civilization," *Am. Journ. Sociol.*, XIX(1913), 170.

[62] I must not give the impression of an unctuous strain of Victorian optimism in Lloyd by saying that for him the environment is always 'cooperative.'   In Lloyd a universe is actually torn by dichotomy and internal perversity. He is really maintaining here that such perversity is not found in the environment but in the straining, growing, and intergrowing relations between man and his environment. His point is *not* that a world exhibits no recalcitrancy but that the obstacle to man lies in the relations between him and his environment, rather than in a deficiency of the environment. It is not the environment that is to be 'overcome' or 'conquered'; it is the adaptive relations between man and his world that are to be more effectively developed.   See Chapter II, sections 12 and 14.

[63] "Incarnation: An Essay in Three Parts," *Am. Journ. Theol.*, XX(1916), 51.

[64] *Ibid.*, p. 52.

[65] *Ibid.*

[66] See "Monuments," *Inlander*, III(1892), 133–36.

[67] See "Five Great Battles of Civilization," *Am. Journ. Sociol.*, XIX (1913), 169.

[68] *Philosophy of History*, p. 72.

[69] *Ibid.*, p. 73.

[70] "Evolution and Immortality," *Monist*, X(1900), 412.

[71] See "Incarnation: An Essay in Three Parts," *Am. Journ. Theol.*, XX(1916), 55.

[72] "Psychophysical Parallelism: A Psychological Episode in History," *Journ. Philos.*, XIV(1917), 563.

[73] Lloyd says that "the Natural World is man's whole past as a memory outwardly recorded in all the various forms of nature and in their arrangement and sequence" ("Incarnation: An Essay in Three Parts," *Am. Journ. Theol.*, XX[1916], 52).

[74] See *Dynamic Idealism*, p. 88.

[75] See *ibid.*, p. 87.

[76] Person and faction are a polarity, but the gap between individuals is not so wide and deep as that between factions (see "The Personal and the Factional in the Life of Society," *Journ. Philos.*, II[1905], 338).

[77] *Dynamic Idealism*, p. 92.

[78] "The Stages of Knowledge," *Psych. Rev.*, IV(1897), 174.

[79] *Ibid.*, p. 176.

[80] *Dynamic Idealism*, p. 84.

[81] *Ibid.*, p. 186.

[82] *Ibid.*, p. 185.

[83] *Ibid.*, p. 184.

[84] *Ibid.*

[85] See "Five Great Battles of Civilization," *Am. Journ. Sociol.*, XIX (1913), 171.

[86] See *Dynamic Idealism*, p. 188 n. Lloyd distinguishes the "afterimage" understood as an underlying principle from its "ordinary applications."

[87] See *ibid.*, p. 188.

[88] See Chapter II, section 9.

[89] "The Stages of Knowledge," *Psych. Rev.*, IV(1897), 174.

[90] *Ibid.*

[91] *Dynamic Idealism*, p. 190.

[92] See "Five Great Battles of Civilization," *Am. Journ. Sociol.*, XIX (1913), 169. Language apparently can "mediate" all things (see *ibid.*, pp. 176–77); hence, whatever is, can be spoken about.

[93] See "Negation and Direction," *Philosoph. Rev.*, XXV(1916), 383–406; see also "Five Great Battles of Civilization," *Am. Journ. Sociol.*, XIX(1913), 166–87. And note, for example, that Lloyd understands the environment as a "universal language, and therefore the common mediating agency of all living beings" ("The Organic Theory of Society," *Am. Journ. Sociol.*, VI[1901], 590).

[94] *Dynamic Idealism*, p. 189.

[95] *Ibid.*, pp. 178–90.

[96] *Ibid.*, p. 186.

[97] Lloyd finds the creationalistic theory of language historically associated with a contract theory of society.

[98] "The Organic Theory of Society," *Am. Journ. Sociol.*, VI(1901), 589.

[99] *Ibid.*

[100] For Lloyd, a universe thinks; all things are "conscious" (see Chapter I, section 11).

[101] "The Organic Theory of Society," *Am. Journ. Sociol.*, VI(1901), 590.

[102] Lloyd, incidentally, is most consistent in his own use of functional descriptions when concerned with practical matters. He never deals, for example, with the *nature* of scholarships, but always with their function, never with the *nature* of philosophy, but always with the function of the philosopher.

[103] *Dynamic Idealism*, p. 111. For a general account see *ibid.*, pp. 111–22.

[104] *Ibid.*, p. 122.

[105] "Five Great Battles of Civilization," *Am. Journ. Sociol.*, XIX(1913), 171.

[106] *Dynamic Idealism*, p. 19.

[107] See "Pragmatism and Metaphysics," *Journ. Philos.*, XIV(1917), 477–83; see also "Psychophysical Parallelism: A Psychological Episode in History," *Journ. Philos.*, XIV(1917), 561–70.

[108] See "Negation and Direction," *Philosoph. Rev.*, XXV(1916), 383; see also "Science and Mystery," *Scient. Monthly*, XXII(1926), 519.

[109] "The Mathematician Pascal, as Philosopher and Saint, 1623–1662," *Scient. Monthly*, XX(1925), 152.

[110] In his unpublished work "History of the Humani," an account of which appears in section 5 of Chapter V.

[111] See "Radical Empiricism and Agnosticism," *Mind*, N.S., XVII(1908), 175–92; see also section 6 of this chapter.

[112] See "Dualism, Parallelism and Infinitism," *Mind*, N.S., XX(1911), 212–34.

[113] See "Conformity, Consistency, and Truth: A Sociological Study," *Journ. Philos.*, X(1913), 281–96.

[114] See "The Passing of the Supernatural," *Journ. Philos.* VII(1910), 533–53.

[115] See "Philosophy in the Service of Science," *Scient. Monthly*, X(1920), 471.

[116] "Five Great Battles of Civilization," *Am. Journ. Sociol.*, XIX(1913), 184.

[117] *Ibid.*, p. 187.

[118] *Ibid.*, p. 181.

[119] It is significant that Whitman is the only poet to whom Lloyd gives more than passing attention. I selected the adjective with this in mind. For Lloyd's remarks on Whitman, see "History and Materialism," *Am. Hist. Rev.*, X(1905), 728, and also "The Institution and Some of its Original Sins," *Am. Journ. Sociol.*, XIII(1908), 533–34.

[120] "Incarnation: An Essay in Three Parts," *Am. Journ. Theol.*, XX (1916), 78.

[121] *Ibid.*, p. 64.

[122] "Conformity, Consistency, and Truth: A Sociological Study," *Journ. Philos.*, X(1913), 281.

[123] "The Possible Idealism of a Pluralist," *Am. Journ. Theol.*, XIV(1910), 421.

[124] "Pragmatism and Metaphysics," *Journ. Philos.*, XIV(1917), 482.

[125] *Ibid.*

[126] *Ibid.*, p. 480.

[127] "The Case of Purpose against Fate in History," *Am. Journ. Sociol.*, XVII(1912), 510.

[128] "Alfred H. Lloyd (1864–1927)," *Philosophia*, III(1938), 21.

[129] "Physical Psychology," *Psych. Rev.*, VII(1900), 172.

[130] See "Conformity, Consistency, and Truth: A Sociological Study," *Journ. Philos.*, X(1913), 296.

[131] "Luther and Machiavelli; Kant and Frederick," *Journ. Philos.*, XVI (1919), 236.

[132] Lloyd says that "in spite of the persistent Kantianism in modern thought, form and its content are one" ("Evolution Evolved—A Philosophical Criticism," *Monist*, IX[1899], 212).

[133] "The *used* idea is wiser, even than its knowing, since it always *transcends* what can be known" (Lloyd's lecture notes for his course Introduction to Philosophy [1913]; italics mine); again, "Knowledge as used, as applied is informed with Reality" (*ibid.*).   For Lloyd's use of the term "transcendence" in this connection, see "Kant and after Kant," *Journ. Philos.*, XII(1915), 373–81; "The Possible Idealism of a Pluralist," *Am. Journ. Theol.*, XIV(1910), 406–21; and "The Passing of the Supernatural," *Journ. Philos.*, VII(1910), 533–53.

CHAPTER IV

[1] "The Doctrinaire in Time of Crisis," *Internat. Journ. Ethics*, XXVI 1916), 485.

[2] Lloyd confuses the psychologically unclear with the logically unintelligible and believes that the speculative thinker violates "logical consistency."

[3] *The Will to Doubt* (London: Swan Sonnenschein and Co., 1907), p. 277.

[4] "Conformity, Consistency, and Truth: A Sociological Study," *Journ. Philos.*, X(1913), 283.

[5] *Ibid.*, p. 284.

[6] In discussing this Lloyd twice uses Dewey's example of the problem of crossing a brook (see "Psychophysical Parallelism: A Psychological Episode in History," *Journ. Philos.*, XIV[1917], 563, and "Ethics and Its History," *Am. Journ. Sociol.*, XI[1905], 245).

[7] See "Conformity, Consistency, and Truth: A Sociological Study," *Journ. Philos.*, X(1913), 281–96.

[8] *Ibid.*, p. 288.

[9] *Ibid.*, p. 292.

[10] *Ibid.*, p. 296.   Note also Lloyd's statement that language is a "standard medium of exchange" and that Kant's categories are a "bureau of standards, a priori" (*ibid.*, p. 295).

[11] *Dynamic Idealism* (Chicago: A. C. McClurg and Co., 1898), p. 113.

[12] See *ibid.*, p. 122.

[13] From Lloyd's lecture notes for his course Introduction to Philosophy (1913).

[14] From Lloyd's lecture notes for his course Problems of Human Conduct.

[15] *Ibid.*

[16] *The Will to Doubt,* p. 195.
[17] *Ibid.,* p. 250.
[18] "Kant and after Kant," *Journ. Philos.,* XII(1915), 377.
[19] See Chapter I, section 12.
[20] "The Possible Idealism of a Pluralist," *Am. Journ. Theol.,* XIV(1910), 421. Italics mine.
[21] From notes taken on Lloyd's History of Philosophy course by Professor A. C. Benjamin in 1919–20. Italics mine.
[22] Title page of *The Will to Doubt.*
[23] See "Five Great Battles of Civilization," *Am. Journ. Sociol.,* XIX (1913), 167.
[24] See Chapter V, section 7.
[25] "Conformity, Consistency, and Truth: A Sociological Study," *Journ. Philos.,* X(1913), 293.
[26] *Ibid.,* p. 294.
[27] "The Glory of Democracy—Poetry, Comedy and Duty," *Internat. Journ. Ethics,* XXVIII(1918), 194.
[28] *Ibid.,* p. 184.
[29] See "The Case of Purpose against Fate in History," *Am. Journ. Sociol.,* XVII(1912), 510.
[30] "Scholars of the Cloister: A Defense," *Internat. Journ. Ethics,* XII (1902), 483.
[31] See Chapter I, section 2.
[32] Language, for Lloyd, arises in the use of environment (see Chapter III, section 10).
[33] *Dynamic Idealism,* p. 36.
[34] *Ibid.,* p. 38.
[35] *Ibid.,* p. 39.
[36] Lloyd actually makes only casual reference to the principle of identity and never thoroughly argues his position.
[37] "Relativity and Reality," *Journ. Philos.,* I(1904), 662.
[38] See *ibid.,* pp. 660–64; "The Poetry of Anaxagoras's Metaphysics," *Journ. Philos.,* IV(1907), 85–94; and *The Will to Doubt,* pp. 193–203.
[39] See "The Possible Idealism of a Pluralist," *Am. Journ. Theol.,* XIV (1910), 419.
[40] See "The Passing of the Supernatural," *Journ. Philos.,* VII(1910), 539.
[41] See "The Organic Theory of Society," *Am. Journ. Sociol.,* VI(1901), 586.
[42] "The Doctrinaire in Time of Crisis," *Internat. Journ. Ethics,* XXVI (1916), 485.
[43] "The High Comedy of Philosophy," *Monist,* XXIII(1913), 526.
[44] *Ibid.,* p. 533.
[45] *Ibid.,* p. 535.
[46] *Ibid.,* p. 537.
[47] *Ibid.*
[48] *Ibid.,* p. 533.
[49] Lloyd argues against utilizing new terms either for philosophy in general or for the "new wares" of idealism in particular on these grounds (see "The Mathematician Pascal, as Philosopher and Saint, 1623–1662,"

Scient. Monthly, XX[1925], 152, and "Evolution Evolved—A Philosophical Criticism," *Monist,* IX[1899], 197–218).

[50] "The High Comedy of Philosophy," *Monist,* XXIII(1913), 535–36.

[51] "A Study in the Logic of the Early Greek Philosophy: Pluralism—Empedocles and Democritus," *Philosoph. Rev.,* X(1901), 262.

[52] See *ibid.,* p. 262 n.

[53] "Some Unscientific Reflections upon Science," *Science,* N.S., XIV (1901), 13–14.

[54] See "Conformity, Consistency, and Truth: A Sociological Study," *Journ. Philos.,* X(1913), 281–96.

[55] Lloyd compares the liberation of science from an overemphasis on technique with the decline of sectarianism in religion, which frees it from the bondage of ritual. He maintains that an overtechnical science and an overritualized religion occur at the same historical time ("Some Unscientific Reflections upon Science," *Science,* N.S., XIV[1901], 20).

[56] *Ibid.,* p. 13.

[57] *Ibid.,* p. 15.

[58] See Chapter III, section 9.

[59] See "Some Unscientific Reflections upon Science," *Science,* N.S., XIV(1901), 19.

[60] See "Monuments," *Inlander,* III(1892), 133–36.

[61] "Some Unscientific Reflections upon Science," *Science,* N.S., XIV (1901), 21.

[62] See "Phi Beta Kappa, Alpha of Michigan," *Michigan Alumnus,* XIV (1907), 100–103.

[63] "Some Unscientific Reflections upon Science," *Science,* N.S., XIV (1901), 15.

[64] *Ibid.,* p. 16.

[65] *Ibid.,* p. 14.

[66] "The Doctrinaire in Time of Crisis," *Internat. Journ. Ethics,* XXVI (1916), 486.

[67] "Evolution Evolved—A Philosophical Criticism," *Monist,* IX(1899), 199.

[68] See "Epistemology and Physical Science," *Philosoph. Rev.,* VII(1898), 374–81.

[69] "Some Unscientific Reflections upon Science," *Science,* N.S., XIV (1901), 17.

[70] *The Philosophy of History* (Ann Arbor: George Wahr, 1899), p. 9.

[71] "Some Unscientific Reflections upon Science," *Science,* N.S., XIV (1901), 18.

[72] *Ibid.*

[73] From Lloyd's manuscript "Notebooks."

[74] "Philosophy in the Service of Science," *Scient. Monthly,* X(1920), 468.

[75] In this respect Lloyd exhibits a Kantian strain. He is not content, however, either with a noumenon apart from experience, or yet with the Kantian conclusion that the antinomies prove the impossibility of knowledge about a whole.

[76] "Philosophy in the Service of Science," *Scient. Monthly,* X(1920), 467.

[77] See "The Glory of Democracy—Poetry, Comedy and Duty," *Internat. Journ. Ethics,* XXVIII(1918), 183.

[78] *Ibid.*

[79] "The High Comedy of Philosophy," *Monist,* XXIII(1913), 523.

[80] Lloyd's use of psychologistic terms is deliberate: ". . . anthropomorphism is not a reproach, if one does but see the man, to whom the world is likened, in his essential and world-wide, world-deep characteristics" (*Dynamic Idealism,* p. 59; see also "Science and Mystery," *Scient. Monthly,* XXII [1926], 521).

[81] See "Negation and Direction," *Philosoph. Rev.,* XXV(1916), 383–406.

[82] This paragraph sums up the burden of *The Will to Doubt.*

[83] See "The Doctrinaire in Time of Crisis," *Internat. Journ. Ethics,* XXVI(1916), 486.

[84] "Monuments," *Inlander,* III(1892), 133–34.

[85] "Some Unscientific Reflections upon Science," *Science,* N.S., XIV (1901), 16.

[86] "Philosophy in the Service of Science," *Scient. Monthly,* X(1920), 466–74.

[87] Lloyd relates psychology and pragmatism, not because he follows James and therefore interprets Jamesian pragmatism as psychologistic, but because, for psychology, man and nature are one. Philosophy's two roles, that of psychology and that of a natural science, are so mingled that they melt into each other. For this reason, "current philosophy, essentially psychologistic, knows not whether it is idealism or realism" (*ibid.,* p. 474).

[88] "The Doctrinaire in Time of Crisis," *Internat. Journ. Ethics,* XXVI (1916), 487.

[89] "Philosophy in the Service of Science," *Scient. Monthly,* X(1920), 466.

[90] *Ibid.,* p. 467.

[91] "The Doctrinaire in Time of Crisis," *Internat. Journ. Ethics,* XXVI (1916), 486.

[92] See "Evolution Evolved—A Philosophical Criticism," *Monist,* IX(1899), 199.

[93] "The Possible Idealism of a Pluralist," *Am. Journ. Theol.,* XIV(1910), 418.

[94] "Philosophy in the Service of Science," *Scient. Monthly,* X(1920), 467. Italics mine.

[95] *Ibid.,* p. 473; see also "The Doctrinaire in Time of Crisis," *Internat. Journ. Ethics,* XXVI(1916), 486.

[96] "The Doctrinaire in Time of Crisis," *Internat. Journ. Ethics,* XXVI (1916), 486.

[97] "The High Comedy of Philosophy," *Monist,* XXIII(1913), 527.

[98] See *ibid.,* p. 530.

[99] *Ibid.,* p. 532.

[100] Lloyd was once president of the Western Division of the American Philosophical Association.

[101] "The High Comedy of Philosophy," *Monist,* XXIII(1913), 525.

[102] *Ibid.,* p. 529.

[103] *Ibid.,* p. 541.

[104] *Ibid.,* p. 530.

[105] *Ibid.*, p. 539.

[106] *Ibid.*, p. 538.

[107] From a poem by Ben King (see *ibid.*, pp. 538–39).

[108] This is another of Lloyd's negatives, meaning not only 'practical,' but 'practical' in a new and qualitatively different way.

[109] See "Pragmatism and Metaphysics," *Journ. Philos.*, XIV(1917), 482.

[110] See "The Doctrinaire in Time of Crisis," *Internat. Journ. Ethics,* XXVI(1916), 487.

[111] "The High Comedy of Philosophy," *Monist,* XXIII(1913), 541.

[112] *Ibid.*, p. 523.

Chapter V

[1] See *Philosophy of History* (Ann Arbor: Geoge Wahr, 1899), p. 121.

[2] See "The Social Will," *Am. Journ. Sociol.*, VIII(1902), 336–59.

[3] See "The Case of Purpose against Fate in History," *Am. Journ. Sociol.*, XVII(1912), 511.

[4] *Leadership and Progress and Other Essays of Progress* (Boston: The Stratford Co., 1922), p. 101.

[5] "The Organic Theory of Society," *Am. Journ. Sociol.*, VI(1901), 601.

[6] "The Case of Purpose against Fate in History," *Am. Journ. Sociol.*, XVII(1912), 510–11.

[7] See *Philosophy of History,* p. 118.

[8] "The Time of Day," *Scient. Monthly,* XVII(1923), 574–75.

[9] "History and Materialism," *Am. Hist. Rev.,* X(1905), 742.

[10] "The Social Will," *Am. Journ. Sociol.*, VIII(1902), 348.

[11] *Ibid.*, p. 356.

[12] *Ibid.*

[13] See "The Doctrinaire in Time of Crisis," *Internat. Journ. Ethics,* XXVI (1916), 496.

[14] "The Allies as a League to Enforce Peace," *New York Times,* April 4, 1916, p. 12.

[15] "The Doctrinaire in Time of Crisis," *Internat. Journ. Ethics,* XXVI (1916), 497.

[16] "The Allies as a League to Enforce Peace," *New York Times,* April 4, 1916, p. 12.

[17] See "The Organic Theory of Society," *Am. Journ. Sociol.*, VI(1901), 577.

[18] *Ibid.*, pp. 577 ff.

[19] *Ibid.*, p. 601.

[20] *Ibid.*

[21] "The Social Will," *Am. Journ. Sociol.*, VIII(1902), 345.

[22] *Ibid.*

[23] *Ibid.*, p. 337.

[24] See *ibid.*

[25] *Ibid.*, p. 347.

[26] *Ibid.*, p. 346. Cf. C. H. Cooley, *Social Organization* (New York: C. Scribner and Sons, 1909). Lloyd and Cooley were colleagues at Michigan and on several occasions appeared in symposia together. The intellectual relations between them deserve special study. Lloyd refers to Cooley in

connection with the use of the term "social" in "History and Materialism," *Am. Hist. Rev.*, X(1905), 728.

[27] For an account of the processes of alienation and restoration of a society, see *Philosophy of History*, pp. 143–200.

[28] For example, in the books *Citizenship and Salvation, or Greek and Jew* (Boston: Little, Brown and Co., 1897) and *Philosophy of History* and in many articles, the most important of which are: "The Reign of Science in the History of a Race," *Mind*, N.S., XXI(1912), 486–507; "The Philosophy of Plato as a Meditation on Death," *Harvard Theol. Rev.*, I(1908), 325–45; and "Luther and Machiavelli; Kant and Frederick," *Journ. Philos.*, XVI (1919), 225–36.

[29] "The Reign of Science in the History of a Race," *Mind*, N.S., XXI (1912), 486.

[30] See *Philosophy of History*, p. 211.

[31] See "Scholars of the Cloister: A Defense," *Internat. Journ. Ethics*, XII(1902), 486.

[32] *Ibid.*

[33] See *Philosophy of History*, pp. 143–67; see also Lloyd's manuscript "History of the Humani," p. 126.

[34] See "Five Great Battles of Civilization," *Am. Journ. Sociol.*, XIX (1913), 171–73; see also "The Glory of Democracy—Poetry, Comedy and Duty," *Internat. Journ. Ethics*, XXVIII(1918), 182 ff.

[35] "History and Materialism," *Am. Hist. Rev.*, X(1905), 727.

[36] *Ibid.*, pp. 727–750.

[37] *Ibid.*, p. 731.

[38] *Ibid.*, p. 732.

[39] See *ibid.*, p. 727.

[40] *Ibid.*

[41] *Ibid.*, p. 736.

[42] See Chapter III, section 9.

[43] Lloyd's article "Scholars of the Cloister: A Defense," *Internat. Journ. Ethics*, XII(1902), 477–86, attempts to support this contention by removing some of the 'darkness' from the medieval period.

[44] "History and Materialism," *Am. Hist. Rev.*, X(1905), 735.

[45] *Ibid.*, p. 743.

[46] See Chapter III, section 9.

[47] "History and Materialism," *Am. Hist. Rev.*, X(1905), 750.

[48] In *Mind*, N.S., XXI(1912), 486–507.

[49] "Five Great Battles of Civilization," *Am. Journ. Sociol.*, XIX(1913), 166–87, attempts to summarize his stages of value; "The Function of Philosophy in Reconstruction," *Journ. Philos.*, XVI(1919), 505–18, and "The Power behind the Throne," *Journ. Philos.*, XI(1914), 673–80, each contain a brief account. An early, unexplained diagram of the order and succession of values appears in the *Philosophy of History*, and *Citizenship and Salvation* and "The Philosophy of Plato as a Meditation on Death," *Harvard Theol. Rev.*, I(1908), 325–45, become more meaningful in the light of this idea. In "Some Important Situations and Their Attitudes," *Psych. Rev.*, XIV(1907), 37–53, Lloyd's "occupations" again appear, this time with the five stages condensed to four.

[50] See *Philosophy of History*, p. 120; see also "The Reign of Science in the History of a Race," *Mind*, N.S., XXI(1912), 486–507.

[51] See *Citizenship and Salvation*, p. 41.

[52] See "Some Important Situations and Their Attitudes," *Psych. Rev.*, XIV(1907), 37–53.

[53] See *Philosophy of History*, pp. 131–41 and 154–55; also "Five Great Battles of Civilization," *Am. Journ. Sociol.*, XIX(1913), 166–87; and "The Reign of Science in the History of a Race," *Mind*, N.S., XXI(1912), 486–507.

[54] "Five Great Battles of Civilization," *Am. Journ. Sociol.*, XIX(1913), 172–73.

[55] *Ibid.*, p. 173.

[56] *Ibid.*, p. 172.

[57] See *ibid.*, pp. 167 ff.

[58] *Ibid.*, p. 170.

[59] From the manuscript "History of the Humani," p. 13.

[60] "Five Great Battles of Civilization," *Am. Journ. Sociol.*, XIX(1913), 167.

[61] From the manuscript "History of the Humani," p. 27.

[62] *Ibid.*, p. 83.

[63] "Five Great Battles of Civilization," *Am. Journ. Sociol.*, XIX(1913), 167.

[64] From the manuscript "History of the Humani," p. 77.

[65] See "Five Great Battles of Civilization," *Am. Journ. Sociol.*, XIX (1913), 182–83.

[66] *Ibid.*, p. 167.

[67] See "Evolution and Immortality," *Monist*, X(1900), 400.

[68] See "Five Great Battles of Civilization," *Am. Journ. Sociol.*, XIX (1913), 154–55.

[69] See "Some Important Situations and Their Attitudes," *Psych. Rev.*, XIV(1907), 38.

[70] "The Function of Philosophy in Reconstruction," *Journ. Philos.*, XVI (1919), 510.

[71] See "The Reign of Science in the History of a Race," *Mind*, N.S., XXI(1912), 486, and the manuscript "History of the Humani," p. 4.

[72] See *Philosophy of History*, p. 128.

[73] See "Some Important Situations and Their Attitudes," *Psych. Rev.*, XIV(1907), 38.

[74] See *Philosophy of History*, p. 130.

[75] "The Function of Philosophy in Reconstruction," *Journ. Philos.*, XVI (1919), 510.

[76] *Ibid.*, p. 511.

[77] "The Reign of Science in the History of a Race," *Mind*, N.S., XXI (1912), 486.

[78] See Chapter II, section 11.

[79] "Negation and Direction," *Philosoph. Rev.*, XXV(1916), 399; see also pp. 383–87.

[80] See "Five Great Battles of Civilization," *Am. Journ. Sociol.*, XIX(1913), 166–87.

[81] *Ibid.*, p. 184.

[82] *Ibid.*

[83] See *Philosophy of History*, p. 201; see also "The Philosophy of Plato as a Meditation on Death," *Harvard Theol. Rev.*, I(1908), 325–45.

[84] See "The Institution and Some of Its Original Sins," *Am. Journ. Sociol.*, XIII(1908), 535.

[85] "Five Great Battles of Civilization," *Am. Journ. Sociol.*, XIX(1913), 186.

[86] *Ibid.*, p. 187.

[87] See "The Time of Day," *Scient. Monthly*, XVII(1923), 562–63 n.

[88] See Chapter III, section 10.

[89] See "Incarnation: An Essay in Three Parts," *Am. Journ. Theol.*, XX(1916), 45–80.

[90] See "Evolution Evolved—A Philosophical Criticism," *Monist*, IX (1899), 207–13.

[91] *The Will to Doubt* (London: Swan Sonnenschein and Co., 1907), p. 160.

[92] *Ibid.*, p. 164.

[93] "The Personal and the Factional in the Life of Society," *Journ. Philos.*, II(1905), 340; see also "History and Materialism," *Am. Hist. Rev.*, X(1905), 727–50.

[94] See "History and Materialism," *Am. Hist. Rev.*, X(1905), 744.

[95] *Ibid.*, p. 743.

[96] *Ibid.*, p. 744.

[97] *Citizenship and Salvation*, p. 28; see also "The Personal and. the Factional in the Life of Society," *Journ. Philos.*, II(1905), 337–45.

[98] *Citizenship and Salvation*, p. 70.

[99] "The Case of Purpose against Fate in History," *Am. Journ. Sociol.*, XVII(1912), 511.

[100] See *Philosophy of History*, pp. 118 and 230.

[101] "The Institution and Some of Its Original Sins," *Am. Journ. Sociol.*, XIII(1908), 524.

[102] "The Personal and the Factional in the Life of Society," *Journ. Philos.*, II(1905), 340.

[103] See "The Institution and Some of Its Original Sins," *Am. Journ. Sociol.*, XIII(1908), 523.

[104] See *Philosophy of History*, pp. 174–75.

[105] "The Reaction," *Inlander*, V(1895), 315.

[106] *Philosophy of History*, p. 140.

[107] *Ibid.*

[108] Lloyd would object to the spatiality of the term.

[109] George Santayana, *Soliloquies in England and Later Soliloquies* (New York: Charles Scribner's Sons, 1922), p. 2.

[110] One's body is part of one's environment, according to Lloyd. See *Philosophy of History*, p. 33 n.

[111] *Leadership and Progress*, p. 36.

[112] See *ibid.*, p. 35.

[113] *Citizenship and Salvation*, p. 5.

[114] *Ibid.*, p. 30.

[115] *Ibid.*, p. 45.

[116] *Ibid.*

[117] *Ibid.*, pp. 77–80.

[118] See "The Duplicity of Democracy," *Am. Journ. Sociol.*, XXI(1915), 1–14.

[119] *Ibid.*, pp. 1–2.

[120] "The Glory of Democracy—Poetry, Comedy and Duty," *Internat. Journ. Ethics*, XXVIII(1918), 194.

[121] See "The Duplicity of Democracy," *Am. Journ. Sociol.*, XXI(1915), 6; see also "Incarnation: An Essay in Three Parts," *Am. Journ. Theol.*, XX(1916), 79–80.

[122] See *Leadership and Progress*, p. 85.

[123] "The Duplicity of Democracy," *Am. Journ. Sociol.*, XXI(1915), 6.

[124] *Leadership and Progress*, p. 85.

[125] *Ibid.*, pp. 87–88.

[126] "The Duplicity of Democracy," *Am. Journ. Sociol.*, XXI(1915), 14.

[127] *Ibid.*, p. 11.

[128] *Ibid.*

[129] *Ibid.*, p. 10.

[130] *Ibid.*, p. 14.

Chapter VI

[1] "Enlightened Action the True Basis of Morality," *Hibbert Journ.*, VI(1908), 824.

[2] See "When Gods Are Born," *Internat. Journ. Ethics*, XXIX(1919), 272–83.

[3] See "Ethics and Its History," *Am. Journ. Sociol.*, XI(1905), 229–51.

[4] *Ibid.*, p. 235.

[5] "Some Important Situations and Their Attitudes," *Psych. Rev.*, XIV (1907), 52.

[6] *Ibid.*, p. 40.

[7] "Incarnation: An Essay in Three Parts," *Am. Journ. Theol.*, XX(1916), 62.

[8] "Ethics and Its History," *Am. Journ. Sociol.*, XI(1905), 234.

[9] See Chapter III, section 10.

[10] "Ethics and Its History," *Am. Journ. Sociol.*, XI(1905), 234.

[11] *Philosophy of History* (Ann Arbor: George Wahr, 1899), p. 226.

[12] "Luther and Machiavelli; Kant and Frederick," *Journ. Philos.*, XVI (1919), 235.

[13] *Ibid.*

[14] See *ibid.*, pp. 225–36.

[15] See "Ethics and Its History," *Am. Journ. Sociol.*, XI(1905), 232 ff.

[16] *Ibid.*, p. 232.

[17] See *ibid.*

[18] See *Dynamic Idealism* (Chicago: A. C. McClurg and Co., 1898), pp. 219–23.

[19] "Ethics and Its History," *Am. Journ. Sociol.*, XI(1905), 246.

[20] *The Will to Doubt* (London: Swan Sonnenschein and Co., 1907), p. 202.

[21] *Philosophy of History*, p. 224.

[22] "Incarnation: An Essay in Three Parts," *Am. Journ. Theol.*, XX(1916), 60.

[23] *Philosophy of History*, p. 224.   Italics mine.

[24] See Chapter II, section 3.

[25] *Philosophy of History*, p. 226.

[26] See *ibid.*, p. 233.

[27] See "Ethics and Its History," *Am. Journ. Sociol.*, XI(1905), 229–51.

[28] See "The Thinker's Idea of God," *Inlander*, IX(1899), 192–201.

[29] See "Enlightened Action the True Basis of Morality," *Hibbert Journ.*, VI(1908), 820.

[30] From Lloyd's manuscript "Notebooks."

[31] "Science and Mystery," *Scient. Monthly*, XXII(1926), 519.

[32] See "The Philosophy of Plato as a Meditation on Death," *Harvard Theol. Rev.*, I(1908), 327.

[33] See "The Mathematician Pascal, as Philosopher and Saint, 1623–1662," *Scient. Monthly*, XX(1925), 151.

[34] See "Incarnation: An Essay in Three Parts," *Am. Journ. Theol.*, XX(1916), 62.

[35] See "Ethics and Its History," *Am. Journ. Sociol.*, XI(1905), 229–51.

[36] "Incarnation: An Essay in Three Parts," *Am. Journ. Theol.*, XX(1916), 64.

[37] "When Gods Are Born," *Internat. Journ. Ethics*, XXIX(1919), 282.

[38] "Incarnation: An Essay in Three Parts," *Am. Journ. Theol.*, XX(1916), 55.

[39] *Ibid.*, p. 59.

[40] "Ethics and Its History," *Am. Journ. Sociol.*, XI(1905), 238.

[41] See *ibid.*

[42] *Ibid.*, p. 236.

[43] *Ibid.*, p. 237 n.

[44] See *ibid.*, p. 239.

[45] *Ibid.*, p. 237.

[46] *Ibid.*, p. 239.

[47] *Ibid.*, p. 229.

[48] *Ibid.*

[49] "Enlightened Action the True Basis of Morality," *Hibbert Journ.*, VI(1908), 813.

[50] See "Ethics and Its History," *Am. Journ. Sociol.*, XI(1905), 250.

[51] See Chapter V, section 7.

[52] See "Enlightened Action the True Basis of Morality," *Hibbert Journ.*, VI(1908), 822 ff.

[53] *Ibid.*, p. 811.

[54] "Games of Chance," *Monist*, XXI(1911), 296.

[55] See *ibid.*, p. 301.

[56] *Ibid.*, p. 296.

[57] See *ibid.*, p. 304.

[58] See *ibid.*, p. 299.

[59] See "Enlightened Action the True Basis of Morality," *Hibbert Journ.*, VI(1908), 820; see also Chapter V, section 7.

[60] "Enlightened Action the True Basis of Morality," *Hibbert Journ.*, VI(1908), 820; see also *Philosophy of History*, pp. 234–39.

[61] *Philosophy of History*, p. 229.

[62] "Enlightened Action the True Basis of Morality," *Hibbert Journ.*, VI(1908), 821.

[63] See "The Relation of Righteousness to Brute Facts," *Internat. Journ. Ethics*, XVIII(1908), 432.

[64] *Ibid.*

[65] "Enlightened Action the True Basis of Morality," *Hibbert Journ.*, VI(1908), 825.

[66] "The Time of Day," *Scient. Monthly*, XVII(1923), 575.

[67] "Incarnation: An Essay in Three Parts," *Am. Journ. Theol.*, XX(1916), 61.

[68] *Ibid.*, p. 62.

[69] "The Time of Day," *Scient. Monthly*, XVII(1923), 570.

[70] "The Reaction," *Inlander*, V(1895), 311–15, and "The Thinker's Idea of God," *ibid.*, IX(1899), 192–201.

[71] *Citizenship and Salvation, or Greek and Jew* (Boston: Little, Brown and Co., 1897), p. 65.

[72] *Dynamic Idealism*, pp. 227–41.

[73] *Philosophy of History*, pp. 211–21.

[74] In an account of the modern era he says that the doctrine of the consubstantiality of Father, Son, and Holy Ghost was a "splendid symbol" sanctioning what was later to become materialism, naturalism, and humanism ("Science and Mystery," *Scient. Monthly*, XXII[1926], 514). Furthermore, Lloyd often uses the term "Christendom" as synonymous sometimes with "society" and sometimes with "religion" (see "The Power behind the Throne," *Journ. Philos.*, XI[1914], 673–80; see also "Science and Mystery," *Scient. Monthly*, XXII[1926], 507–21).

[75] Thought should not be understood as "the conceit of knowledge nor the mere accumulation of knowledge . . . but it is the valuation of knowledge for life" ("The Thinker's Idea of God," *Inlander*, IX[1899], 197).

[76] From the manuscript "Notebooks."

[77] *The Will to Doubt*, p. 128.

[78] See "Games of Chance," *Monist*, XXI(1911), 303.

[79] "Enlightened Action the True Basis of Morality," *Hibbert Journ.*, VI(1908), 825.

[80] "The Thinker's Idea of God," *Inlander*, IX(1899), 192–201.

[81] *Ibid.*, p. 193.   Italics mine.

[82] *Ibid.*

[83] *Ibid.*

[84] *Ibid.*, p. 194.

[85] *Ibid.*, p. 195.

[86] "The Reaction," *Inlander*, V(1895), 313.

[87] See *Citizenship and Salvation*, pp. 28 ff.

[88] See "The Personal and the Factional in the Life of Society," *Journ. Philos.*, II(1905), 337–45.

[89] See "History and Materialism," *Am. Hist. Rev.*, X(1905), 727–50.

[90] "The Passing of the Supernatural," *Journ. Philos.*, VII(1910), 534.

[91] See "History and Materialism," *Am. Hist. Rev.*, X(1905), 727–50.

[92] "The Time of Day," *Scient. Monthly*, XVII(1923), 571.

[93] See "Incarnation: An Essay in Three Parts," *Am. Journ. Theol.*, XX(1916), 45–80.

[94] See "When Gods Are Born," *Internat. Journ. Ethics*, XXIX(1919), 283.

[95] "The Thinker's Idea of God," *Inlander*, IX(1899), 196. A further attack on the literal symbols used by the Church occurs in "The Passing of the Supernatural," *Journ. Philos.*, VII(1910), 533–53.

[96] "The Thinker's Idea of God," *Inlander*, IX(1899), 195.

[97] *Ibid.*, p. 196.

[98] See "The Reaction," *Inlander*, V(1895), 311–15.

[99] See "The Thinker's Idea of God," *Inlander*, IX(1899), 192–201.

[100] See "The Time of Day," *Scient. Monthly*, XVII(1923), 564.

[101] Apparently all ritual—civil, political, and the like—is subject to this stigma.

[102] See Chapter IV, section 3.

[103] See "The Personal and the Factional in the Life of Society," *Journ. Philos.*, II(1905), 337–45.

[104] See "The Thinker's Idea of God," *Inlander*, IX(1899), 192–201.

[105] See the manuscript "The Romance of the University."

[106] See "The Thinker's Idea of God," *Inlander*, IX(1899), 196.

[107] From the manuscript "The Romance of the University."

[108] *Ibid.*

[109] See Part I, section 4, of this chapter, and "Incarnation: An Essay in Three Parts," *Am. Journ. Theol.*, XX(1916), 45–80.

[110] See "The Institution and Some of Its Original Sins," *Am. Journ. Sociol.*, XIII(1908), 523–40.

[111] "The Thinker's Idea of God," *Inlander*, IX(1899), 196.

[112] See *ibid.*, p. 197.

[113] See "History and Materialism," *Am. Hist. Rev.*, X(1905), 727–50; see also "The Institution and Some of Its Original Sins," *Am. Journ. Sociol.*, XIII(1908), 523–40, and *Dynamic Idealism*, pp. 132–33.

[114] See *Philosophy of History*, p. 114; see also "The Reign of Science in the History of a Race," *Mind*, N.S., XXI(1912), 486–507.

[115] "The Relation of Righteousness to Brute Facts," *Internat. Journ. Ethics*, XVIII(1908), 421.

[116] From the manuscript "Is America Obsessed with Occupationalism?"

[117] In the manuscript "Clannism and Republicanism."

[118] See *Dynamic Idealism*, pp. 129–46.

[119] See "Evolution Evolved—A Philosophical Criticism," *Monist*, IX (1899), 211.

[120] See "The Thinker's Idea of God," *Inlander*, IX(1899), 197–98.

[121] "The Reaction," *Inlander*, V(1895), 315.

[122] "The Thinker's Idea of God," *Inlander*, IX(1899), 195–96.

[123] *Ibid.*, p. 198.

[124] "Enlightened Action the True Basis of Morality," *Hibbert Journ.*, VI(1908), 821.

[125] See "The High Comedy of Philosophy," *Monist*, XXIII(1913), 523–42.

[126] "Science and Mystery," *Scient. Monthly*, XXII(1926), 520.

[127] "The Time of Day," *Scient. Monthly*, XVII(1923), 458.

[128] "The Passing of the Supernatural," *Journ. Philos.*, VII(1910), 550.

[129] See *ibid.*, p. 547.

[130] From the manuscript "History of the Humani."

[131] "Enlightened Action the True Basis of Morality," *Hibbert Journ.*, VI(1908), 814.   Italics mine.

[132] See "The Thinker's Idea of God," *Inlander*, IX(1899), 199.

[133] "The Social Will," *Am. Journ. Sociol.*, VIII(1902), 358.

[134] See Chapter V.

[135] See "Enlightened Action the True Basis of Morality," *Hibbert Journ.*, VI(1908), 810–25.

[136] "When Gods Are Born," *Internat. Journ. Ethics*, XXIX(1919), 275.

[137] From the manuscript "Problems of Human Conduct."

[138] See *ibid.*

[139] See "The Relation of Righteousness to Brute Facts," *Internat. Journ. Ethics*, XVIII(1908), 426.

[140] See "The Thinker's Idea of God," *Inlander*, IX(1899), 193.

[141] *Philosophy of History*, p. 140.

[142] "The Relation of Righteousness to Brute Facts," *Internat. Journ. Ethics*, XVIII(1908), 428.

[143] From the manuscript "Notebooks."

[144] See Chapter II.

[145] "The Reaction," *Inlander*, V(1895), 314.

[146] "Incarnation: An Essay in Three Parts," *Am. Journ. Theol.*, XX (1916), 62.

[147] See "The Passing of the Supernatural," *Journ. Philos.*, VII(1910), 548.

[148] "Evolution and Immortality," *Monist*, X(1900), 420.

[149] *Dynamic Idealism*, p. 237.

[150] "Evolution and Immortality," *Monist*, X(1900), 421.

[151] "Science and Mystery," *Scient. Monthly*, XXII(1926), 520.

[152] See "Incarnation: An Essay in Three Parts," *Am. Journ. Theol.*, XX(1916), 76 ff.

[153] "The High Comedy of Philosophy," *Monist*, XXIII(1913), 528.

[154] See "The Power behind the Throne," *Journ. Philos.*, XI(1914), 673–80.

[155] See "When Gods Are Born," *Internat. Journ. Ethics*, XXIX(1919), 283.

[156] I infer this from Lloyd's attitude toward pragmatism, which I have indicated in previous chapters. Furthermore, he says that "pragmatism, while possibly not satisfying any known metaphysician, is, nevertheless, really big with the metaphysical" ("Pragmatism and Metaphysics," *Journ. Philos.*, XIV[1917], 482).

[157] Lloyd does not want to reduce naturalism to materialism and he does not want to abandon the term 'supernaturalism,' which here means

'more than physicalistic.' 'Naturalism' is an inclusive negative which redefines the meanings of both the physicalistic and the nonphysicalistic and includes both in a theory of organism.

[158] See Lloyd's theory of knowledge (Chapter III, above), his theory of the function of the person (Chapter V), his defense of psychologistic categories (Chapter II), and his defense of anthropomorphism (Chapter I).

[159] "The Power behind the Throne," *Journ. Philos.*, XI(1914), 677.

[160] See "The Passing of the Supernatural," *Journ. Philos.*, VII(1910), 548.

[161] See *ibid.*, p. 549.

[162] See "The Relation of Righteousness to Brute Facts," *Internat. Journ. Ethics*, XVIII(1908), 427.

[163] "Science and Mystery," *Scient. Monthly*, XXII(1926), 514–15.

[164] *Ibid.*, p. 519.

[165] "The Time of Day," *Scient. Monthly*, XVII(1923), 452.

[166] *Ibid.*, p. 576.

[167] *Ibid.*, p. 574.

[168] *Ibid.*, p. 576.

[169] "Evolution and Immortality," *Monist*, X(1900), 409.

[170] "Incarnation: An Essay in Three Parts," *Am. Journ. Theol.*, XX(1916), 78–80.

[171] "Five Great Battles of Civilization," *Am. Journ. Sociol.*, XIX(1913), 184.

[172] *Philosophy of History*, p. 140.

BIBLIOGRAPHY

PRIMARY SOURCES: LLOYD'S PUBLISHED WORKS AND UNPUBLISHED MANUSCRIPTS

(The books, articles, and reviews are in chronological order. The manuscripts, except for Lloyd's doctoral dissertation, are in the Michigan Historical Collections, at the University of Michigan.)

I. BOOKS

Citizenship and Salvation, or Greek and Jew. A Study in the Philosophy of History. Boston: Little, Brown and Co., 1897.

Dynamic Idealism. An Elementary Course in the Metaphysics of Psychology. Chicago: A. C. McClurg and Co., 1898.

Philosophy of History. An Introduction to the Philosophical Study of Politics. Ann Arbor: George Wahr, 1899.

The Will to Doubt. An Essay in Philosophy for the General Thinker. London: Swan Sonnenschein and Co., 1907.

Leadership and Progress and Other Essays of Progress. Boston: The Stratford Co., 1922.

II. ARTICLES

"Monuments," *Inlander*, III (Dec., 1892), 133–36.

"The Reaction," *Inlander*, V (June, 1895), 311–15.

"A Psychological Interpretation of Certain Doctrines in Formal Logic," *Psychological Review*, III (July, 1896), 422–26. (Read at a meeting of the American Psychological Association, 1895.)

"The Stages of Knowledge," *Psychological Review,* IV (March, 1897), 164–79.

"Epistemology and Physical Science," *Philosophical Review,* VII (July, 1898), 374–81. (Read in part at a meeting of the American Psychological Association, Dec., 1897.)

"Germany and the Germans," *Springfield Daily Republican, ca.* 1899.

"Evolution Evolved—A Philosophical Criticism," *Monist,* IX (Jan., 1899), 197–218. (Read before the Katholepistemiad Klub of the University of Michigan faculty and before the University of Michigan Philosophical Society, Oct., 1898.)

"Time as a Datum of History," *Philosophical Review,* VIII (Jan., 1899), 40–48.

"The Thinker's Idea of God," *Inlander,* IX (Feb., 1899), 192–201.

"George A. Hench—In Memoriam," *Michigan Alumnus,* VI (Oct., 1899), 8–11.

"Physical Psychology," *Psychological Review,* VII (March, 1900), 172–77.

"Evolution and Immortality," *Monist,* X (April, 1900), 397–421.

"The Organic Theory of Society," *American Journal of Sociology,* VI (March, 1901), 577–601.

"A Study in the Logic of the Early Greek Philosophy: Pluralism— Empedocles and Democritus," *Philosophical Review,* X (May, 1901), 261–70.

"Some Unscientific Reflections upon Science," *Science,* N.S., XIV (July 5, 1901), 13–22. (Read in part at a meeting of the American Psychological Association, Dec., 1900, and *in toto* before the Research Club of the University of Michigan, in May, 1901.)

"Professor Fullerton on 'The Doctrine of Space and Time,'" *Psychological Review,* IX (March, 1902), 174–80.

"A Study in the Logic of the Early Greek Philosophy: Being, Not Being, and Becoming," *Monist,* XII (April, 1902), 404–15.

"Scholars of the Cloister: A Defense," *International Journal of Ethics*, XII (July, 1902), 477–86.

"The Social Will," *American Journal of Sociology*, VIII (Nov., 1902), 336–59.

"The Contribution of the Theory of Evolution to the Science of Teaching," *New York Teachers' Monographs*, IV (Dec., 1902), 56–62.

"Relativity and Reality," *Journal of Philosophy, Psychology and Scientific Methods*, I (Nov. 24, 1904), 660–65.

"Academic Avocations," *Inlander*, XV (April, 1905), 235–41.

"The Personal and the Factional in the Life of Society," *Journal of Philosophy, Psychology and Scientific Methods*, II (June 22, 1905), 337–45.

"History and Materialism," *American Historical Review*, X (July, 1905), 727–50.

"Ethics and Its History," *American Journal of Sociology*, XI (Sept., 1905), 229–51.

"Some Important Situations and Their Attitudes," *Psychological Review*, XIV (Jan., 1907), 37–53.

"The Poetry of Anaxagoras's Metaphysics," *Journal of Philosophy, Psychology and Scientific Methods*, IV (Feb. 14, 1907), 85–94.

"Phi Beta Kappa, Alpha of Michigan," *Michigan Alumnus*, XIV (Dec., 1907), 100–103.

"The Institution and Some of Its Original Sins," *American Journal of Sociology*, XIII (Jan., 1908), 523–40.

"The Meaning of $\sqrt{-1}$," *Journal of Philosophy, Psychology and Scientific Methods*, V (March 12, 1908), 141–50.

"Radical Empiricism and Agnosticism," *Mind*, N.S., XVII (April, 1908), 175–92.

"Enlightened Action the True Basis of Morality," *Hibbert Journal*, VI (July, 1908), 810–25.

"The Philosophy of Plato as a Meditation on Death," *Harvard Theological Review*, I (July, 1908), 325–45.

"The Relation of Righteousness to Brute Facts," *International Journal of Ethics*, XVIII (July, 1908), 418–33.

"The Possible Idealism of a Pluralist," *American Journal of Theology*, XIV (July, 1910), 406–21.

"The Passing of the Supernatural," *Journal of Philosophy, Psychology and Scientific Methods*, VII (Sept. 29, 1910), 533–53.

"Dualism, Parallelism and Infinitism," *Mind*, N.S., XX (April, 1911), 212–34.

"Games of Chance," *Monist*, XXI (April, 1911), 296–304.

"The Logic of Antithesis," *Journal of Philosophy, Psychology and Scientific Methods*, VIII (May 25, 1911), 281–89.

"The Case of Purpose against Fate in History," *American Journal of Sociology*, XVII (Jan., 1912), 491–511.

"The Reign of Science in the History of a Race," *Mind*, N.S., XXI (Oct., 1912), 486–507. (Chapter III of the manuscript "History of the Humani.")

"Conformity, Consistency, and Truth: A Sociological Study," *Journal of Philosophy, Psychology and Scientific Methods*, X (May 22, 1913), 281–96.

"Five Great Battles of Civilization," *American Journal of Sociology*, XIX (Sept., 1913), 166–87.

"The High Comedy of Philosophy," *Monist*, XXIII (Oct., 1913), 523–42.

"Roger Bacon the Philosopher," *Open Court*, XXVIII (Aug., 1914), 486–93.

"The Power behind the Throne," *Journal of Philosophy, Psychology and Scientific Methods*, XI (Dec. 3, 1914), 673–80.

"The Duplicity of Democracy," *American Journal of Sociology*, XXI (July, 1915), 1–14.

"Kant and after Kant," *Journal of Philosophy, Psychology and Scientific Methods*, XII (July 8, 1915), 373–81.

"Expediency of an Academic Call to Arms," *New York Times*, Nov. 26, 1915, p. 12.

"Incarnation: An Essay in Three Parts," *American Journal of Theology*, XX (Jan., 1916), 45–80.

"The Allies as a League to Enforce Peace," *New York Times*, April 4, 1916, p. 12.

"Negation and Direction," *Philosophical Review*, XXV (May, 1916), 383–406. (Paper in honor of Josiah Royce on his sixtieth birthday.)

"The Doctrinaire in Time of Crisis," *International Journal of Ethics*, XXVI (July, 1916), 482–99. (Presidential address, Western Philosophical Association, April, 1916.)

"Pragmatism and Metaphysics," *Journal of Philosophy, Psychology and Scientific Methods*, XIV (Aug. 30, 1917), 477–83.

"Psychophysical Parallelism: A Psychological Episode in History," *Journal of Philosophy, Psychology and Scientific Methods*, XIV (Oct. 11, 1917), 561–70.

"The Glory of Democracy—Poetry, Comedy and Duty," *International Journal of Ethics*, XXVIII (Jan., 1918), 179–96.

"Luther and Machiavelli; Kant and Frederick," *Journal of Philosophy, Psychology and Scientific Methods*, XVI (April 24, 1919), 225–36.

"When Gods Are Born," *International Journal of Ethics*, XXIX (April, 1919), 272–83.

"The Function of Philosophy in Reconstruction," *Journal of Philosophy, Psychology and Scientific Methods*, XVI (Sept. 11, 1919), 505–18. (Read at a meeting of the Western Philosophical Association, April, 1919, Iowa City.)

"Democracy," *Detroit Free Press, ca.* 1920.

"Education," *Detroit Free Press, ca.* 1920.

"The New Death," *Detroit Free Press, ca.* 1920.

"A New Nationalism," *Detroit Free Press, ca.* 1920.

"The Supernatural," *Detroit Free Press, ca.* 1920.

"Tolerance," *Detroit Free Press, ca.* 1920.

"Vital Phases of the Spiritual Reconstruction," *Detroit Free Press, ca.* 1920.

"The World and the Individual," *Detroit Free Press, ca.* 1920.

"Philosophy in the Service of Science," *Scientific Monthly*, X (May, 1920), 466–74.

"The Philosophy of Herbert Spencer," *Scientific Monthly*, XI (Aug., 1920), 97–111. (One of three papers read at a memorial meeting of the Research Club, University of Michigan, celebrating the centenary of John Tyndall and Herbert Spencer.)

"Charles Beylard Guerard de Nancrede, 1847–1921," *Michigan Alumnus* (June, 1921), 567–73. (Memorial delivered jointly by Lloyd and two others before the Senate of the University of Michigan on May 16, 1921.)

"Newspaper Conscience—A Study in Half-Truths," *American Journal of Sociology*, XXVII (Sept., 1921), 197–210. (Later incorporated in *Leadership and Progress*, Chapter III.)

"Fellowships and Their Relation to Teaching," *Educational Review*, LXII (Oct., 1921), 197–209. (Revised version of a paper read before the Association of American Universities, Nov., 1920.)

"Leadership and Progress," *International Journal of Ethics*, XXXII (Jan., 1922), 167–92.

"The Time of Day" (first part), *Scientific Monthly*, XVII (Nov., 1923), 449–61.

"The Time of Day" (second part), *Scientific Monthly*, XVII (Dec., 1923), 562–76.

"The Mathematician Pascal, as Philosopher and Saint, 1623–1662," *Scientific Monthly*, XX (Feb., 1925), 139–52.

"Science and Mystery," *Scientific Monthly*, XXII (June, 1926), 507–21.

"Also the Emergence of Matter," *Journal of Philosophy*, XXIV (June 9, 1927), 309–32.

III. Reviews

"Professor Münsterberg's Essays" (Hugo Münsterberg's *Psychology and Life*), in *Harvard Graduates' Magazine*, VIII (Dec., 1899), 178–81.

Hugo Münsterberg's *Grundzüge der Psychologie*, in *Psychological Review*, VIII (May, 1901), 282–95.

I. Woodbridge Riley's *American Philosophy: The Early Schools*, in *American Journal of Theology*, XII (July, 1908), 505–7.

Albert Leclère's *La Morale rationelle dans ses relations avec la philosophie générale*, in *Journal of Philosophy, Psychology and Scientific Methods*, V (Oct. 8, 1908), 577–80.

W. Benett's *The Ethical Aspects of Evolution Regarded as a Parallel Growth of Opposite Tendencies*, in *Journal of Philosophy, Psychology and Scientific Methods*, VI (Sept. 16, 1909), 524–28.

"The Philosophy of Values" (Hugo Münsterberg's *The Eternal Values*), in *American Journal of Theology*, XIII (Oct., 1909), 634–37.

W. Benett's *Justice and Happiness*, in *Journal of Philosophy, Psychology and Scientific Methods*, IX (June 20, 1912), 360–61.

Giorgio del Vecchio's *The Formal Bases of Law*, in *Michigan Law Review*, XIII (June, 1915), 713–15.

George T. Whitney and Philip H. Vogel's *An Introduction to Kant's Critical Philosophy*, in *Journal of Philosophy, Psychology and Scientific Methods*, XIV (Aug. 2, 1917), 446.

William Mackintosh Salter's *Nietzsche, the Thinker: A Study*, in *Journal of Philosophy, Psychology and Scientific Methods*, XV (Feb. 14, 1918), 103–10.

Walter Goodnow Everett's *Moral Values: A Study of the Principles of Conduct*, in *Journal of Philosophy, Psychology and Scientific Methods*, XVI (June 5, 1919), 330–33.

Hartley Burr Alexander's *Nature and Human Nature. Essays Metaphysical and Historical*, in *Journal of Philosophy*, XXIII (June 10, 1926), 328–31.

IV. Manuscripts

"An Address at a Funeral" (5 pp.).

"At the Barber's—Two Trips" (as acting president and after the new president was selected) (6 pp.).

"Clannism and Republicanism" (5 pp.).

Commencement addresses: two untitled ones (17 pp. and about 25 pp.).

"Duty: Rights: Power" (22 pp.).

"Education and Personality" (commencement address) (25 pp.).

"Facts and Values" (45 pp.).

"Freedom" (doctoral dissertation, Harvard, 1892).

"Freedom of the Modern City" (commencement address) (22 pp.).

"The Great Issue at Its Crisis" (an address before the Quadrangle Club, Jan., 1917) (11 pp.).

"History of the Humani: A Study of Civilization and Personality":
Book 1, "The Line of Succession" (pp. 1–186)
Book 2, "The War of the Classes" (pp. 187–363)
Book 3, "Personality in the Making" (outlined)

"In the Cause of Reality—An Essay between Reason and Fancy" (14 pp.).

"Is America Obsessed with Occupationalism?" (4 pp.).

"The Laborer Is Worthy of His Hire" (27 pp.).

"Leadership" (subtitled "For All Those Who Have a Country, by a Compatriot") (49 pp.).

"Modern Adventure" (commencement address) (19 pp.).

"Mystery, Simulated or Real, Important to Religion?" (13 pp.).

"Normalcy, Dormancy and Deviltry" (8 pp.).

"On Universities' Education" (5 pp.).

"The Passing of 'Theodore Roosevelt' " (3 pp.).

"Poetry, Comedy and Duty" (31 pp.).

"Problems of Human Conduct" (5 pp.).

"The Romance of the University" (about 22 random pages).

"Space, Time and Motion" (5 pp.).

"The Time of History and Its Challenge" (Phi Beta Kappa address at Vassar, 1923) (54 pp.).

"To the Class of 1929" (an address to the freshmen when Lloyd was serving as acting president, in 1925) (3 pp.).

"Tocianism" (33 pp.).

V. NOTEBOOKS AND LECTURE NOTES

Notebooks (diary of student days in Germany, *ca.* 1889–91). (In the possession of the Lloyd family.)

Lecture notes for History of Philosophy:
  (1) Modern Philosophy (1895–96)
  (2) Medieval and Modern Philosophy (1902)
  (3) Modern Philosophy (1902)
  (4) Modern Philosophy (1920)
  (5) Spinoza
  (6) Ancient Philosophy (1907)
  (7) Ancient Philosophy (1909)
  (8) Introduction to Philosophy (1913)

Lecture notes for Political Philosophy (1904, 1906–7, 1912–13, 1913).

Synopsis of course on History of Political Theories.

Synopsis of course on Problems of Human Conduct.

SECONDARY SOURCES

BATES, E. S., article on Lloyd in *Dictionary of American Biography*, XI (1933), 328–29.

CROSS, ARTHUR LYON, DeWitt H. Parker, and R. M. Wenley, "Alfred Henry Lloyd, 1864–1927," *Journal of Philosophy*, XXV (March 1, 1928), 124–30.

PERRY, CHARLES M., "Alfred H. Lloyd (1864–1927)," *Philosophia*, III (1938), 12–22.

SCHNEIDER, HERBERT W., *A History of American Philosophy*, pp. 478–81. New York: Columbia University Press, 1946.

WHITE, MORTON G., *The Origin of Dewey's Instrumentalism*, pp. 113–19. New York: Columbia University Press, 1943.